The Empire Strikes Back

To Be an American:
Cultural Pluralism and the Rhetoric of Assimilation
Bill Ong Hing

Negrophobia and Reasonable Racism:
The Hidden Costs of Being Black in America
Jody David Armour

Black and Brown in America:
The Case for Cooperation
Bill Piatt

Black Rage Confronts the Law
Paul Harris

Selling Words:
Free Speech in a Commercial Culture
R. George Wright

The Color of Crime:
Racial Hoaxes, White Fear, Black Protectionism, Police
Harassment, and Other Macroaggressions
Katheryn K. Russell

The Smart Culture:
Society, Intelligence, and Law
Robert L. Hayman, Jr.

Was Blind, But Now I See:
White Race Consciousness and the Law
Barbara J. Flagg

American Law in the Age of Hypercapitalism:
The Worker, the Family, and the State
Ruth Colker

Heretics in the Temple:
Americans Who Reject the Nation's Legal Faith
David Ray Papke

The Empire Strikes Back:
Outsiders and the Struggle over Legal Education
Arthur Austin

The Empire Strikes Back

Outsiders and the Struggle over Legal Education

Arthur Austin

NEW YORK UNIVERSITY PRESS

New York and London

NEW YORK UNIVERSITY PRESS
New York and London

Library of Congress Cataloging-in-Publication Data
Austin, Arthur, 1932–
The empire strikes back : outsiders and the struggle over legal
education / Arthur Austin
p. cm. — (Critical America)
Includes bibliographical references and index.
ISBN 0-8147-0650-9 (clothbound : acid-free paper)
ISBN 0-8147-0651-7 (paperback : acid-free paper)
1. Law—Study and teaching—United States. 2. Critical legal
studies—United States. 3. Sociological jurisprudence. I. Title.
II. Series.
KF272.A93 1998
340'.071'173—ddc21   98-9046
                            CIP

10 9 8 7 6 5 4 3 2 1

Dedicated to the men of the First Platoon,
Love Company, 32nd Infantry Regiment,
who went up Porkchop Hill on July 10, 1953.

Contents

Acknowledgments

I confess to reacting with considerable surprise when Richard Delgado and Jean Stefancic, editors of the Critical America series, invited me to submit a manuscript. They obviously knew that I had written articles critical of Critical Race scholarship, describing it as a manifestation of the politically correct fashion. In fact, that was exactly what appealed to them; they wanted an authentic critical series—a real dialogue. I appreciate their interest and support and nothing that I write can diminish their contribution to the dialogue. Likewise, the encouragement and counsel of Niko Pfund, Director of NYU Press, has been invaluable.

While numerous people supplied advice and made helpful suggestions as the manuscript evolved and matured, a few went beyond the call of duty. Patricia Chambers, ace writing doctor, served as a caution on style excesses. As usual, Judge Oscar Bealing made sure that the culture of objectivity was recognized and adhered to, while John Masters, Esquire, provided the pragmatic judgment of the practitioner. Brian Brown and Eric Chang, Class of '94, were with me at the beginning and did the initial grunt work. Jenna Ingersoll, Class of '95, took the manuscript through the next stage by helping me organize the material into chapters, while Laura Nelms and Jared Ray spent the summer proofreading. Becky Hill transcribed the first several chapters. The most onerous task was assumed by Ventrice Cadette, who converted my handwritten pages into print and made sure that the manuscript complied with the publisher's guidelines.

Note to the Reader

The genesis of this book dates to the winter of 1968. Kathy Boudin, a graduate of Bryn Mawr and a student in my contracts class at Case Western Reserve University School of Law, walked into my office to announce she was withdrawing from law school. Kathy mentioned that it was time to think about going underground and added that she was in trouble for something that had happened in Chicago. In my naiveté, I assumed that "underground" meant Kathy was taking the rapid transit to the airport. I gave her my best wishes and offered to provide any help I could. She gave me a quizzical look, smiled, and left.

Kathy had been indicted for disrupting the Democratic Convention in Chicago during the Four Days of Rage. She was a founding member of the Weather Underground and the daughter of the prominent civil rights lawyer Leonard Boudin. She left law school to become a fugitive. I next heard about Kathy from a news report that identified her as one of two naked women seen running from the explosion of a house in New York City. One of her Weatherman colleagues had set off the explosion while making bombs to blow up randomly selected buildings at Columbia University. The two women got clothes from Henry Fonda's ex-wife, who lived in the neighborhood. Both escaped. While on the run, Kathy and her accomplices committed numerous violent acts, culminating in a shootout in upstate New York where a Brinks guard and two police officers were killed. Tried for her role in the murders, Kathy is serving time in prison until the year 2001.

Kathy became the outsider as revolutionary. She and her Weatherman comrades were determined to reject their privileged liberal bourgeois status by using violence to free the oppressed. Instead, as Lucinda Franks wrote in 1981, they perverted "every purpose they ever had: the children of the rich killing the less privileged in the name of revolution."

Two years after Kathy went underground, Kent State University, a two-hour drive from the Case Western Law School, erupted with a confrontation that resulted in the shooting of four students. Within hours the conflagration spread to other schools in the region, closing classes with sit–ins and riots. The stars of the radical chic circulated among Ohio schools, appropriating student radio stations to demand revolution and the end of meritocracy. While the University canceled classes and ceased functioning, the Law School remained open for exams. This was the national pattern; law schools were not seriously affected by the passions and upheavals of the 1970s.

Law students, who had impending careers to consider and had more to lose than a B.A. in literature, stayed on the periphery of the insurrection. But the most formidable obstacle to radicalization was cultural. The core values of legal education—analytical evaluation, rationality, and objectivity—do not tolerate intellectual populism. Ideological gamesmanship is anathema to the Socratic method—the symbol of individualist merit. Unlike the fad-conscious arts and humanities, the law academy adhered to the rule of law. Through the 1970s, legal education remained a monolithic institution beyond the reach of the revolution.

While law schools remained aloof, the undergraduate sector was radicalized according to political correctness—a set of rules designed to terminate Liberal principles. In the 1980s academics replayed the consciousness-raising lyrics of the 1970s. Steppenwolf's *Born to Be Wild* became required reading in History 101. Adopting George Orwell's *Newspeak* strategy, radicals subverted the Liberal vocabulary. To be rational and objective is to reject the positive influences of emotion and empathy. Hierarchy denies the existence of equality. Authoritarianism translates into male dominance and oppression. Individualism connotes materialism and greed, while white male implies homophobia and patriarchy.

Speaking for outside consumption, PC academics call for multiculturalism and racial and gender diversity. This is for show; inside the tent they impose race and gender separateness. PC Newspeak decrees that oppression by Liberal white males has given females and people of color victimhood status, providing them with the experience to produce distinctive scholarship valued on its own terms. Guiding the PC apparatus is the principle that everything is political; scholarship had better be ideological or it doesn't exist.

We in the law academy were living on borrowed time. By the mid-1980s, law schools were no longer monoliths of Liberalism, having been infiltrated by young post-Woodstock instructors of a different culture. As products of PC they are sympathetic to a pop culture vision of scholarship and law. They are joined by the new wave of students trained in a postmodern undergraduate milieu. The infiltration has not been a replay of the successful PC revolution of the undergraduate program. The Liberal infrastructure is still strong enough to control the agenda—but while they are winning the war they are losing enough battles to raise doubts about the long-term future.

Kathy Boudin was an outsider, albeit one who carried her rebellion to the extremes of violence. In 1968, the Liberal hegemony did not tolerate dissent in the law academy. Seminars and law and a banana courses were years away as professors delivered Hessian Socratic training in the basics. Law students became lawyers. Around 10 percent of Kathy's class were females (identified on my seating chart by Miss); the class also included a sprinkling of Blacks. Times changed; Black enrollment hovers around 15 percent, while women are at 45 percent. These figures have contributed to another change; the Liberal will has been eroded by years of agitation and ideological politics, opening up the opportunity for outsiders to participate in the dialogue. Unlike Kathy's revolution, today's struggle is guerrilla warfare to subvert Liberal ideals and canons. Moreover, today's outsider prefers the perquisites of the bourgeois lifestyle over the underground of rancid food, grubby clothes, and life in a vacuum.

The reader should be alerted to the blend of writing methods and styles I use. The major parts of the book adhere to the conventional academic format—descriptive, linear, and analytical. To embellish my critique of storytelling as legal scholarship, I include counterstories at appropriate places. Like Outsider writers, I rely on autobiographical references to personal experiences to give perspective. Finally, do not be surprised to encounter commentary from fictional(?) characters who function as voices of the chorus.

A final note. Do not expect footnotes because there aren't any. Referencing is important; notes validate scholarship. But a surplus of notes can be a distraction, draining consciousness from the text. I compromise by compiling an extensive bibliography.

The Empire Strikes Back

1

The Outsiders vs. the Empire

The Players: Empire, Crits, Feminists, and CRT

The Empire is composed of academic traditionalists—the Kingsfields of legal education. The dominant theme dates to 1870 when Christopher Columbus Langdell introduced the casebook method to Harvard Law School. Since then, the study of law has been conducted according to the scientific model, which relies on rigid analysis to lead the student inevitably to neutral judgments. Scholarship adheres to the doctrinal method that informs decision makers and colleagues with objective analysis of legal problems. Until the appearance of the Outsider movement, the Empire had never been seriously challenged. Now it faces extinction.

According to conventional wisdom, the prevalence of back-stabbing in academics is due to the triviality of the rewards. Fights over curriculum changes, word processors, or tenure for a protégé are what academics call real politics. The Outsiders vs. the Empire is not trivial law school politics. Over the past decade legal education has exploded with vicious trashing, incendiary fax exchanges, and the return of the abuse tactics of the 1960s. This is not an academic sideshow; at issue is a brute power conflict over control of legal education and the future of the legal system.

On one side stands the Empire, composed mostly of Liberal white males. Joining them is a small group of females and minorities who share the Empire's commitment to the Liberal tradition. The Empire is the Establishment. Challenging them is a coalition of three groups; the Crits of Critical Legal Studies, Feminists, and Critical Race Theorists (CRT). They are the Outsiders who accuse the Empire of refusing to acknowledge the unique contributions of their cultures and scholarship.

The Crits initiated the revolution. They defiantly threw down the gauntlet by attacking core Liberal values and by listing various Liberal atrocities committed against everyone from law students to minorities. Instead of benevolent protectors of the public trust, the Liberals were profiled as elitist

1

oppressors who twisted the legal system to aggrandize power. To the Empire, the Crits were snot-nosed ingrates, nothing more than leftist rabble-rousers. Law school Jerry Rubinses. Harvard Professor (now Dean) Robert Clark called the Crits "Huns" whose sole objective was "the ritual slaying of the elders."

Young, bright, with egos to match, the Crits saw law as the gateway to power, which had been exploited by the Empire to engage in class oppression. The ostensible objectivity of the legal system protects a market system that marginalizes the underclass, particularly minorities and women. Laws, decisions, and regulations are indeterminate, full of choices and options that are denied the oppressed. The solution: topple the Establishment, break up the monopoly on objectivity, and institute communitarianism. The first strike was aimed at the perceived source of the corruption—the law schools.

While the appearance of females in classes was still a novelty in the 1970s, by the 1980s it had become a tidal wave. With the substantial increase in population, feminists began to assert themselves, influencing administration, curriculum, and scholarship. Two of the most influential feminists, Carol Gilligan and Catharine MacKinnon, produced new—and differing—perspectives on the new feminism. In developing the thesis that women and men "speak" in "different voices," Gilligan provided a persuasive justification for a distinct feminist ideology. The voice argument was to be borrowed by the Crits and the Critical Race Theorists. MacKinnon, a law professor, gained a national reputation for her antipornography campaign and for her writing on sex as a form of male oppression. Gilligan's argument "infuriates" MacKinnon, who argues that male oppression is the sole reason women speak in a different voice. So long as man's "foot is on her throat," no woman can be part of the power equation.

Feminists argue that the Empire's exclusive reliance on the analytical and objective problem-solving model excludes the female voice of empathy and nurturing. They counter this form of oppression with highly subjective critical scholarship designed to dismantle the white male hegemony of anti-women canons.

They are the Gangsta rappers of legal education. They titillate, provoke, and censure the canons of the Empire. Deans shudder when a CRT person makes an appointment for a "visit." Deans have reason to blink; CRT is the most energetic and focused wing of the Outsider movement. They describe themselves as a "people of color" institution—a collective designation that includes everyone except white males.

CRT ideology is based on a voice thesis: centuries of oppression gives minorities a distinctive vision of agony and the capacity to describe the experiences of the Outsiders of society. They scorn the Empire for presiding over a plantation culture in which people of color are relegated to a peripheral status. CRT challenges Empire doctrinal scholarship with storytelling, a term that includes narrative, allegory, parable, autobiography, and poetry.

While Harvard Law School enjoys fame as the home of the great names in legal education and as the birthplace of the casebook method, it shudders at its notoriety as the site of the Outsiders' most aggressive and sweeping attacks on the Empire—and the Empire's equally vigorous response. Things got so bad that Harvard was labeled "the Beirut of legal education." The Harvard experience is the most thorough and revealing case study of the Outsiders-vs.-Empire conflict and will be used to introduce some of the players, the issues, and the consequences.

Led by the young and charismatic Duncan Kennedy, the Crits at Harvard adopted a multilayered strategy. The immediate objective was to "turn" the students away from the usual drift into fashionable law school liberalism by exposing its callous victimization of women and minorities. In class, Crits used the indeterminacy argument to show how fields like contracts and property were used to conduct class war. Faculty meetings and committees became battlegrounds as Crits pushed for curriculum change and sought to terminate the Socratic Method, to take control of admissions, and to recruit new Crit faculty. On a broader and more ambitious level, they joined Crits at other schools to publish scholarship critical of Liberal tyranny.

The Harvard conflict revealed much about power, motive, and strategy. Even with support from a circle of sympathetic friends, the Crits did not have the numbers to pose a serious threat. On the Liberal side, the bitterness cut deep, prompting Liberals to retaliate against the Crits with the ultimate academic weapon: a lockout on promotion and tenure. As a tactic it was successful; as strategy it was a disaster. The Crits wrapped themselves in the cloak of martyrdom, yelled about academic class warfare, and accused the dominant Liberal authoritarians of beating up on the vulnerable Critical Legal Studies people. They played the oppression game of victimology politics. Within a short time the oppressed category was expanded to include feminists and minorities.

Feminism Emerges: The Dalton Case

Out of six new faculty of the class of 1981, three were women and one was Black. When everyone in the group made tenure except Clare Dalton (even after a two-year extension), the gender issue flashed into faculty politics at Harvard. It became an extremely divisive controversy, characterized by rowdy sit-ins and press conferences. A disgruntled student charged that Professor Dalton used her final contracts exam to solicit legal advice from her students: "[S]he was exploiting us just as surely as the worst capitalist exploits his workers." Reports out of Harvard indicate that her tenure rejection left such a bitter division that some faculty still refuse to talk to each other. Her husband, Robert Reich, a member of the faculty of the Kennedy School of Government who was to become President Clinton's secretary of labor, was indignant; the day after her rejection Reich phoned one of her opponents, "an old curmudgeon, as arrogant as he is smart, without the slightest sense of the irony lying in the epithet I chose to hurl at him; I called him a son of a bitch."

On the official level, the tenure decision involved a simple question of merit, and when Dalton's scholarship was judged intellectually flawed, she was gone. (An energetic opponent wrote an eighty-page negative critique of her work.) One of her tenure pieces, "An Essay in the Deconstruction of Contract Doctrine," was written in the Fem-Crit style, including references to deconstruction and storytelling, techniques anathema to Liberals. Instead of the standard Liberal form of practical doctrinal analysis, Dalton's work was a partisan piece of advocacy, reflecting what Harvard Law Professor Mary Ann Glendon called the Fem-Crit "zany passion for novelty [and] a confusion of advocacy with scholarship."

Who won? The Harvard Empire got rid of Dalton. On the other hand, she eventually accepted a $250,000 settlement in a sex discrimination suit. The real significance of the Dalton incident was that it highlighted scholarship as the main issue in the fight for control of legal education.

For the Empire, it was tantamount to a show trial to deliver a message to the law school community: strait is the gate to tenure, and only certified Liberals need apply. The Liberal majority circled the wagons around the Empire scholarship criteria of analysis and objectivity. Implicit was another message: raises, status, and perquisites come from acceptable scholarship, so get in line, all of you outnumbered tenured Crit sympathizers. When Robert Clark became dean, he was explicit: "I don't want to stamp out the CLS people. I just want to domesticate them."

The Dalton incident was a learning experience for Outsiders—including those at other schools. It confirmed the suspicion that the Liberal agenda used scholarship to maintain the illusion that the system of law and education is neutral when, in reality, it is oppressive and exclusionary. On the other hand, there was a positive consequence—the recognition that the Outsider movement was a legitimate threat and that defiance of the Empire style of scholarship was the way to achieve parity and ultimately gain control. It was time for a new Fem-Crit-Black voice in scholarship.

The Voice of Derrick Bell

The most defiant and contentious Outsider at Harvard was Derrick Bell, the school's first Black professor. Bell is quoted as saying, "Derek Bok [dean of the Law School and later president of Harvard] hired me, and we have disappointed each other ever since. I have not been grateful, which is about the most serious thing a black person can do to a white person." Bell's agitation is always on or near the surface; high profile and sometimes volatile, he conducted a four-day sit-in at his office to protest the denial of tenure to two Crits, was one of the most vocal supporters of Clare Dalton, and made diversity the main issue of the 1980s by accusing the Liberal majority of using its version of merit to rationalize the exclusion of Blacks. As for several Black colleagues Bell suspected of supporting Empire views, he frostily observed that while they "look black, they think white."

While Bell, who is presently at NYU, keeps his options open by operating as an independent agitator, selecting his causes with care, his career has defined the aspirations and the strategy of the Racial Critique Theorists. In 1985, the *Harvard Law Review* published Bell's *The Civil Rights Chronicles*, a series of parable-narratives that described race and gender oppression. The parable style was a direct challenge to the Liberal doctrinal linear, analytical article.

The Civil Rights Chronicles quickly became the Critical Race Theorists' model for stories of the evils of the Empire. Storytelling increased in popularity to become the accepted vehicle to demonstrate to the community that the experiences of Blacks, feminists, and other minorities in a white-male-dominated world produce a distinctive perspective and attitude. The narrative and the unique voice of the author merge to create a new and dynamic form of legal scholarship. According to Outsiders, it is this distinctive voice that justifies the use of nontraditional criteria in evaluating narrative as scholarship for hiring, promotion, and tenure.

The Implications

The Outsiders did more than merely survive; they persevered to become a presence that the administration decision makers must now consider in making policy. Even Dean Clark made an effort to ease tensions; he designated Professor Roger Fisher, known for his unsuccessful efforts to get Kuwait and Iraq together, as a faculty-student go-between. In an effort to soften his image, Clark shaved off his beard. The growing leverage of feminists and Blacks took up the slack left by the dwindling Crit influence. The students are always on call for support. Moreover, if the Liberal majority is serious about avowed efforts to recruit women and minorities, its numerical advantage will probably go down.

The Outsiders achieved a major victory when they outflanked the faculty by going to the pages of the *Harvard Law Review* to publish nontraditional scholarship. To the Liberal scholar, the *Review* is an institution; while Yale indulges in publishing trendy chic work, Harvard is the keeper of the grand style. That certainly was my assumption—until I compiled a ranking of the top ten politically correct law journals and discovered that Harvard had a lock on number ten. Everyone knew Stanford, Yale, and Michigan had succumbed to the politically correct winds—but Harvard!

Because of its prestige, when the *Review* opens its pages to the Outsider scholarship genre, it makes a major statement of approval. Bell's *Chronicles* was a beneficiary of the *Review's* endorsement and is now canon in the Outsider movement. Another example of the use of student editors to feed Outsider scholarship into the system is Cynthia Bowman's "Street Harassment and the Informal Ghettoization of Women." Bowman advocates fining harassing men who "intrude or attempt to intrude upon the women's attention in a manner that is unwelcome to the woman, with language or action that is explicitly or implicitly sexual." Harassment would include wolf whistles, leers, winks, grabs, pinches, catcalls, and street remarks. Then there was the Mary Joe Frug article.

It had been a good day for Professor Kingsfield. Damn near perfect. He had devoted the hour to the Allegheny College decision, using logic-chopping analysis like a scalpel to guide students to the inescapable conclusion that Cardozo used a form of intellectual deception to impose an irrational contract theory on that poor widow. It was always a pleasure to expose that lightweight Cardozo. Why, he mused, did those crazy females in the back of the classroom start whispering and chanting oppression, oppression.... "I wish those women would acquire some manners—and some decent clothes. Probably riffraff Yalies. It's about time I took care of that bunch." This slight irritation was soothed by a note from Erik Jensen who wrote that Kingsfield's recent article, "Relational Theories in Contracts: Subverting Intention with Subjective Fallacies," was the ultimate counter to the ranting of the anti-rationalist opportunists. I like that young Jensen; he values style. Maybe he carries it too far. Too much Maxwell Perkins in him.

As was his custom, Kingsfield was relaxing with a glass of Château Lagrezette. After an extended sigh to let the drink take its soothing effect, he extracted a recent copy of the Harvard Law Review *from the top of his desk. Ever since the* Review *had published that subversive aberration by Derrick Bell, he kept a sharp eye on what those student fools were publishing. Parables—what the hell was going on? Next it would be stories. He was glad when Bell took his oppression politics and left for New York. What Kingsfield had been reading in the* Review *was a gradual but steady decline in quality. The young people were into that dreadful interdisciplinary nonsense. But what else could you expect from student editors—people just out of an undergraduate experience of politically correct chaos. Berkeley, Columbia—even Penn. It did not make sense. Then Kingsfield saw it: "A Postmodern Feminist Legal Manifesto (An Unfinished Draft)" by Mary Joe Frug. After the first page he was sweating and at page 1072, he felt vomit nearing his mouth, then a stabbing pain tried to get out of his chest.... Kingsfield glanced up at an oil portrait of his mentor....*

A Postmodern Feminist Legal Manifesto is the most controversial law review article ever published. Mary Joe Frug, a forty-nine-year-old professor at New England Law School, the wife of a Harvard Crit law professor and the co-founder with Clare Dalton of the Fem–Crit movement, was brutally murdered near her home in an exclusive area of Cambridge. Although the decision to publish her uncompleted manuscript was not unanimous, the editors concluded that the preservation of her voice justified relaxing "traditional editorial policy." After its publication, the dissenting editors publicized their reservations in a parody at the *Review's* annual banquet that triggered a fax firefight among the faculty. Lawrence Tribe wanted the dissenters disciplined. Alan Dershowitz responded with charges of "a McCarthy witch hunt." Elizabeth Bartholet's reply: "This incident shows something very scary about male anger toward women at this institution." Charles Fried, the house conservative: "If you are a leftist, this has not been a good decade for you."

If the Bell article was a challenge to the limits of credible scholarship, the Frug article was treason. To the Kingsfields of the Empire it was the final insult—postmodernism in the *Harvard Law Review*! An epochal term, postmodernism is a pop culture theory that favors the assumption that reality is ultimately unknowable. Under postmodernism, everything is relevant, meaning that Donald Duck and Shakespeare get equal status. It blends microtheory, micropolitics, plurality, fragmentation, and indeterminacy. As Bernard Rosenberg said: "In short, the postmodern world offers man everything or nothing. Any rational consideration of the probabilities leads to a fear that he will be overtaken by the social furies that already beset him."

Frug's postmodern manifesto is a collection of fragments of indeterminacy on the relationship of law to the female body. To remind the reader that everything is nothing, she endorsed the postmodern style and then said: "[B]ut I don't think feminist legal activists need to adopt the postmodern medium in order to exploit the postmodern message; my point about the style is simply that it doesn't require us, strategically, to dismiss postmodernism as an influence on our work." After citing Madonna, Frug made law review history by invoking the F and C words: "In pornography, women get fucked." "Now, women get 'fucked' in the workplace, too, where we do 'women's work' for 'women's wages,' working for male bosses and working on male schedules." "We are raped at work or on route to work because of our sex, because we are cunts." These references are obviously the sources of Professor Kingsfield's consternation.

The Outsiders applauded the Frug article as an effective form of oppositional writing, that is, an example of feminist advocacy using postmodern imagery to mock the Empire. The use of the "F" and "C" words forces the dominant male system to confront the most graphic effects of its oppression on the female body. It's a verbal kick to the Establishment's groin, a gesture that gained the approval of the feminist Martha Minow, who, writing in response to Frug's article, said: "I get a charge thinking about . . . certain four-letter words appearing in a law review." While a reader dedicated to the linear analytical style of the Liberal scholar may disdain Frug's disjointed syntax, it is consistent with the objectives of postmodernism, in which, as she says, the medium is the message. "When style is salient," according to Frug, "it is characterized by irony and by wordplay that is often dazzlingly funny, smart, and irreverent. Things aren't just what they seem." And she proved it.

The experiences of Harvard Law School challenge, in varying ways, every law school. White male Liberals dominate. While the identity of the opposition group, or combination of groups, varies, the core issues are the same. Even when a group, such as the Critical Race Theorists, is numerically small, students often act as surrogates. Sometimes the visit of one of the nationally known players like Catharine MacKinnon or Derrick Bell can turn heat on the system. (At my school a visit by the Crit guru Duncan Kennedy inspired demands for CLS and feminist courses. To the chagrin of my colleagues, I volunteered.) The Frug factor, Liberals splitting away to support specific Outsider causes, plays out at middle- and lower-tier law schools. Nevertheless, when push comes to shove over control of power, the line resurfaces between the two major adversaries: Outsiders vs. the Empire.

Push *always* comes to shove when the issue is scholarship. As the Harvard experience demonstrates, scholarship is where the power resides, and control of scholarship is control of the legal academy. Since the turn of the century, Liberals have used the treatise and the analytical style of the doctrinal methodology to educate and guide judges, lawyers, and law professors. Everything in the academy, from hiring, promotion, tenure, and salary to the world of perquisites, depends on adherence to the accepted criteria of scholarship. The Outsider movement aspires to break through and demolish this barrier to gain control of the system. This push-comes-to-shove struggle is what this book is about.

The Preface

Normally prefaces belong in the i to vi pages, which no one except reviewers read. I'm sticking it here.

Things are quiet at Harvard now, at least on the surface. Nevertheless, fragments of what happened are being played out in varying degrees at every law school in the country. Kingsfield lives; I encounter versions of Kingsfield every day. They have a distant look: confusion, dismay, and a touch of resignation. They sense the changes coming. When they hear young professors complain about the white male dominance of legal scholarship, they shudder. It's the cumulative effect of minor incidents: a resolution to declare the Socratic Method patriarchal and insensitive, complaints that casebooks discriminate against women and minorities, that there are not enough portraits of minorities in the library. Then came the storytellers.

Enrollment continues to slide, putting strains on standards and budgets. Pressure from state legislatures to economize makes it difficult for state schools to compete for top faculty talent. The job market for graduates is tough, another reason not to attend law school. The *MacCrate Report* of 1992 exposed a festering tension between law schools and the American Bar Association. The *Report* accused law schools of failing to provide adequate training in practical skills and professional wisdom. Academics saw the *Report* as a power play to assume control of the curriculum and, hence, an effort to subvert academic freedom. It is not pleasant for the Kingsfields to listen to younger professors castigate "real lawyers" for doing what lawyers are supposed to do—represent clients and get paid for it. These are the obvious problems, serious but resolvable. The real challenge comes from the Outsiders.

As keepers of the casebook method, analytical scholarship, and the principle of objectivity, the Kingsfields are puzzled by the Outsiders' antagonism toward traditional culture. Despite some differences in goals and tactics, the Outsiders share one unifying theme—the use of scholarship to subvert the political domination of the Empire over legal education. It is a head-on encounter over scholarship's role in law. It is the Empire's demand for analysis vs. the Outsiders' reliance on empathy and subjectivity; the rational discourse vs. the unique voice of women and minorities; the linear style of the conventional doctrine article vs. the narrative of storytelling; neutral discussion vs. proselytizing.

It was a fluke, a whim, that attracted me to the scholarship wars. For twenty years, I did traditional doctrinal and interdisciplinary work in antitrust. In keeping up with the various indexes of publications, I noticed the growing presence of odd titles and nontraditional topics: "Roll Over Beethoven." "Everything Great Stands in the Storm that Blows from Paradise." "Judaism and Postmodernism." "Popular Legal Culture." Reading the new genre articles conjured up Timothy Leary and his psychedelic trips. It was aggressive advocacy—practically every sentence was a political statement, and even bland footnotes had been politicized. A new vocabulary was spitting out words like trashing, intersubjective zap, masking, and depersonalization. There were heated debates over esoteric things like whether the failure to capitalize the word feminist constitutes sexist marginalization. Or, is it elitist to capitalize Crit? There were thoughts from new stars like Stanley Fish, who made statements like: "On my analysis, the Constitution cannot be drained of meaning, because it is not a repository of meaning." One young professor wrote of the need for "moral terrorism" in faculty meetings: "We can disrupt faculty meetings with various acts of civil or, preferably, uncivil disobedience." A Crit advanced the proposition that postmodernism means that "law is right up there with other cultural forms and we lawyers have no reason to feel bashful about being compared to Madonna."

At first it was a distraction from other more tedious tasks, something to get through boring committee meetings. The *Cornell Law Review* published a poem called "Vietnam Haiku." What was next? It got to be a hobby—

grab the most recent periodical index and check out the titles. By the time the Mary Joe Frug article came out, it was clear that these pieces were not aberrations. The authors were deadly serious about what they were writing, and, more important, they were gaining a presence, publishing in the best law reviews on a regular basis. "Roll Over Beethoven" was published in Stanford.

I was hooked on the scholarship wars. Compared to the Outsiders and the Kingsfields from the Empire circling each other like two junkyard dogs growling and baring their teeth, antitrust is watching grass grow. I even did what many Outsiders do; I wrote narratives—stories about storytellers and political correctness. I got some nasty glances; one colleague told me that if I wanted to do fiction I should go into television. I also did some deconstruction, quickly learning that, as for deconstruction, Henri Mensonge was right when he said, "[T]here is no about about for anything to be about." Mensonge, the laureate of absence, went on to accomplish the ultimate in deconstruction flamboyance—he deconstructed himself.

The Empire Strikes Back is a study of how legal scholarship is used to aggrandize and protect political power in legal education. I critically analyze the factions and players who control the struggle, their use of writing to spread the message and gain power, and the success or failure of the strategies. There are multiple issues involved in the conflict, such as whether a vocational field like law needs the type of scholarship produced by law professors. How can scholarship have credibility in the university community when it is not subjected to peer review and is edited by student editors?

Much of the conflict centers on objectivity and how that term plays out in legal scholarship. Scholars are in agreement that doctrinal research and writing are not objective as that term is defined in the hard sciences. When law professors refer to doctrinal objectivity and neutrality, they are talking about a methodology that guides legal analysis. It is not the same technique used by physicists for problem solving. Instead it is the process of evaluating data, cases, laws, and commentary, then synthesizing the analysis to make a normative judgment or a recommendation. Throughout the process, the author makes judgments on what to ignore, what to emphasize, and levels of priority. These are judgments based on experience and normative beliefs. While the analysis and arguments may be persuasive to a majority of the audience, the conclusion is not necessarily correct. Outsiders see this paradox as the vulnerable spot in doctrinal scholarship. It is the justification for the arguments that law is indeterminate and that the Empire uses false objectivity as a cover for maintaining the status quo of an oppressive system.

Debate over uncertainty and subjectivity in law has always been part of the dialogue. Practitioners deal with shades of indeterminacy every day. Judges must choose between competing precedent. The Realist movement of the 1930s and 1940s, cited frequently by Crits for support, argued that law is based on the delusion of logic and predictability. Jerome Frank wrote about idiosyncratic results of court results, while advocating closer ties with other disciplines to get a better understanding of law.

While Realists wanted to revise elements of the Empire from within, Outsiders want to get rid of the entire Empire apparatus and start anew. Outsiders introduce a new factor; the rules of the debate over objectivity are being heavily influenced by the race and gender. Instead of arguing that the Empire is resistant to change as the Realists did, the Outsiders accuse the Empire of using exclusionary tactics to oppress females and minorities.

The battering ram of Outsider strategy is storytelling. The sociology of storytelling defines the Outsider movement. Outsiders use the emotion and subjectivity of parables, autobiography, and narrative to repudiate the accepted methodology of legal scholarship. The unique feature, perceived to be an advantage by storytellers, is that its method is its message. An autobiographical slice of an author's experiences invariably flushes out racism and/or sexism. A female's description of birthing exploits subjectivity and emotion to deliver a message of patriarchal interference. This produces an obvious contrast to conventional scholarship in which the message of norms is often in open conflict but the methodology of objectivity and analysis is constant.

I target four layers of readers. *The Combat Zone* is composed of the players from the Outsider movement and the Empire who would be extremely interested in a critical survey of the conflict. If nothing else, they can use the book for cite material to trash their opponents. *Puzzled Observers* constitute a second layer of observers who are sitting at the edge of the combat zone trying to figure out what the shouting is all about. This is a rather large group, one that includes traditional types who work in different areas, teaching corporate law courses like securities and tax, administrators at various levels, and interested students who are pulled back and forth in class. It is an audience that is puzzled by the partisan shouting and sniping. *The Bench and Bar* comprises a large pool of judges who deplore nontraditional scholarship, particularly the work of Outsiders. Federal Judge Harry Edwards condemns the elite law schools for abandoning "their proper place by emphasizing abstract theory at the expense of practical scholarship and pedagogy." On the other hand, there is an emerging group of younger judges who developed an interest in Outsider work in law school. The same dichotomy exists among practitioners, with older lawyers agreeing with Judge Edwards. *The Interdisciplinary Crowd* is a relatively new and expanding audience, cultivated when legal scholarship went interdisciplinary in fields such as economics, literature, and history. This is a cross-over group, with people from other disciplines writing articles in law journals that exert some influence over the law curriculum. This group has a vital interest in the outcome of the dispute: its members are closely associated with the Empire, and an Outsider victory would diminish their influence.

Finally, I also assume the interest of the public intellectual group that follow the debate in media like *The Nation, The New Republic*, and the *New York Times*.

2

The Empire

The Indulgences of the Eighties

"There has not been an indulgence we have not enjoyed. Everything she could have wanted, our marriage has given her." Yet, despite this glorious life, something was wrong. "This very morning she said to me, haltingly, 'We must speak tonight after the guests depart.'" Sure that he had lost her to another, he agonized through the day and, when the guests were gone, faced his love, "my fears at their peak, as she said to me, 'Darling, my loved one, my life, I want to go to law school.'" This is a Ralph Lauren advertisement for fur coats that ran in the 1980s. It is titled "Reflection on a Marriage."

The 1980s were the *go-go* years for legal education, the best of times and a period unlikely to be duplicated. Applications, test scores, and enrollment went through the ceiling. They were the "best and the brightest students," so much so that Derek Bok complained that the brain drain into legal education was "a massive diversion of exceptional talent into pursuits that often add little to the growth of the economy, the pursuit of culture, the enhancement of the human spirit."

The money flowed in and out. For the first time, law schools could subsidize an influx of young professors, most of whom had limited practical experience. Once on board, they were allowed to develop their own interests, regardless of the consequences. No longer did faculty have to justify new classes or research programs on the basis of need, student demand, or some other rationalization. Seminars sprouted like crabgrass. Every law school in the country benefited from stories of mega-law firms hiring graduates at the $80,000 level and then giving them the opportunity to get the front-line experience of participating in leveraged-buyout battles. On the other hand, maybe Bok was right. For example, there is the story about the former law review editor who was assigned to latrine patrol, a euphemism for hanging around restrooms to pick up gossip from the insiders to LBO negotiations.

Dickens's comment about the best of times also included a reference to the worst of times—and so it was. By the late 1980s the cracks in the boom were evident. The glory days were ending for the LBO crowd, mega-law firms were forced to cut young and middle-level associates by the dozens, and, in some instances, by groups of forty. As the economy went soft, enrollment dropped; the brain drain was over. Law schools faced budget problems, including salary freezes and contract buyouts. The reign of the scholar deans ended as they were replaced by people who were adroit at shaking alumni money trees. There was more fallout; the budget squeeze deflected attention from significant events that were occurring on the academic side of the ledger. As everyone watched the books, the Outsider movement started its campaign to topple the Empire.

The signals were as evident as mortar shell holes on a battlefield: the *Stanford Law Review* symposium on Critical Legal Studies came out in 1984, Bell's allegory *The Civil Rights Chronicles* was published in 1985, while the *Michigan Law Review* symposium on storytelling appeared in 1987. Concentrating on their private fiefdoms, the bulk of Empire people ignored the threatening omens. The more alert faculty considered the signs aberrations, reflections of the to-be-expected rebellion of some members of the new group of young professors who would eventually mature into producing more traditional work. By the late 1980s, however, the Outsider movement was too vigorous and widespread to ignore.

The traditionalists detected another disquieting signal; young members of the Empire spent less time on core subjects and more time and effort on nonlaw fields like anthropology, literary criticism, and linguistics. To the old guard, this constitutes the "delawing" of scholarship by celebrating nonlegal disciplines at the expense of law. Delawing could not get worse than the symposium on *Popular Legal Culture* published by the *Yale Law Journal* in 1989.

In the academic world of political correctness, popular culture scholarship is taken seriously for its anti-elitist and anti-intellectual content. "It is all over the map and means everything and nothing." Papers and articles deal with the impact of Madonna on sex, gender, and religion; her fans are "enriched through identification with [her] image of control and self-possession." Donald Duck is an imperialist. Pop culture conveys a subtle message in an Andy Warhol response to a request asking why he painted a Campbell soup can: "Tell him . . . I wanted to paint nothing. I was looking for something that was the essence of nothing, and that was it."

What in God's name, query the Empire traditionalist, does popular culture have to do with law? How about the Nielson winner, *L.A. Law*, the TV lawyer drama some admissions people believe to be an influential factor in the student brain drain to law schools? Writing in the *Yale Law Journal*, Stephen Gillers concluded, "Overall, *L.A. Law* has managed to be a beneficial influence on popular conceptions of law and legal ethics." Its plots are like classroom hypotheticals, viewers are challenged by unresolved issues, and, unlike real lawyers, "*L.A. Law* uses the actor's and the storyteller's arts to entertain, not to fool, people." Empire traditionalists would no doubt approve the direct and somewhat disdainful response by the practitioner adviser to the show to the concept of *L.A. Law* as a classroom: "From my perspective as an 'insider,' however, the show is less a conscious attempt by the writers to influence how people feel about the law or lawyers than it is an effort to create interesting drama with law as its stage."

Yale's "Popular Legal Culture" edition is not likely to have been a hot topic in the court house or with the practitioner. And one can hardly imagine the chagrin of Kingsfield and his Liberal friends if they read Professor Macaulay's contribution on the subject: "We may choose to put aside our latest issue of the *Harvard Law Review*, or even, for that matter, the *Yale Law Journal*, and watch an episode of *L.A. Law*. As I have said before, '[p]erhaps, best of all, I no longer need feel guilty as I watch the Badgers, Bucks, Brewers, and Packers struggle with so little success. It's not wasting time. It's research.'"

Evita Syzygy

When Professor Lester P. Bile read Macaulay's comment about popular legal culture and researching the Packers, he went into a big-time funk—he avoided his colleagues, wrote a forty-page article on the admissibility of junk science, and eschewed sex with his wife (which didn't seem to bother her). He simply could not comprehend how someone could make, much less publish, a statement like that. Eventually he came out of the funk, only to be challenged by something even worse. It started at the Barking Spider while he was enjoying a few beers with some students—his kind of students, people who despised this sensitivity-consciousness baloney the young professors were into and instead focused on preparing for the tough demands of practice. Reflecting on how Scoff Law School had been coopted by those whining, wimpy public-interest types, Bile drifted back to the conversation with a jolt. It was about Evita Syzygy, a young professor in her third year of teaching.

"That squeeze is definitely wired, she comes on like Cathy MacKinnon and Molly Yard combined. Her Evidence course is . . . is . . . like one of these touchy-feely retreats you read about." Bile groaned; retreats were made in Hell by diversity zealots. It was

multiculturalism in drag. "*Everyone had to keep a diary—our daily thoughts on how the course affected our lives. Then there was the circle; she had the desks arranged in a circle— 'no hierarchy, no hierarchy, no Socratic torture,' she kept saying. So we rapped on the patriarchal effects of the rules of evidence while Syzygy drilled us on the hearsay rule as racism. The best came on the last day, when she announced that she was going to imitate that Nesson guy at Harvard and give all As! The class went crazy.*" *[Syzygy was almost correct; Professor Nesson did in fact give all As, except one B, to his Evidence class. "I told them," he said, "that I would tell them what was on the exam, and I proceeded to do so." Nesson is famous for another innovation, "leading his Evidence class in a fifteen-minute calisthenics program to loud music projecting from the portable stereo he brings with him to class."]*

It was back to funk time for Bile. This was unbelievable. He had put his name on the line by recommending that the Law School extend an offer to Syzygy. She was to be his protégé, a female who had the understanding of what Law, in the grand tradition, meant. The first year he patiently counseled her in the nuances of the Socratic Method, especially on how to compel the student to spit out the correct answer. The bottom line was no pass! Never let them take a pass. By the end of the year Syzygy was successfully creating a Kingsfield-Hart confrontation atmosphere in class; her logic chopping was in the grand tradition.

Bile had a mean streak, which he tried to subdue when he confronted Syzygy in her office. He got bad vibes when he saw the feminist posters that now covered the formerly faded white walls. Bile almost left when he saw Andrea Dworkin smiling at him. It was more smirk than smile. "Why—why did you repudiate the Method in exchange for that fem knee-jerk nurturing nonsense? We are supposed to train lawyers, not baby sitters." Bile waited.

"I thought you would be around for a visit." She was coming on with a big smile. There was no question about Bile's attraction to her. He pictured them attending ABA meetings together. Who knows what could happen? "As they say in the spy novels, which I know you read, I was turned, I came in from the cold. It was the student evaluations. The first year they shot my kneecaps off: 'a nasty, mean-spirited way of teaching.' 'No respect for personhood.' 'It's student vs. student.' 'You treat us like the enemy.' 'Ralph Nader is right; it's a game in which the professor always wins.'

"Bile, the Method never bothered me at Yale; I never went to class enough during the first year to feel its effects and after that it was all seminars. Mostly in environmental law. Face it, Bile, the Method is an anachronism, morally corrupt, a capitalist tool to condition the student's mind to a system that excludes women and minorities. There is another aspect that your generation has been able to hide under Liberal propaganda; the Method is a tool for profscams. Most professors don't prepare like you do, and the Method allows them to get away with it. In fact, the Method is an illusion.

In the typical class, the professor either lectures (boring, boring), tells war stories, or throws out off-the-wall questions.

"It gets worse. The Method is responsible for the casebook, an embarrassment that devalues us in the eyes of everyone in the university. A casebook is an intellectual wasteland, a fraud. You know what it is, Bile, a scissors-and-paste compilation of cases, notes, and trivia, simply to make it longer. A chimp could produce a casebook. But, under the influence of the Method, it comes out as a great intellectual effort, and the editors become authors who then conspire with publishers to sell the product to a captive audience at monopolistic prices. And there is the planned obsolescence of having a new edition every four years. It's unethical."

She kept smiling; God damn it, it was like Bile was a school boy. His lecture was clearly a lost cause, so he was now, like a good lawyer, speaking for the record.

"You have been seduced into the victim and voice game of slogans and vacuous accusations. How are you going to conduct a trial in a circle? Get Marcia, Darden, the Dream Team, and O. J. in a circle around Ito and see what the hell happens. So what if students have their egos bruised—that's the price for learning. That's the Tradition."

Syzygy slowly shook her head, obviously losing patience with Moot's intransigence. "It's hierarchy. . . ."

"Of course it is, and that is what civilization is all about. The Method is the foundation of legal education. Is it efficient? Damn right. And that's why you can teach seminars and that's why you get paid twice as much as those worthless slugs in Liberal arts. There is another factor that you fail to appreciate: it is the Method that gives legal education its unique status. Other fields, like business, try to imitate us but fail. You know why? We Have Tyranny." Bile's eyes were bulging, and he was shouting. "It is tyranny that creates the impression that law schools offer a unique experience and a special challenge. On one point I agree with you, Syzygy—the Method is at risk in a world of fems, crits, and the likes of Matsuda and Delgado. I'm sure Christopher Columbus Langdell is churning in his grave."

Like most of the traditionalists, Bile does not fathom the new generation. Imbued with the orthodoxies of the Empire, he rejects any departure from the conventions of established wisdom. An attack on the Method is blasphemy. A symposium on popular legal culture is counterscholarship. Students sitting in a circle in a law school class is something out of nursery school. Nevertheless, these were ominous signs, sufficiently ominous to cause Bile to become introspective about why he was so protective of the Empire. Was it worth it? Bile didn't know; he had never made the effort to trace the roots of the Empire.

Power

The Empire can attribute its power and its unique role in American society to the vicissitudes of history. It started with America's separation from England, which terminated its adherence to an established model of legal training and practice. Freedom from English control and interference enabled American lawyers to develop a system compatible with emerging customs, economics, and politics. Responding to the needs of a developing nation, the profession grew numerically to achieve a status unmatched in any nation. Status and power came from a cluster of factors: each state organized a court system, thereby creating demand for more practitioners, while a growing population and middle class enlarged the consumer base. The industrial revolution carried the practice of law into the twentieth century by compelling lawyers to combine into firms capable of handling complicated corporate business. The emergence of the large law firm gave lawyers access to the highest levels of power in business, government, and politics. The status of the lawyer had a self-feeding effect; young people saw the profession as a quick vehicle for upward social and economic mobility. Robert Stevens makes the point about lawyer status in America: "In his observations of American society made in 1831 and 1832, Alexi de Tocqueville could express the views that have now become truisms—that the 'aristocracy of America occupies the judicial bench and bar' and that 'scarcely any political question arises in the United States that is not resolved, sooner or later, into a judicial question.'"

An economist once said that the comments of Karl Marx are like bats; from one perspective they look like birds, while from another angle they look like mice. The same can be said about law as a profession; from one angle it is a bird of rules, traditions, and institutions, whose objective is to maintain and improve competency and professionalism. On the other hand, there is the mouse perception, which has monopoly and exclusion as its goals.

Whatever the angle, legal education and the profession are packed with exclusions or, in economic terminology, barriers to entry. The history of legal education is a study in the persistent erection of economic barriers, beginning with efforts to replace office training (apprenticeship) with a more formal lecture method. Despite its tenacity, apprenticeship is now a relic of the populist era. Over the years, educational barriers have expanded: from a one-year to the present three-year degree requirement, from direct entry into law school to the prerequisite of an undergraduate degree. (When I attended law school, many schools allowed admission after three years of undergraduate, with the student earning two degrees after completing law school.) As a barrier, LSAT scores play a critical role in admission. A high score guarantees acceptance by one of the elite schools, virtually assuring a job at one of the higher-paying law firms.

Adopting the economic strategy of oligopolists, the entrenched and financially sound schools sought to deter the entry of new competition. To justify exclusionary tactics, they rationalized the necessity of high professional standards to protect the public from incompetence. When for-profit proprietary schools threatened the elite schools by appealing to the working-class and the immigrant markets, the established schools opened fire. The for-profits were accused of employing part-time instructors, elevating profit over teaching, and operating in inadequate facilities (especially the library, an effective charge since books were expensive). Worst of all, they were too bar-pass-oriented, which, ironically, was deemed a liability by the elites. All of this harping was capped with the smug charge that proprietary school graduates were likely to become ambulance chasers.

Almost total control over entry was achieved when the American Bar Association and the American Association of Law Schools (a trade association of law schools) formed an accreditation joint venture to impose educational standards on schools and to determine who could enter the market. The justification was that law is a public calling, like the practice of medicine, and therefore needs standards to elevate law from a vocation to a learned profession. Accreditation power permitted the law school club to become a mature oligopoly with its own ethos. It fit Justice Burton's description of the tight oligopoly in the tobacco industry: "Such a community of interest in any industry, however, provides a natural foundation for working policies and understandings favorable to the insiders and unfavorable to outsiders."

That is the way it worked in the legal education industry. Schools not affiliated with a university were disfavored, forcing them to negotiate for a university connection or risk denial of entry. The standards favored instruction of academic theory over skills training. Periodic inspections by the accrediting agency were used by law school deans to pressure university administrations for budget favors or new buildings. Arguing that professors could earn more money by practicing law, accreditors helped law schools justify higher-than-average salaries. According to the Department of Justice, they went even further; schools were required to supply the ABA inspectors with faculty salary records, which were then used to stabilize, that is, fix, salaries at higher levels, thereby artificially inflating the costs of legal education. Although it vehemently denied government charges that it was violating the

Sherman Antitrust Act, the ABA settled by signing a consent decree in which it agreed to stop using wage data in the accreditation process. The consent decree also prohibits the ABA from adopting any standard that prohibits a school from being organized as a for-profit entity. Responding to the ABA denials of wrongdoing, Dean Ronald Cass of Boston University Law School said: "Practitioners in Antitrust are just astounded that the ABA was looking at salaries [as a criterion for accreditation]. . . . Justice had a slam dunk."

The Massachusetts Law School litigation demonstrates that the ABA law school joint venture, like any cartel, will not tolerate deviant forms of competition. When MLS ignored the prevailing ABA admission criteria by adopting cost-cutting programs, thereby lowering cost and tuition, it was denied accreditation. MLS argued that its policies—not giving sabbaticals, allowing professors to practice, making professors work twelve months rather than nine, requiring bar review courses for students, eliminating the LSAT, and permitting students to work full-time—are cost-cutting practices that do not interfere with the training of students in the practical skills necessary for legal practice. The dean of MLS made this point: "Law schools are not filled with lawyers. They're filled with law professors, and there is a big difference."

It is a tautology that cartel members invariably rebel against tight control by cheating, which leads to dissension and, ultimately, to self-destruction. Even the powerful and profitable OPEC oil cartel succumbed to bickering and cheating through black market sales. There are signals that the ABA certification barrier to entry is following this historical pattern; in 1994, 16 deans from schools like Harvard, Yale, Stanford, Texas, and Virginia released a letter criticizing the intrusive, inflexible, inefficient, and costly certification process. The main complaint was that the cartel inhibited diversity of programs and smothered competition. One of the rogue deans said: "It's not that different an educational experience [no matter which school you attend]. Most textbooks are the same, and the courses are the same."

Miracle, Mystery, and Authority

"Mr. Fox, will you state the facts in the case of *Payne v. Cove?*" With that request, Christopher Columbus Langdell announced the birth of the Empire.

Langdell was not your typical charismatic and flamboyant crusader. He was by all accounts a mediocre New York lawyer for twenty years until Harvard President Eliot named him dean of Harvard Law School in 1870. He looked like a nineteenth-century nerd; dressed in a dark suit, wearing granny glasses, and often wearing green eye shades, he was an unprepossessing figure in class. Outside class, Langdell was the classic bookworm. His critics suggested that he hid in the library to avoid coping with reality.

The year Langdell came to Harvard, Oliver Wendell Holmes Jr. and Arthur Sedgwick wrote an article in which they concluded that the Law School was "almost a disgrace": "So long as the possession of a degree signified nothing except a residence for a certain period in Cambridge or Boston, it was without value." A major disgrace was the erratic performance level of the lecture system. It ranged from boring—the professor reading a chapter from a treatise—to an incomprehensible delivery on some obscure point. If the listener lost a single step in a string of logic, it was all over. Langdell's response was genius; he excised the past methods by announcing that law is a science. "Law, considered as a science, consists of certain principles or doctrines. To have such a mastery of these as to be able to apply them with constant facility and certainty to the ever-tangled skein of human affairs, is what constitutes a true lawyer; and hence to acquire that mastery should be the business of every earnest student of law."

Dostoyevsky's Grand Inquisitor said: "There are three powers, three powers alone, able to conquer and to hold captive forever the conscience of these impotent rebels for their happiness—those forces are miracle, mystery, and authority." These forces are inherent in the Socratic Method and help account for its hold on legal education. This hold has important ramifications for Outsiders; the Method is the source of the Empire's spirit, methods, and scholarship style.

What had been a grab bag of seemingly irreconcilable decisions with result-oriented judgments became a science of universal principles. As a science, where the final word is miracle, mystery, and authority combined, legal education assumed a new respectability. The authority of the scientific technique is expressed in the Socratic Method's use of objective and neutral analysis. To the Outsider, this is the Tyranny of Objectivity; to the Empire, it is logic chopping and thinking like a lawyer.

The Method and its imprimatur of respectability were important factors in spreading the Empire's influence. To second-tier law schools, it was an opportunity to speak the same language as the elite. A Tulane dean said: "In a effort to make the law school equal to the best in the country, the method used at Harvard in teaching will be adopted." Law professors rarely discuss another reason for the Method's success. The Method can cover a cluster of less than honorable purposes. The professor uses a question-and-answer dialogue and inductive reasoning to develop general principles, but the rest of the exercise, the details of performance, is left to the discretion of the professor.

There is no correct Socratic Method, making it the ideal format for some profscams. There is the busy professor who prefers reading the *Village Voice* or fondling a computer to preparing for class. He knows he can go to class cold and then put the burden on the students. Let them extract the grand principles. Gordon Gee, the president of Brown University, confessed that when he was a law professor, "we knew we could 'get by' if necessary by a close reading of the casebook just before class. We knew that, if we chose to, we could simply follow the course set by the casebook editor."

To the storytellers, each case reminds them of an experience from practice or from consulting. Students prefer storytellers because storytellers free them from the burden of responding to questions. While Outsiders profess to hate the Method, they use it for their own scams. The grand principles they extract from the cases include sexism, racism, patriarchy, hierarchy, elitism, and capitalism. Do not underestimate the power of a politicized Method. More than thirty-five years ago, I had a contracts professor who analyzed every case as a conflict between the proletariat and capitalism, with capitalism using devious tactics to win the struggle. Every time I read a case, I hark back to his politicized interpretation and shudder.

Finally, there are the sadistic people who get their kicks humiliating and browbeating students under the pretext of teaching them to think like lawyers. These are the Clapps of the profession. Clapp, a fictional character in Michael Levin's *The Socratic Method*, conducted his classes like a torture session, breaking students into babbling wrecks, finally slicing someone up so badly she committed suicide. Clapp's response was that he was merely "having fun with her, strictly Socratic Method stuff." Clapp is the Outsider's stereotype of the evil Empire professor.

The most compelling reason for the persistent commitment to the Method is its efficiency. A lecture system sucks resources out of a law school in the form of salaries and investment of time in preparation, plus other individual contact sessions with students. This contrasts with the Method, which fills up a lecture hall without the need for quizzes, recitation, or follow-up contact. Moreover, costs are significantly reduced when one professor can handle more than 100 students per class. In addition, the lecture is a delivery system where the student is passive, while the Method offers an element that attracts students—a feeling of involvement, challenge, and participation. It is, as Professor Bile opines, the Method's unique experience that effectively differentiates the educational product of law schools from graduate programs in other disciplines, such as economics and history.

The Empire used the Method to spread its influence among the second-tier schools. It was an offer the schools could not afford to refuse. To many schools, the economics of the Method meant survival, enabling them to become self-sufficient by providing leverage in dealing with the central administration. Its success gave a boost to legal education and law as a legitimate profession, thereby justifying demands for salaries above the typical academic scale. Universalizing the Method among all law schools was the first step in building a cartel type of mentality. The Method circulated a common theme and set of values, bringing elite and second-tier schools together. There was a *quid pro quo*: in exchange for the wisdom and economics of the Method, the Empire received a tacit admission of leadership— an acknowledgment that it was the source of legal education's ideology.

The Method's values blossomed into the dominant theme of legal education. The scientific method is the anchor, the certainty of principles the objective. The law professor, student, and lawyer use the analytical technique, which subsumes neutrality and objectivity, to describe general principles. From the beginning, Langdell and his followers saw the Method as a problem-solving device, thereby satisfying the practical demands of the practitioner. Outsiders abhor these values and abominate the rugged individualism inherent in the Method. Students are forced to test their analytical abilities under the interrogation of a professor while simultaneously competing with other students to uncover the most rational statement of a principle. It is a version of free-market competition in the classroom; may the best and brightest student win and go on to success in practice.

The Method is the inspiration for the doctrinal article. It was an obvious and inevitable transaction; professors adopted a writing style derived from the method they used in class. They applied the Method to specific areas by flushing out the key cases, then synthesized the holdings to generate principles applicable to practical problems. As we shall see, it is a methodology that still dominates legal scholarship.

The Class System

Legal education is obsessed with class distinction in schools, fields of instruction, publications, and scholarship. Classism starts with the controversy over ranking. The most influential ranking is the annual survey from *U.S.*

News and World Report, which divides the industry into five groups, with the top twenty-five constituting the elite class. While deans deplore the rankings as unscientific and irrelevant, every year the magazine's March edition is a sellout. A drop in ratings is a serious event; at Harvard the dean reportedly went "ballistic" when told his school had dropped to number five. He indignantly called the survey "Mickey Mouse," "just plain wacko," "totally bonkers," and "crazy." Demanding that *U.S. News* terminate its ranking, the AALS has called the practice "a deceiving misuse of information" and "irresponsible journalism."

You are on the tenure treadmill. Two articles will get you into the club. Publication in which law reviews ensures passage through the gate? The answer is a proxy for an identification of the Elite law schools. Elite schools command authority over legal education. For Harvard, Yale, Columbia, and Pennsylvania, it was a long and sustained presence that converted what started as a vocational system into the law academy. Michigan, Chicago, and Stanford educated their regions to the Eastern model. These schools are the Elite. While there may be a top twenty-five, not all of the twenty-five are elite.

"Let me give you some advice about teaching here. Our students are different; they're older, some have full-time jobs, and they pay their own way. Another thing— they don't give a damn about your theories, so don't preach. You are teaching guys who have one objective—to pass the bar. And don't underestimate them. They will make good lawyers who are willing to scratch and fight all the way. Most of the judges in this city come from here and not that private school down the road. One final word— and this is important—don't play absurd Socratic tricks on them. You're not dealing with college kids. Play games, and they will turn on you."

This was the advice I got from a colleague when I started teaching at a Skills law school over thirty years ago. Many of these schools are legacies of the night-law-school era that have survived by getting ABA certification. Others are relatively new schools that emerged to take advantage of the prosperous market of the 1980s and 1990s. They have developed a distinct market of lower-income students who may lack the necessary credentials for a "better" school or who have to work. Faced with the necessity of having to immediately earn an income upon passing the bar, the students want practical training, not theory. The Socratic Method is a nuisance to people who often have to cram reading cases into a work schedule. Because they can tell it like it is, adjunct professors are preferred.

Despite bad-mouthing from some of the upper-tier schools, Skills schools are a positive movement in legal education. They provide an opportunity for capable people to serve a client group that is otherwise ignored. By preference, faculty at Skills schools are not active in scholarship. Except for those people who seek to move up, publication is not a priority. For the Skills faculty, publishing how-to-do-it vocational material is enough to get tenure and keep the ABA accreditation people happy.

The mainstream is located in the second and third tiers of the *U.S. News* ranking, which constitutes more than a third of the 155 ABA-accredited schools. Around two-thirds of this group are state-supported. Mainstreamers are the pretenders to the top-tier group. They break down into two subcategories. *Pretenders I* like to think it is possible to develop a strategy that could enable them to push into the select group. Members of this group are likely to be susceptible to new programs, including Outsider advocacy and scholarship, as a way of outflanking the competition by getting quick media attention. The second group, *Pretenders II*, is more realistic and recognizes its limitations; its goal is to go after the *Pretenders I*.

Historically, Mainstream schools have functioned as a satellite system for the Elite. They measure performance according to the Elite model. The relationship started with the universalization of the Socratic Method as the dominant teaching technique. Since the wisdom of the Method came from Harvard and the other Elites, it was inevitable that these schools would be the primary source of instruction. And they were, thus confirming the superiority of an emerging Empire of Elites. What evolved was colonization: the circulation of Elite graduates around the country to show the natives how to use the Method.

"The pressure comes from alumni, the central administration, and even some faculty. It was always there; we had to hire someone from the Northeast establishment or we weren't respectable. Either we get some of those people or, they said, we would always be a regional school, a cut above the Skills shops. So what did we do? We let the bright people from the Utahs, North Carolinas, and Wisconsins slip through; we simply ignore them, never interview them, and hire people from the bottom of the barrel from Yale, Harvard, and the rest. And those professors from the Eastern schools would give their people rave recommendations, knowing that they were lying through their teeth. But it didn't make a damn difference to them; all they wanted was to colonize us." (Professor explaining his negative vote on hiring a young Yale graduate)

When the Elite schools started requiring a faculty commitment to scholarship, Mainstream schools tracked along. It was an easy decision because it gave them the opportunity to use scholarship to emphasize a dedication to theory and thus put more distance between them and the Skills schools. They could polish the national law school image by publishing articles on the same topics as the other national schools. Some of the more astute deans and faculty discerned another benefit: scholarship was a quick and efficient way of getting a jump on rivals in the reputation game. Hire bright young people and motivate them to publish by dangling salary and perquisites in their faces. The strategy worked for schools like Duke, now ensconced in the *U.S. News* top twenty-five. There was another advantage—it cost less to underwrite scholarship than to initiate flashy programs that rarely produce a profit.

The consequence was the transformation of the role of scholarship in legal education and law. To keep up with the competition, schools had no choice but to produce scholarship. While vocational writing was tolerated, it was the doctrinal article that emerged as the model for most authors. The subject was law, not economics, psychology, or sociology; the primary audience was the bar and the judiciary. Publication became the most important factor in the allocation of salary and grants. The production of scholarship gave law professors semirespectability with colleagues in other disciplines.

The scholarship wave was responsible for the existence of the law review system as the primary outlet for legal writing. Mainstream schools had a heavy stake in subsidizing a journal: it ensured an outlet for its faculty. In addition, without a journal, a school could not expect to be a player in the new competition. The standard peer review journal was out of the question; the cost of a full-time editor and staff to proof and cite-check was well beyond the budget. The substitute was already in place at the Eastern Elite schools like Harvard and Penn—the low-cost student-edited journal. A student journal served another purpose: it could be hyped as a valuable teaching tool and a résumé asset. Professors had reason to support the student-controlled system; unlike other disciplines, which are dominated by a small cluster of journals, the large number of law journals virtually ensures publication, regardless of quality.

The Personality of Power

From the late 1800s until World War II, Harvard Law School was the center of authority. It had influential faculty, the Socratic Method, and the best students. Harvard's sphere of influence expanded over the years to embrace Yale, Columbia, Pennsylvania, Michigan, and Stanford into the elite core of the Empire. This is not to suggest that everyone slavishly imitated Harvard. There was an aggressive challenge by the Legal Realists at Columbia and Yale. Advocating the use of empirical social science methods, the Realists probed the authority of traditional legal scholarship. They anticipated the Outsider movement by questioning doctrinal assumptions on certainty and objectivity.

The Traditionalists and the Realists were more alike than different. As a group, they stood with the fictional Kingsfield, dedicated to law as a profession and committed to fulfilling their responsibilities as priests. Some may not have come from New England (Dean Pound of Harvard came from Nebraska), but they soon acquired the Brahmin view of life and law. One did not apply for a teaching position; one was called. And one followed orders. Grant Gilmore: "At the end of World War II, I gratefully accepted an invitation to join the faculty of Yale Law School. When I reported for duty in New Haven, Dean Wesley Sturges said to me, 'You will teach sales.' I said, 'Yes, sir.'"

Those who were called to teach were expected to replicate the work and perspectives of their predecessors. The process left nothing to chance. New faculty were nominated by a select group of senior people who had a vested interest in maintaining the prevailing culture. It was not participatory democracy. The gate into the club was narrowed by the mandatory credentials: degree from the right school, law review, a significant clerkship, followed by employment at a white-shoe law firm or respectable government service. If judges and lawyers were, by de Tocqueville's reckoning, the aristocracy, then the Kingsfield law professors were the elite of the aristocracy.

There was another type of replication: *Williston, Leach, Seavy, Cardozo, Wigmore, Loss, Beale, Pomeroy, Frank, Frankfurter, Warren, Ballantine, Osborne, Clark, Gray, Chafee, Douglas, Holmes, Llewellyn, Fuller, Pound, Corbin, Goebel, Wambaugh, Currie, Thayer, Ames, Arnold, Cook, Lasswell, Patterson, Hutchins, Cavers, Bogert, Freund, Bigelow.*

This is a list of some of the players who dominated the *Kingsfield Period*, 1900–1945. They provided the scholarship and wisdom of legal education. Some of the names—Corbin, Williston, and Wigmore, for example—still resonate in classrooms and research. There is, however, an interesting fact: there are no women or Blacks on the list.

The Elite schools synergized to establish productive connections to government, politics, and practice. It started with admissions strategy. In a conversation with an Elite admissions director, I jokingly suggested that wealth beat merit in determining who got into his school. He gave me a good-natured grin, a mixture of smugness and caginess, and allowed that as the best law school in the world, his place had an obligation to educate those who would eventually shape national policy. He added: "It doesn't hurt our endowment."

He was serious. It might sound arrogant, but it is a strategy that works. In contemporary vernacular, it is a version of diversity; minorities are admitted to create a sociological mix, while the rich and powerful are admitted for the same reason. This does not interfere with the Elites' ability to get the best students. There is another way to spread influence—a geographical diversity program. By reserving slots for geographical admissions ("we need someone from Montana to circulate our influence in the Western region"), a school like Harvard touches every obscure part of the country and the world.

Synergism flourishes as faculties use contacts to channel the best students to prestigious clerkships or to white-shoe law firms. A few are called back to be faculty or recommended to teach at other law schools, while the bulk go on to financially successful and influential careers. They perpetuate the network and underwrite the endowment. The result is a law school–controlled network of lawyers, law firms, and judiciary. To the Outsiders, the network is the glue that binds the Elite schools to the evil world of the mega-law firms. It is a Mephistophelian quid pro quo deal; the megas reserve slots for the best and brightest, while the law schools teach what Chris Goodrich calls "law think—the ability to play a game without caring who wins or loses, or even whether the game is completed."

The sociologist Robert Granfield writes that the network encourages the top-tier schools to produce money-grubbing elite lawyers at the expense of public-interest defenders. His study of Harvard Law School concludes that students enter school with ideologically Liberal-left mind-sets and public-interest motivations but at graduation jump to the power firms engaged in protecting capitalism. What happens to youthful idealism? It is drained away by the capitalist lacky professors who teach the "ideology of neutrality" and "capitalist logic." "Students were taught the ability to justify their opinions on legal grounds as opposed to ideological or substantive ones." They are conned into comprehending tax law as something other than "dirty," while discovering that corporate law can actually be interesting. Instead of the polar positions of good or bad, students "see more gray areas." In short, they become professionals and, as a result, lose touch with "an orientation toward social justice."

To the Corbins and their colleagues, legal education was law—a preface to practice. Government and politics were of peripheral interest, something to consider with brandy when discussing the most recent judicial appointment. If anything, their politics were conservative Northeastern Republicanism. Then came the massive political energy of the New Deal.

More than members of any other profession, lawyers and law professors were the beneficiaries of Franklin Roosevelt's victory. The New Deal produced a new government crammed full of agencies, all requiring the skills of lawyers. The stampede of law professors to Washington, D.C., added the word "Liberal" to white male. It was an illustrious group, people like Thurman Arnold, William O. Douglas, and James Landis. Landis's experience made it look easy. He started as a Harvard student, then clerked for Justice Brandeis. He was called back to teach at Harvard, where he drafted legislation for the New Deal, then took a leave of absence to serve on the Federal Trade Commission. He went on to chair the Securities and Exchange Commission and completed the cycle by returning to the Law School as dean.

The model for the law professor as Liberal political operative was Felix Frankfurter, who dedicated a career to spreading the influence of New Deal Liberalism. He traveled in the highest circles, going from Harvard law professor to Supreme Court Justice. Frankfurter knew Franklin Roosevelt on a first-name basis. Perhaps his greatest achievement was a generation of "happy hot dogs," the numerous former students imbued with Liberal ideology whom he helped position with the newly created agencies. His explanation for success in getting hot dogs placed: "Why? Because I'd been at the Harvard Law School from 1914, and this was 1933, and because of the kind of people the Harvard Law School was turning out. . . . I was doing for the administration what I had been doing for big offices from the time I was at the Harvard Law School, year after year after year."

The underground railroad from the law academy to the federal empire in the nation's capital is now accepted custom. Years ago one of my deans, a Harvard man, sent me packing to the Department of Justice, advising me that one cannot have a career in legal education without the experience of government service. "It is tradition," he said.

If there was any doubt about the law academy's commitment to Liberalism, it was erased in the fight over Robert Bork's nomination to the Supreme Court. Never before had so many law professors been mobilized to influence a nomination. In the process of fighting against the nomination, Liberals were forced to do some embarrassing convolutions and weaseling when it came to the attack on Bork's scholarship.

As a nationally recognized antitrust scholar at Yale Law School, Robert Bork persuasively challenged the populist school of antitrust that had prevailed during the Warren Court years. Cutting against the conventional wisdom, he and a few colleagues used writing to elevate the Chicago School of Economics to the level of a competing mainstream view. If Bork had continued to compete for dominance of antitrust ideology and stayed away from constitutional law, he would be sitting on the Supreme Court.

When Bork entered the constitutional law field, he had to deal with the ideological center of Liberalism. The inefficiency of the administration agency system forced Liberals to turn to the judiciary to control the economy. Academic scholarship encouraged judicial activism as the quickest and most effective way of mainlining Liberalism into society. From the 1970s on, constitutional law has been *the* course, a Mecca for Liberal-left students and a course that young professors fought to teach. The course was, and is, the vehicle for Liberal value judgments and for trashing conservative views. When Robert Bork published scholarship with a conservative theme, he was an automatic outcast. He dropped from a lofty reputation as an antitrust scholar to the outsider status of conservative zealot.

Although the opposition was composed of a broad collection of leftists, feminists, and various Liberal groups, the law professors conducted the attack on Bork's paper trail. The most manifest evidence of Liberal dominance in legal education came from opposition letters. Senator Edward Kennedy introduced opposing letters from thirty-two law deans and seventy-two constitutional law professors. Senator Joseph Biden submitted a list of 1,925 law professors (40 percent of all full-time faculty) who opposed Bork's nomination.

In the promotion and tenure context, Liberals ostensibly adhere to the conventional rule of objectivity, an evaluation process that focuses on the depth and thoroughness of research and the success of the author in rebutting challenges. So long as it meets analytical and research criteria, criticism of accepted wisdom is encouraged. As a professor, Bork met the criteria. When he became a Supreme Court nominee, however, his work was evaluated by a political test: was it consistent with mainstream Liberal interpretation?

It was obvious manipulation of scholarship criteria. Max Lerner wrote that after Bork's rejection: "[T]he word went forth to every law school that those with federal court ambitions must travel a safe constitutional journey, with no paper trial and no bite to their tongue or pen." The Bork conflict also confirmed a festering suspicion held by Outsiders, who assume that the Liberal establishment relies on a political mainstream test to keep them out of the loop: write about feminism or take up the racial critique cause and get "Borked."

The story within the story of the Bork imbroglio was the splintering of the New Deal Liberal establishment. Mary Ann Glendon of Harvard divides law faculties into left and right: "The right is composed mainly of New Deal Democrats and libertarians, who are traditionalists with regard to scholarship and standards." Her Liberal rightists are the Buffaloes—white males in their fifties who added affirmative action to New Deal economics. They are the last group to have studied under New Deal mentors. To them, the Socratic Method defines the grand tradition of law. The Buffaloes are split on interdisciplinary writing; the law and economics work is acceptable (economics is, after all, a science), but the law and a banana writing is disdained as fluff.

Buffaloes protect their turf by screening new hires. Most faculties have added young people who share the Liberal view on scholarship. There are subtle but critical differences between Buffaloes and the new traditionalists. The latter are more tolerant of Outsider ideology, especially when it comes to teaching law and a banana courses. The Buffalo influence is much stronger in the second-tier schools. Close ties to the bar and bench precludes experimentation in nontraditional types of courses. In more than twenty-five years at my school, I have never seen Liberal dominance diluted, even with the addition of women and minorities. It is simply a matter of careful screening.

What accounts for Outsider infiltration of the club? First, some of the new traditionalists are turning, that is, being converted; their experiences are more congenial to the Outsiders. It is more chic to play the role of Tenured Radical. Second, as Richard Delgado suggests, the rational strategy is to play the possum role. Get tenure with conventional work, then go after the Empire rascals. Third, the Liberals have always been naive about threats from within the big tent. All right-thinking Liberals have the same vision; how can anyone reject the wisdom of the Empire?

The deans are staunch supporters of the Buffaloes. They know where they come from; the Buffaloes recommend them, and the administration and trustees with Liberal instincts approve their hire. Because Buffalo Liberals are predictable and easier to handle, Buffalo deans prefer a Buffalo faculty. Alumni support Liberal deans because they are from the same mold—and who could tolerate a Duncan Kennedy or Derrick Bell type of dean?

3

Empire Scholarship: What Are They Protecting?

"It Is the Best Law Review Article I Have Ever Read!"

Ignatius B. Moot knew it was a stacked committee. Everyone owed the Dean a favor. Moot's debt was big time. When that crazy feminist entrapped me on the couch and threatened harassment charges, sexual idiosyncrasies, she said, the good old Dean shut her up with a nice clerkship with one of his buddies. Now it is payback time. It was simple. The Dean needed a Black woman. It was nonnegotiable. The Provost's word was final—get one or I cut your budget. Moot's orders were equally direct. A unanimous Promotion and Tenure recommendation for Professor Evelyn Allegory.

What the hell was going on? Moot could not believe it. What should have been a cinch, a short, perfunctory meeting, was now a shouting match and so far a three-two vote against Allegory. It was that weirdo Peabody Snopes. What was he so obstinate about—he had not published a sentence in fifteen years. He would not shut up!

"Don't you get it, Moot, she writes stories. STORIES!" Snopes was in his early sixties and overweight, which added to his Ben Franklin appearance. "This is supposed to be legal scholarship and what does she do—gives us a tale about some incident at a grocery store, something about someone cutting in front of her at the checkout line. What did she call it, a soul crime! Hell, that happens to me all the time. I don't waste time writing articles about it."

Moot knew the old goat was right, but he owed the Dean. "You don't understand what her genre is. It's agony experience. It's about the gaps in the system that the oppressed fall into. Allegory uses the agony of a racial insult to flush out what has to be done. For God's sake, Snopes, articles don't have to be crammed full of footnotes to be scholarship."

Snopes exploded. "Don't you ever tell me about footnotes, and never lecture me about legal scholarship, you poseur."

Now Moot remembered. Snopes was a one-article phenomenon who had published a major piece early in his career and that had been it. He was frozen in that one burst of glory. Realizing he could never duplicate the flash of genius or, as he sometimes admitted to himself in a drunken stupor, the flash of luck, Snopes wrote nothing. It was the only way to maintain a slice of dignity.

Snopes was now subdued and continued in a near-reverential tone. "My article [everyone in the room knew that he was talking about The Article] was modeled after a piece by Don Turner, and, listen to me, Moot, the Turner piece is the best law review article I have ever read!

"The Turner article had something that none of you people are acquainted with, a quality that was lost in the 1970s shuffle of values. It made a statement about a legal problem. Let me explain. Most of what comes out now is either scrambled eggs—saying what is already known but mixing it into an incoherent style—or incremental, which is adding superficial and irrelevant analysis or vacuous comments to accepted wisdom. Moot, everything you publish is incremental. You spit trivial things out to pad your résumé, get cites from your buddies, and justify hiring bimbo student assistants to play couch music with you. I admit, it works; you are one of the highest paid poseurs on this faculty.

"The first rule of legal scholarship is that it has to deal with something of consequence. That's what Turner did. He went after some formidable puzzles of the black hole of antitrust. Consider the mysteries of oligopoly, Moot. How can three firms in a market get away with charging virtually the same prices? Remember when Ralph Nader raised hell about the Big Three auto makers in the fifties; he wanted the Antitrust Division to break them up. But how? The Sherman Act requires conspiracy: he could never get it through his stubborn mind that there may be one hell of a conspiracy problem.

"This is the problem that Turner discusses—what to do in a market in which rational oligopolists will settle on uniform prices without meeting in a smelly bar at midnight to conspire. They don't need to go to a bar; if one raises prices and the others do not, the price raiser loses business to the others, and obviously it is in everyone's interest not to lower prices. Turner's discussion undoubtedly did not placate Nader, but it gave the people responsible for dealing with the problem a clear guide for decision making.

"The next rule is analyze, analyze, and analyze. It's hard to beat Turner on analysis. He covers every twist and issue of the oligopoly pricing problem. For example, he acknowledges that it ostensibly makes sense to characterize oligopoly parallel pricing as illegal; in other words, Nader may have a case against the Big Three. But, as a practical matter, a victory would have been a superfluous gesture because there is no effective remedy.

"Let me ask you a question, Moot. Who is Allegory writing for? We know that she is writing about herself; that is why she calls her story an agony experience. It's auto-

biographical. That's what I get when I scan what she is really writing, long op-ed pieces on her agony. But who is her audience? The readers of Ms., *the* Village Voice, *or* The New Yorker? The Nation *would love her op-ed stuff. But her audience is sure as hell not anyone in this law school or anyone I know in the legal community."*

Snopes's question interrupted Moot's thoughts of his new student assistant. This was the first Asian he had recruited. *"I told you that she is writing for you and everyone here. We have to cut through our white male biases to. . . ."*

Waving his arm to cut off Moot's nonsense, Snopes continued. *"No, Allegory ignores rule three—know your audience. Even your incremental trivia is targeted to someone, obviously of modest intellect, in the legal community. Scholars like Don Turner always start with a primary audience, a group that will understand every nuance of the work. The primary market for the Turner article was the antitrust enforcement community—the Antitrust Division and the Federal Trade Commission. His message was that what looks like reasonable policy is instead impractical. The secondary audience was his colleagues in the academy, people that he can engage in an ongoing dialogue."*

"There is something else. Where are her footnotes? Let me tell you about. . . ."

Moot looked at the ceiling. *The hell with the Dean; it's a lost cause. That old fool will never let up.*

The Politics of the Zone

When Michael Jordan is in a zone, he scores at will. Every player will hit a zone at least once in his life. Snopes was in a zone when he wrote his career article. Unfortunately, zones are always followed by dry periods. A player reacts by persistent adherence to what got him in the zone, knowing that his efforts may be wasted. It is instinct. The same pattern holds for academics like Snopes. He is in an extended dry period, but he still knows the correct form for getting back into the scholarship zone. He therefore disdains Moot's incrementalism as pseudoscholarship. To Snopes, it's better not to do anything than to sink into the sewer of ignominious incrementalism.

The disagreement over the correct zone of scholarship is an inevitable part of the politics of legal education. To paraphrase George Orwell's *Animal Farm* characters, some type of work is more equal than others. What would, for example, Moot and Snopes do with Professor Clare Dalton's tenure piece "An Essay in the Deconstruction of Contract Doctrine"? She endeavors to show objectivity in contract law as a sleight-of-hand facade that hides the pressures of subjectivity, substance, and intent. Dalton uses cases and literature to revise contract doctrine into various types of indeterminacy, concluding: "Thus our concern with form and substance, and manifestation and intent, are but particular expressions of our inability to resolve the tension between public and private, self and other."

As an incrementalist, Moot would argue that Dalton goes too far by rejecting the certainty and direction of precedent. Snopes would accuse Dalton of playing Critical Legal Studies politics: the dominant system uses ostensible objectivity to hide oppression, hierarchy, and patriarchy. A colleague of mine, a Harvard Law graduate, called it one of the best articles on contract theory he has read. On the other hand, a substantial number of Dalton's colleagues at Harvard Law School concluded that it did not measure up to their tenure standards.

Which is the best advice—Moot's incrementalism, Snopes's code of The Article, or Dalton's Critspeak? What about Bell's narratives—is that legal scholarship? The answer starts with the *Harvard Law Review*.

The commercial journals that first serviced the profession specialized in practical articles for practitioners. The student-edited law reviews revolutionized the market by shifting focus to the academic style. Doctrinal writing became a reality with the first edition of the *Harvard Law Review* in 1887. Trading on an 1861 English decision, J. B. Ames examined the problems of protecting a purchaser for value without notice of a defect in title. It took him sixteen pages, with cites to six treatises plus English and American decisions, to conclude that "The purchaser of any right, in its nature transmissible . . . acquires the right free from all equities of which he had no notice at the time of its acquisition." Simeon Baldwin's article on voting trusts in the first *Yale Law Journal* in 1891 followed the same form—fifteen pages, but fewer footnotes and no treatise cites.

The University of Pennsylvania started publishing in 1896, followed by Columbia in 1901. It was evident that scholarship was entering a new level. The student reviews were achieving their goal of producing an indigenous body of American academic legal scholarship. In Columbia's first edition, Professor William Keener mediated the differing views of Dean Langdell and Samuel Williston, the emerging expert in contracts. The ascendancy of the law review article signaled the end of the English influence and, as time elapsed, reduced reliance on treatises.

As a group, the early articles were succinct and practical; each article focused on a specific problem. It was a steady diet of common law: equity, trusts, and contracts. The first Harvard edition included an article entitled "Tickets": "The use of tickets by railroad companies has in the last thirty years given great and increasing legal significance to that species of document." Articles were characterized by basic lawyerlike analysis; as with any good scientist, the objective was to uncover a guiding principle or rule of law. Footnotes were for tell, not for show.

The articles were well written and problem focused and could serve today as models for a first-year writing course. However, neither Moot nor Snopes would accept them as scholarship: "Too vocational, too simplistic; there is no there there." "Those old guys," according to Moot, "didn't know how to play the footnote game, to get the reader's attention with obscure references or hot quotes. Another thing—look at how many of those old men ended up with a footnote of an even number—which is feminine. Maybe there is a message there." "Where is the advocacy? They are too neutral." "The things they wrote about are as exciting as growing grass." In fact, Moot and Snopes are correct: the first wave of law review scholarship survives as historical references, guaranteed to get frowns and rejection from a contemporary promotion and tenure committee.

In 1933, the University of Chicago joined the law review market by publishing an array of articles that confirmed a tilt away from common law topics. It was New Deal time; the focus was on the government regulation of economic recovery. Also in 1933 Harvard published seven of a total of twenty-four articles on New Deal regulation, while Yale covered the Securities Act of 1933 (including a piece by Assistant Professor William O. Douglas). The typical article lengthened, doubling the average fifteen pages of the early reviews. In the interval, writers had learned to use footnotes for more than source reference. Impertinence arrived when Barton Leach of Harvard used a footnote to slam the esteemed John Chapman Gray: "It is hard to be deferential in suggesting that this doesn't make sense." It was clear that, by 1933, it was the best of times for the doctrinal article.

The 1933–34 law review season included the publication of Duke Law School's David Cavers's "A Critique of the Choice of Law Problem," an early model for doctrinal scholarship. The scholar's responsibility is to identify and resolve problems exemplified in the rules-versus-precedent controversy. Finding chaos in the battle of rules, Carvers sought to demonstrate the "fresh appeal" of shifting focus to fact analysis. In a burst of candor, he confessed in a footnote that he was "not without sin" for having previously supported a rules solution.

With articles like the Cavers piece, the doctrinal formula was set. It starts with the statement of a problem, followed by the identification and discussion of prevailing perspectives and solutions. Objectivity rules; the existing positions have to be acknowledged and thoroughly explored. The ultimate direction can veer toward Moot's incrementalism, which adds gloss but sticks with the prevailing view. Snopes wants something more dramatic—a new solution or, like Professor Cavers, a dramatic shift in the focus of the scholarship on the problem. Footnotes played a critical role by providing an opportunity to engage in additional layers of analysis and criticism. In contemporary terms, this is called the "barking from the bottom of the page."

When a colleague publishes in a top journal, Snopes has two reactions: the observation that its acceptance was pure luck, followed by a tirade against the subversive effects of incremental work. Sooner or later, he targets Moot, accusing him of producing law versions of *Cliff Notes*, only "not as thorough and understandable. Moot is strictly a Grub Street hack. He is embarrassing us with a constant stream of what is essentially *vocational* writing!"

Vocational is the most basic form of legal scholarship. The objective is to describe law as it is: no policy ruminations, avoidance of extensive analysis and synthesis, and certainly no Moot incrementalism. Vocationalism dominated the early stages of scholarship, mainly through practitioner-oriented journals and treatises. The first wave of law reviews contributed to the movement by publishing outlines from selected lectures. In the first edition of 1887, the *Harvard Law Review* published its version of *Gilbert's* outline in the form of *Lecture Notes* from Ames, Langdell, Thayer, and Gray.

Contempt for vocational work is often merciless. No one in his right mind would take the chance of relying on anything resembling vocational writing to get tenure at a good school. As a cross is the kiss of death to a vampire, so is the word "descriptive" anathema to the law academic. Scholars must do more than merely describe fads, arguments, and what judges say. Critics associate certainty with description. Certainty is what Jerome Frank of Yale called *The Basic Myth*: "Lawyers do not merely sustain the vulgar notion that law is capable of being made entirely stable and unvarying; they seem bent on creating the impression that, on the whole, it is already established and certain."

The Law in decisions, statutes, regulations, and facts can never achieve finality or definiteness, and to Frank this is not an "unfortunate accident" but the genius of social growth. "Law, in attempting a harmony of these conflicting demands, is at best governed by the 'logic of probabilities.'" Anything, such as vocational writing, that contributes to the Myth is untenable and to be repudiated. In contemporary times, Outsiders consider vocationalism as a variant of doctrinal writing, which they consider to be a vehicle for maintaining the myth of determinacy.

The doctrinalists of the Empire are extremely sensitive to the Outsider charge that they use scholarship to perpetuate false determinacy. To even tolerate vocational writing with its reputation for manufacturing pseudocertainty is to risk guilt by association. The obvious way to avoid this risk is to condemn and suppress vocationalism as nonscholarship, something comparable to what Outsiders produce.

Efforts at suppression have failed. A harvest of vocational writing comes off law review pages each year. For many lower-tier law schools committed to skills training, practical-oriented scholarship is a logical corollary and suffices for promotion and tenure. By use of copious footnoting and obfuscation, vocational writing can be recast to come across as doctrinal. Professor Moot often does this, except that he calls it incrementalism. Much of vocational work is superficial and best ignored, but the same can be said about the bulk of doctrinal writing. What the doctrinal people choose to brush aside is that there is a demand for vocationalism and that it can be, on its own terms, a valid form of scholarship.

Although he died in 1985, Melville B. Nimmer is the authority on copyright. His treatise, *Nimmer on Copyright* (updated by his son David), is both practical and elegant. It is practical because it counsels lawyers how to advise clients and try cases. Judges go to *Nimmer* first. He brings definition to black holes like the conflict between the First Amendment and copyright.

In a short article on copyright infringement, Nimmer refutes the criticism that vocational writing is simply stringing cases together. To establish liability, courts require the plaintiff to prove that the defendant made a substantial appropriation of the copied work. But why? In responding to this question, Nimmer does what all good vocationalists do: he goes to history to bring light to the gaps and puzzles.

Initially plagiarism actions were brought in equity which required proof of substantial injury for relief. If a plaintiff could not show a substantial injury, the action went to a court of law for damages. This procedural requirement became moot with the passage of the Copyright Act of 1909, which combined actions for injunction, damages, and profits. Yet the courts continued to require proof of substantial appropriation for *any* relief, thereby converting a procedural requirement into a substantive requirement.

Nimmer may be stringing cases together, but he does it to expose an anomaly and to ask "whether there is any rationale which warrants the conversion of the equity principle into a substantive rule of copyright law." He refers to two problem areas in copying: infringement of embellishments and plots. He starts with three embellishment decisions in which the court denied relief even though there was evidence of substantial appropriation. Nimmer concluded that the courts' denial was intentional; courts feared that "the progress of the arts would be hampered if writers were not allowed to copy such embellishments, for to some extent, the protection of embellishments would retard the production of literature." This conclusion does not make sense to Nimmer, since hindering the creative process is the inevitable result of any copyright system. The real issue is whether the copier should be granted a free ride at the expense of the creative author.

Plot protection is one of the mysteries of copyright. Confusion reigns in separating an unprotectable idea from a protectable expression. To Nimmer's chagrin, courts use the substantial appropriation principle in an effort to cut through confusion. The cases show that authors are denied protection even for a dramatic work that is "sufficiently developed so as to be more than a mere idea or one of the few irreducible plots."

Hence, as to both embellishment and plot, the existence of the substantial injury rule results in discrimination against authors while favoring copiers. The practical effect—and the irony—of the rule is that authors who can prove *actual* appropriation are denied *any* recovery even though the copyright law permits damages.

Nimmer's work explains why the vocational genre is defended by a solid minority as the only acceptable form of legal scholarship. He speaks to lawyers and judges in their language. He practices the Langdellian thesis that the final authority comes from a careful reading of the cases. It was the courts, not academics, that converted a procedural rule into a substantive principle.

New Deal Journalism

In 1936, Professor Fred Rodell of Yale Law School came out with a short essay titled "Goodbye to Law Reviews." It became his reputation. Every time someone takes a swing at the law review system, Rodell is a boilerplate cite. The article titillates with an ironical twist—law professor biting the hand that gives him tenure and fame. Rodell was succinct: "There are two things wrong with almost all legal writing. One is its style. The other is its content. That, I think, about covers the ground." Then he gets mean and personal: "The average law review writer is peculiarly able to say nothing with an air of great importance."

The irony of Rodell's essay is that his writing was the best evidence of his criticism. Rodell was a member of the Liberal front that saturated the law reviews with New Deal scholarship. The front's objective was straightforward: rationalize the New Deal. The need for thorough analysis and consideration of the potential negative effects of regulatory operation was obviated by the crisis of depression and inflation. There was a sense of self-righteousness; it would be a waste of time to analyze the new laws for harmful effects since they would likely fall on the class that caused the crisis—the reactionary wealthy and the Wall Street crowd.

Rodell's contributions to the front's legal journalism was his slant on the then new securities regulations. It was formula writing; the reactionary opposition, especially the Wall Street–controlled media, was out to discredit the new regulatory scheme with disinformation about adverse effects on investors who in reality would receive improved protection. The real threat came from a pre–New Deal judiciary, which showed hostility to the unrestrained exercise of agency discretion. Rodell's conclusion stated the obvious: "The Federal Securities Act was passed to protect individuals from losing their money by investing it in unsoundly or unscrupulously financed business enterprises." Three years after making this profound comment, Rodell wrote in "Goodbye to Law Reviews" that it is "the content of legal writing that makes the literature of the law a dud and a disgrace."

In 1965 Justice Douglas delivered a speech to the *University of Washington Law Review* editors in which he condemned articles for hire. He referred to professors who publish ostensibly objective articles that were financed by interested parties. Douglas said: "I fear that law journals have been more seriously corrupted by nondisclosure than we imagine." He recommended that law reviews adopt a policy of full disclosure of relevant affiliation and fees. By focusing on the hired professor, Douglas sidestepped the more prevalent and complex problem of ideological stealth publishing. Perhaps the Justice did not want to touch on something he had been part of—result-oriented advocacy by the New Deal academic front. It was an imaginative and productive group, but few were as effective and persuasive as Thurman Arnold of Yale.

The muscle of New Deal recovery was composed of a labyrinth of agencies and regulations touching every form of economic activity. F.D.R.'s administration had public and congressional support, leaving one formidable obstacle—the federal judiciary. As an institution with core conservative values and lifetime tenure, the federal courts were a serious threat to the regulatory apparatus. It was inevitable that Arnold would go after the last bastion of reactionary resistance. He made a reputation for vigorously challenging what he called myths of conservativism. In a book published in 1935, *The Symbols of Government*, Arnold attacked the court system for its role as an instrument for hit-or-miss conservative social planning, a theme he started in a 1934 *Harvard Law Review* article.

Arnold set the mood with the title: "Trial by Combat and the New Deal." Trial means adversarial engagement, rather than mediation or accommodation. The negatives of trial by combat are emphasized. By focusing on specific parties and narrowing the issues, trials have limited range and effect. Trial-by-combat lawyers script evidence and bend facts to support their client's interests. Truth is expendable; the objective is jury persuasion. In other words, it's an irrational mess. And who rationalizes the mess? "[T]he ordinary teacher of law will insist (1) that combat makes for clarity, (2) that heated arguments bring out the truth, and (3) that anyone who doesn't believe this is a loose thinker."

Outsiders could take lessons in trashing from that good ol' white male Liberal, Thurman Arnold. He first sets up the court system as a "mystical institution," a reflection of the dominant government ideals. If courts function to conduct trials by combat, it's because of a "public psychology which compels them to play that part." And, the "part" courts play is the encouragement of rugged individualism and the opposition of regulation. Arnold reads like a lecture from the Crits, the New Deal's version of Duncan Kennedy. As proxy for the dominant "public psychology," courts encourage "businessmen to fight each other for business . . . litigants to fight each other to obtain law," while "withholding legal rights from those who will not fight." Like the Outsiders, Arnold does not suffer criticism lightly; conservative warnings about regulation "have assumed an indigo hue which is quite pathetic."

The article is a shill for New Deal regulation and bureaucracy, provocative without pretense at balanced analysis and objectivity. Arnold concludes with the sanguine surmise that the "public psychology" is changing, trial by combat will be perceived as absurd in the face of efficient planning and regulation, and there "are signs everywhere that government regulation is becoming an accepted ideal."

More Liberal Advocacy

By 1940 the New Deal was the law of the land, the alphabet agencies were busy regulating, and the Supreme Court, with its newly appointed Justice,

William O. Douglas, was drifting to the left. The focus of New Deal academic writing shifted from proposing regulations to interpretation and fine tuning. The scholar advocates continued to follow a left-Liberal political agenda, eschewing balance or objectivity. There were some differences—two Yale professors disagreed over the effectiveness of the Bituminous Coal Act of 1937—but everyone was on the same page of rationalizing the New Deal.

The war was a year away, and scholars were anticipating the problems with titles such as "The Rule of Law in Total War"; "Neutrality and the European War"; "Legislative Restrictions on Foreign Enlistment and Travel"; "Wartime Conscription and Control of Labor"; and "Some Aspects of Military Service." The war articles tended to be descriptive and heavy on history. "The pay of the Roman soldier, like that of his present compier, was nothing to boast about but he did have special privileges as to marriage, inheritance, and the making of wills." It was nuts and bolts vocational writing.

The Empire cannot escape the persistent appearance of one-sided advocacy writing. In "Trial by Ordeal, New Style," a Yale law professor took on a socially acceptable Liberal cause, defending Bertrand Russell. In a taxpayer's suit, a New York court found Russell's appointment to a philosophy chair at City College "an insult to the people of New York City." Citing "filth" from his books advocating sex before marriage, adultery, masturbation, and toleration of homosexuality, the Court concluded that Russell's presence would seduce young students into violating various penal laws.

It was not exactly a Sacco-Vanzetti cause, but it was a cleaner issue. No one knows whether the immigrants murdered that guard at Braintree, but there is no doubt about the injustice meted out to Russell. Something else made this an appealing cause to a Liberal academic: what was at issue was a philosophical inquiry into the meaning of morality and its role in society. This was an article that was bound to get nods of approval from colleagues at sherry time.

"Trial by Ordeal" reads like a polemic from *The New Republic*. The professor adopts the sneer and assault rhetoric of that magazine's former editor Michael Kinsley. The syntax, incorporating seventy-word sentences, is pretentious and academically correct. The theme is that the judge is an ass "who is superbly unaware of the hazards indigenous to his calling" and who, in the course of his decision, "rises to every error which opportunity presents." The New York judge, more suited for the Bible Belt, was determined to deny Russell "the immemorial right to answer to charges filed." The indignant professor even goes after the plaintiff for "tattling to the court" and using the gimmick of a taxpayer's suit to get standing. In today's climate, his references to her gender would be deemed sexist.

"Trial by Ordeal" is an entertaining exercise in Liberal fervor and indignation at reactionary lapses. It is definitely not in the style that Langdell would have endorsed. On the other hand, the sharp tone would certainly amuse the Outsider people. The piece anticipates the angry-voice style that Derrick Bell and Richard Delgado would use forty years later.

Rebuttal articles were the fashion in the 1940s. There were rejoinders, replications, addendums, demurrers, and postscriptions. In law review practice, rebuttal pieces are generally argumentative and do not adhere to the neutral-objective script that is expected in vocational-doctrinal scholarship. They read more like legal briefs; the author's argument becomes his client, and the objective is to win the argument.

"Sabotage and National Defense," a rebuttal to the Model Sabotage Prevention Act, demonstrates the aggressive crossfire technique. The act was designed to revise state penal codes to accommodate expected Axis sabotage efforts. "Sabotage is far more dangerous now than it has ever been in the past, because in the mechanized war of today the products of the factory are essential to the success of the army." Activities like loosening bolts in machinery or putting emery dust in gear boxes were not covered in a way commensurate with the crime of sabotage. Another problem was the difficulty of legally detaining trespassers on plant property. The act would make it easier to detect, detain, and convict saboteurs.

From a labor union standpoint, the act was an assault on the members' rights. Sabotage and picketing the employer's property were the unions' primary offensive weapons. The act permits, even encourages, "a blitzkrieg on labor and other groups, and in effect a sabotage of the constitutional liberties of the American people." It was a "frame-up" act to ensnare workers. (Frame-up to academicians meant "little more than a logical abstraction called 'perjury' or 'lawless enforcement of the law.'") "Carelessness" by a union member could be converted into sabotage, followed by prosecution by an ambitious prosecutor before "a jury of inflamed farmers, or conservative businessmen."

At the conclusion, crossfire turns to ideological finesse. Forget about the sabotage threat from the Axis and from Fascists. The real threat comes from inside the plant, where breakdowns in defense production come from manufacturers who engage in repressive strikebreaking activities. "This is the first and most important form of sabotage of national defense which must be disposed of." How? Easy—make violations of the National Labor Relations Act by employers criminal violations, and "we might really put a stop to the sabotage of defense on a colossal scale."

The Sabotage Act article was more than a crossfire rebuttal—it was also an oppression piece. It was the minority group that would pay the price at the hands of unscrupulous employers and prosecutors. The Sabotage Act was a declaration of class warfare and the threat of frame-ups "to labor, to the Negro people, and to all minority, underprivileged, or oppressed groups who must struggle to attain their social aspirations."

Finally, there is the intriguing question as to whether the rebuttal subsumed a stealth factor in the sense that there was an undisclosed motive involved. Lee Pressman, one of the coauthors and a former *Harvard Law Review* editor (where he was "Leon"), was a member of the Communist Party. He, along with Alger Hiss and Whittaker Chambers, was a member of the Ware Group, a Marxist study group. Pressman and Hiss had been colleagues on the *Law Review* and had collaborated on a student comment.

The Game

Snopes often thunders in the faculty lounge that Moot plays the "vulgar cite game. He collects cites like he collects bimbos. Every time a decision comes out, whatever the status of the court, he will write something on it. To Moot every case, every time a judge belches, constitutes an apocalypse. The law reviews are his pimps; they publish his op-ed trash, and the courts cite it. It's not the judges but the clerks who are conditioned to the footnote scam; they cite Moot to justify their existence."

Moot's only response is a sneering "When are we going to get an article from you, old buddy?" It was worth it to see Snopes seethe and sputter. Actually Moot took the remark as a compliment. It was acknowledgment that he had learned the rules of The Game. Snopes was a walking case of self-pity, a relic of Langdellism virus. His addiction to the Big Article had ruined his career. Moot knew that lurking underneath Snopes's ideals was a bad case of sloth.

William O. Douglas taught Moot about The Game. Not directly, but through Professor George Screed, his securities professor at Harvard. Screed was one of the youngest chairs in the school's history. He was a regular on King and Geraldo, even Dershowitz existed in his shadow. And, as he frequently confided, "I owe it all to Willie O." Although Screed never explained this cryptic remark, he finally gave Moot the story over a few drinks of Wild Turkey during a night out on the town in Boston.

"After clerking and spending the obligatory two years at Auchinloss, Beekman, and Ehninger, learning the manners of Wall Street practice, I was invited by Dean Gris-

wold to come to Cambridge. Before I left the firm, Robert Service, a young partner and former president of the Law Review, took me aside and very thoughtfully and carefully said: 'Watch out up there, be careful who you run with.' What he meant was this: it is a matter of options. The gate to success is writing; everything depends on that single enterprise. It is a question of strategy, and you need a game plan. So the first thing I did was to look for a model, someone who was successful. Since I was in securities, you would assume it would be Louis Loss, supposedly the Williston on securities. But I soon realized that there was nothing there other than a treatise. A mundane piece of work at best, a relic of the past, and, as a model for scholarship, a sure road to oblivion. Then—it was pure chance—I read that Justice Douglas was getting married again, to some young chick. Eureka! I remembered the story about Douglas, Arnold, and Frank, all young professors at Yale, competing in a friendly contest to see who would get the most recognition—cites, quotations in the media, publications and so forth. And Douglas always won. Willie O. knew how to play the game. So I studied his academic career, and I reviewed the law reviews for trends.

"One thing was clear—those guys at Yale were not your stereotypical detached ivory tower scholars. They were more huckster reformers than professors. Early in the game they latched on to the New Deal and used it as the springboard for articles, books, and publicity. I wonder how Arthur Corbin felt about those young upstarts getting all the attention. Make no mistake about it, Moot, Willie O. and his buddies were Outsiders cutting against the majoritarian influence of the Langdell legacy. Remember the story about Douglas and his interview at Sullivan & Cromwell? He got so mad at John Foster Dulles's patronizing and pontifical manners that he tipped Dulles a quarter when Dulles helped him with his coat.

"Willie O. got more PR points by getting involved in legal realism, which of course was another dig at the establishment. His empirical research on business failures was methodologically flawed, but it got him notice from the right people in the New Deal. Another shrewd move was his work in securities—it was a vital industry but full of crooks and bucket shops—and, coincidentally, the topic of intense media attention. So there it is, Outsider Willie O. tweaks the Langdellian bluebloods, gets a reputation, is appointed to the S.E.C., and finally ends up on the Supreme Court and a poker-playing buddy of F.D.R.

"Had I not spent time pouring over those dusty pages of prewar reviews, I would have gone along with the conventional wisdom that the 1930–40 period was the grand age of legal scholarship. That was the advice junior people got from the old men 'if you want to know how to write pure scholarship, use that period for models.' Not true, Moot, they were perpetuating a world that never existed except in their minds.

"*Maybe it was the unique tension of the times—a nation undergoing a catharsis and facing a war—but I encountered a surprising number of essay pieces. The writers had a point of view and did not allow themselves to get diverted by scholarly refinements. I remember to this day an article by a professor from Duke who gave notice with the first sentence: 'This article is not the outgrowth of scholarly research but of disputation, which the editors of this Review, with the opportunism characteristic of their guild, have diverted to serve their own editorial ends.'*

"*Disputation. There was a lot of that going on, especially when it came to wrangling over the New Deal. The other article I remember is the economist Henry Simons's analysis of Thurman Arnold's book* The Bottlenecks of Business. *Calling Arnold's previous work 'often a bit suspect intellectually,' Simons praised him for advocating a free market and thereby challenging his friends in the Roosevelt Administration. Then came a bullet aimed at Henry Wallace for trading in his free-market views to accommodate the New Deal. 'Any literate person may now identify Mr. Wallace as our leading advocate of the totalitarian or pretotalitarian economy of negotiation among tightly organized, monopolizing functional groups—as the mystical, sentimental, emotional partisan of democracy who zealously upholds it internationally while championing the kind of internal policies that have undermined and destroyed it abroad.' That comment is definitely an early version of what the Critical Legal Studies people call trashing.*

"*Whenever you see something in the media about a new genre of legal writing, ignore it. These guys have already done it. People seem to think the narrative style of Lon Fuller's 'The Case of the Speluncean Explorer' was a unique breakthrough, but eight years earlier Professor John M. Maguire published a short story on, of all things, hearsay. It's damned good. There was an auto collision. The plaintiff was a millionaire-philanthropist 'whose wife was said to have an insatiable yearning for the company of literary lions.' The plaintiff's witness was Bernard Galsworth Wells, an author, who was too traumatized to testify. The young plaintiff's attorneys sought to get Wells's version of what happened through the testimony of Wells's examining physician, Dr. Saner, who would give 'testimony and memoranda of a highly detailed statement or series of statements made by Mr. Wells, while at the sanitarium, with regard to the unfortunate event which caused him to go there for treatment.'*

"*In an obvious counter, the defense attorney, a pompous windbag, objects on the basis of hearsay, disdainfully informing his opponent and the court that 'the nature of hearsay is so well understood that Wigmore does not trouble to define the word.' We learn, through an ingenious story, how the defense lives to regret that comment. In the process, the young attorney cites the case of the 'lifted eyelid' as precedent. Both judge and defense attorney were too embarrassed to acknowledge that they did not have the foggiest notion of the case. 'Mr. Stout certainly smelled a rat but knew not what to do about it. The silence became oppressive.' Then the judge goes into a tirade about the use of footnotes. 'What's that—footnotes?' cried the judge. 'I don't like them.' I recommend it, Moot—it has a Perry Mason ending.*

"So I played it straight, wrote a few long, boring doctrinal, articles, and got tenure, and then went out on my own. I ignored my seniors and played to a wider audience like Willie O. I use whatever style works—op-ed, whatever. But the bottom line is never be boring—that is the kiss of death."

The Article

By the 1960s, the doctrinal style dominated reviews. *Brown v. Board of Education* was decided in 1955 and continued to generate dialogue, usually in advocacy pieces. Nevertheless, the bulk of writing was doctrinal, focusing on mainstream topics. The student law review was a contrast to the English faculty-edited journals, which were fewer in numbers and had fewer pages to the articles and fewer issues (the longest article in the 1960 Cambridge Law Journal was twenty-eight pages with thirty-two footnotes). The English journals focused on practical issues like constructive malice, hire purchase agreements, and the willful neglect to maintain a wife.

In number of pages and brute weight, the American law reviews were self-steroidizing to reach their present size. In 1960, Penn published 1,252 pages, Yale 1,414, Columbia 1,211, and Harvard 1,680. Stanford, which started in 1947, was at 996. Stanford's articles were also competitive in length and in number of footnotes: "Adjustment of Interunion Disputes," 54 pages, 344 footnotes; "Court-Martial of Civilians," 60 pages, 278 footnotes; "Justice Traynor," 61 pages, 236 footnotes.

In 1960, Derek Bok, an assistant professor at Harvard, published "Section 7 of the Clayton Act and the Merging of Law and Economics." It helped him get tenure, which he parlayed into a deanship of the Law School and then into the presidency of Harvard. As the doctrinal model for promotion and tenure, it is The Article.

I cited The Article in a piece for the *Minnesota Law Review* titled "A Priori Mechanical Jurisprudence in Antitrust." I was trying to make sense of Clayton 7, the antimerger statute that was the source of controversy during the merger wave of the late 1960s. It was a period of heated dialogue in antitrust. Robert Bork and the Chicago School had started their attack on the economic populists. Ralph Nader wanted the Justice Department to dissolve General Motors. Helterskelter decisions from the Supreme Court left confusion for lawyers, prompting Justice Potter Stewart to complain that "the sole consistency that I can find is that in litigation under Section 7, the Government always wins." Stewart cited The Article.

I cited Bok for reasons of thoroughness rather than appreciation. I was looking for answers while Bok raised questions, with speculation piled on conjecture. His advice was to listen to economists but ignore their directions. Big firm acquisitions are suspect, but not all the time. Then came the conclusion in the classic Harvard Stutter: "In summary, then, the question of whether or not to employ precise rules is complex, and cannot safely be resolved on the strengths of the data here at hand. The natural tendency for judges and administrators will doubtless be to speak in flexible terms, and . . . the effects of such phraseology may be of no great importance under Section 7." This summary is all the reader has to show for 129 pages.

Later, much later, after getting tenure, I reread The Article. It hit me. My initial impression was off the mark. I had completely missed the genius of the Harvard Stutter. It was not a superficial affectation but instead a method Bok followed to produce the classic model for the Empire doctrinal tenure article. Follow it and any reasonably intelligent young professor is sure to get the votes.

The Harvard Stutter starts with the selection of a topic. The obvious tactic is to select a topic that gives an author range and the opportunity to produce something that "looks like scholarship." If your primary area is Wills and Trusts, you have serious problems and had best consider a new interest. Trusts is a subject that is at best vocational, that is, there is no beef. Young professors fight to teach Constitutional Law; it's hot and Liberal chic, and an author can make outrageous proposals, so long as they fit the Liberal-left line. Con law articles are more likely to get accepted by an impressionable student editor than is a boring tax article.

Although Bok was a labor specialist, he opted to write on antitrust. The antimerger act had been amended in 1952, and in the ensuing eight years the Supreme Court had not reviewed a merger case. An article would provide Bok the opportunity to advise the Justices on interpretation and to pick up a citation. (He got the cite.) Clayton 7's broad language, proscription based on a tendency to lessen competition, left a trail of judicial frustration that would provide a bright young professor with an opportunity to impress. Most important, interdisciplinary writing was beginning to blossom, and antitrust was the ideal subject for Law and Economics. With one article, Bok could satisfy the demands of the traditionalist members of the faculty and impress the interdisciplinary people.

The literary form of the Harvard Stutter is a composition of feint and parry, a bit of show and tell, but thorough in coverage. The idea is to maintain the tone of objectivity. The impressive footnote ornaments (briefs, trial memorandums, and transcripts) are there, along with the obligatory congressional documents. In footnote 137, Bok lets us know that he visited the Federal Trade Commission archives to review a transcript. Finally, Bok adheres to the unwritten rule that tenure pieces have to exceed 300 footnotes by airing it out to 361. The interdisciplinary content is high, with more cites to economists than to law people.

Bok never boxes himself into a corner by unflinchingly endorsing a specific position or rule. He utilizes the "scholars' doubt" technique of using phraseology that, while exalting predictability, reflects a healthy suspicion of certainty. "Hence," says Bok, "the problem of indeterminateness, and how best to deal with it, will pervade much of what is said in the following pages." Finally, knowing that a good Harvard Stutter article always concludes with a plea for "further thought," Bok obliges.

Stories from the Empire

In 1949, doctrinal writing was still the fashion. Volume 62 of the *Harvard Law Review* published articles on venerable topics such as dower, restitution, and unfair competition. There were significant exceptions by two of the academy's top scholars, Karl Llewellyn and Lon Fuller. Complaining that law professors spend all their time studying rules of law, Llewellyn advocated closer ties between sociology and law. Lon Fuller's "The Case of the Speluncean Explorers" was the other exception.

In May of the year 4299, five members of the Speluncean Society, an amateur explorers club, were trapped in a cavern when a landslide covered the only entrance. Additional landslides frustrated rescue and in one instance killed ten workers. On the twentieth day of confinement, wireless contact was established, and the trapped men were told even if no new landslides occurred it would take at least ten days for a rescue team to reach them. Roger Whetmore, their spokesman, requested a conference with the medical people; he advised them they had been trapped with only scant provisions and asked whether they could survive another ten days without food. He was told that there was little possibility of survival. Eight hours later Whetmore reestablished contact and asked what their chances of survival were if they ate one of the group. The answer indicated survival. When asked by Whetmore if it would be advisable to cast lots to determine the victim, the physicians demurred. Whetmore requested advice on the same question from either a judge or a minister (or priest); none was available.

Whetmore proposed the solution for survival and suggested a roll of dice to determine the victim. After other explorers agreed to the plan, Whetmore backed off, countering that he wanted to postpone the roll of the dice for seven days. Charging him with a breach of faith, the group rolled the dice, one of them rolling for Whetmore. His proxy lost, and the group ate Whetmore's flesh. On the thirty-second day, nine days after Whetmore's death, the survivors were rescued. Following an indictment, they were tried, convicted of murder, and sentenced to be hanged. The jurors petitioned the Court to commute the sentence to six months' imprisonment. The case went to the Supreme Court of Newgarth on appeal.

The credibility of fictional opinions by the Newgarth Court depended on the facts coming across as a Greek tragedy. The structure adheres to Aristotelian poetics—the beginning: landslide and entrapment; the middle: the choice between death by starvation or casting the dice, the inquiry and request for advice; closure: the roll of dice, the meal of human flesh. The tragedy is the story of a group of men confronted with the threat *but not the certainty* of death. They succumb to Whetmore's suggestion of a human lottery, force him to play against his will by proxy, and then, when his proxy loses, murder him. Fuller satisfies Aristotle's requirement of *hamontia*, an error or misjudgment that leads the protagonist to the tragedy. The explorers' misjudgment occurred when they were rescued nine days after murdering Whetmore, a day before the predicted time of starvation.

A short story has been defined as an apocalypse served in a very small cup. Fuller fills the cup with subtle pauses that magnify the horror of the tragedy. Why did the rescuers excuse themselves from offering advice? Were they interrogated on this during the investigation or trial? Didn't they have a moral (natural law) obligation to supply advice? Fuller delivers irony; it is only after the facts of the tragedy are described that we learn that Whetmore instigated the lottery resulting in his death. When Whetmore withdrew, the group accused him of a breach of faith. Did the explorers use the breach to rationalize their forcing him to participate against his will in the roll of the dice? Finally, who killed Whetmore?

At the threshold, it is a tragedy that raises tough issues suitable for discussion in legal ethics or jurisprudence courses. Fuller prompts the Newgarth justices to debate how best to interpret statutes to maximize justice. Chief Justice Truepenny's role is to emphasize the difficult choice confronting the Court. He weasels out by suggesting that because of "the tragic situation in which the men found themselves," the Court should emulate the jury by recommending clemency. Justice Keen injects the statutory interpretation issue into the debate by rejecting Truepenny's proposal as flying in the face of Holmes's plain-meaning principle. A judge's personal values or individual notions of justice are irrelevant. Objective meanings control, and the plain meaning of the statute says the explorers are guilty. Realism was a force in the 1940s, and Fuller used Justice Henry to voice the Realist rejection of formalism. To Henry, plain meaning was an error derived from the mistaken notion of the existence of objective principles.

Justice Foster voted to acquit. His opinion is Fuller's centerpiece, a statement of his view on interpretation. Statutes have a purpose, and it is the judiciary's responsibility to find and make sure the purpose is satisfied. The general purpose of all law is to regulate with fairness the coexistence of people, to alleviate the problems of group life. For the Spelunceans, that purpose was inoperative. "When the assumption that men may live together loses its truth, as it obviously did in this extraordinary situation where life only became possible by the taking of life, then the basic premises underlying our whole legal order have lost their meaning and force." When the murder took place, the defendants were in "a state of nature," governed by natural law, which, given the circumstances, would not impose a penalty. "I have no hesitancy in saying that under those principles they were guiltless of any crime."

Justices Keen and Tatting (who withdrew from the case) rejected Foster's purposive doctrine, the latter noting that Foster's opinion overlooked those cases when a statute has many purposes or when its purposes are in dispute. The even split by the court meant that the trial court's judgment was upheld.

Relying on a tragedy of extraordinary circumstances as the anchor, Fuller composed a sophisticated intellectual debate that collected and anticipated prominent theories of law. Subsequent exchanges between academics and members of the U.S. Supreme Court are legacies of "The Explorers." Cited frequently in journals and decisions, it has achieved stature as an authority in statutory interpretation. William Eskridge concludes, "Fuller's fictional exercise must be counted as one of the important jurisprudential documents in the century."

Norval Morris has produced a series of stories around the experiences of Eric Blair (George Orwell's real name) "which Professor Morris claims (although this claim has not been verified) are based upon a set of manuscripts he discovered while retracing the travels Blair made while serving in Burma between 1923 and 1927." In "The Veraswami Story," Blair, as the District Officer in a Burmese Village, is ordered to investigate the illegal distribution of heroin through the local hospital. Incidents parallel to the investigation signal the plot. Troubled about his role in an accident in which a policeman is killed, Blair engages his Indian friend Dr. Veraswami in a conversation over pain. Veraswami explains the difference between physical and psychological pain, using his own childhood experiences of being abused by his nanny. Pain becomes the *motif*. It turns out that Veraswami, who works at the hospital, is the one who is illegally dispensing heroin to relieve the pain of an old friend dying from cancer. He confesses, bluntly telling Blair that his friend's pain is too intense to tolerate and he will continue the treatment until locked up.

Over a beer at the Club, Blair tries to sort out his sympathies for his friend and his responsibility to perform his duty. There is the anomaly that heroin is totally banned for any use in Burma while it is permitted for medicinal purposes in England. Something to do with policy. Then there is Veraswami's sensitivity to pain, possibly strong enough to affect his judgment where a dying friend is concerned.

"Bar Chit," "Bar Chit," "Chit Boy," "Chit Boy." "I filled in my 'chit' for a cold beer; the 'boy' in his mid-forties collected the chit and delivered the beer, the chit remaining at the bar to define my bill, the assumption of the lack of memory and trustworthiness of all 'boys' thus reaffirmed."

The "bar chit, chit boy" reference adds another layer to the story: the pervasive fallout effects from colonialism, an influence that gives Blair another factor in the case to ponder. When first assigned to the Rangoon Hospital, Veraswami was in charge of an emergency team dispatched to treat Burmese and English passengers injured in a train wreck. Casualties were high, including the death of Veraswami's superior, prompting an investigation. Although the purpose of the hearing was to develop methods for improving emergency response, Veraswami came under suspicion for favoring Burmese passengers over English. Blair sees this as a lingering motive by the colonial government for prosecuting Veraswami.

Blair ultimately recommends against prosecution. He invokes the doctrine of necessity to determine that the criminal conduct can be excused as the consequence of the unavoidable choice of two evils. "I believe that his buying and using the heroin was a lesser evil than letting Mr. Chanduri suffer avoidable agony and, further, that there were no otherwise legal means of achieving the end."

The aesthetics of "Veraswami" resonate. Morris effectively uses minor incidents such as the "chit boy" reference, Blair's reservations about operating through an undercover agent, plus a little misdirection (Blair's suspicion that Veraswami is an addict), to feed and build the unity of the plot. In Blair's character, one imagines George Orwell as the reluctant British bureaucrat trying to reconcile cultural differences. When Veraswami tells him that he has been devious and scheming in softening the effects of colonial law on the village, Blair ponders the dilemma of serving two masters—his country and his instincts. The plot may not be as dramatic as "The Explorers," but the story is more fully developed.

Like "The Explorers," there is an obvious crime, but the author's management of the legal implications is quite different. One can make meritorious arguments on either side in both "Explorers" and "Veraswami." There is, however, a singular difference. In "Explorers," we have a vigorous and thoughtful debate on two jurisprudential levels: the appropriate method of statutory interpretation and the vision of what law should be. By using Justice Foster to voice his views of what law should be and is, Fuller expands the debate by putting his ideas into the marketplace. On the other hand, Blair's recommendation (a memo written by a nonlawyer) is all we get from "Veraswami"—no debate, no counterpositions. Instead, Morris attaches a selected annotated bibliography of cases, legislative materials, and commentaries that suggests some of the issues. There is the threshold issue of whether the defense should be allowed. In his memo, Blair suggested that even though the statute was absolute, one could argue the lack of an exception merely meant the legislature had failed to address the problem. There is also the issue of the abuse, that is, the defendant creates the choice of two evils. Another relevant point is the reasonableness of the belief that the choice was necessary. For example, was "Veraswami"'s case similar to that of a protester destroying property in a nuclear plant then arguing that his action was the lesser of two evils and necessary to prevent an imminent nuclear war?

These titillating questions would no doubt energize a criminal law class. But does "Veraswami" take the audience beyond the annotated bibliography? Does the story analyze the problem and furnish new insights? Or has Professor Morris flushed out a heretofore unexplored problem? If these are criteria for legal scholarship, "Veraswami" fails to go beyond a story. The author produced an aesthetically exciting problem or exam, inviting a responsive discussion. Of his collection of Burma stories, a reviewer said:

"Studying knotty legal dilemmas by the case method is nothing new; but it surely has never been done so oddly and cleverly as in this most original book." Norris does, however, leave us with a question he undoubtedly did not anticipate: suppose Dr. Veraswami had written the story; would it then constitute an Outsider perspective piece and therefore constitute legal scholarship?

Louis Auchincloss was a lawyer by trade and is still a writer by profession. He writes about manners among the patrician set, often using lawyers as characters. "The Senior Partner's Ghosts," a short story about perceptions and realities, appeared in the 1964 *Virginia Law Review*. Sylvaner Prime begins to dictate the biography of his mentor, Guy de Grasse, the deceased senior partner of a prominent Wall Street firm. He intends to produce a testimonial to the integrity and achievements of de Grasse. Instead, some unknown force compels him to describe his mentor's evil genius. Every time he dictates, a tale of skulduggery emerges; this leads Prime into a partnership with de Grasse's dark side and the abstract presence of evil becomes real, compelling Prime to cheat a client. When he repents and seeks to correct the ethical breach, his colleagues recommend that he get psychiatric help.

Auchincloss is not interested in adding to our knowledge of law; his objective is to tell a *story* about the manners and morals of lawyers at work and play. To accomplish this, he must satisfy the aesthetic burden of storytelling. The characters, plot, motif (typically the practice of law), and closure must blend into an aesthetic unity in the reader's mind. "The aesthetic object" is, according to Seymour Chatman, "that which comes into existence when the observer experiences the real objective aesthetically. Thus it is a construction (or reconstruction) in the observer's mind." Fulfilling the aesthetic burden in legal storytelling is complicated by the added necessity of satisfying the scholarship element.

A Few Skeletons in the Doctrinal Closet

In 1970 Dean Bok was back with another lesson on how to write The Article. Before departing the Law School for the presidency of Harvard, he published "Reflections on the Distinctive Character of American Labor Law," a final tribute to his specialty. That same year Stanford published "A Parable," by Professor William Baxter, who, a decade later, would become Ronald Reagan's antitrust chief. (The parable was about a corn-on-the-cob monopoly.) Law review bulk was pushing the outer limits of page inflation: Duke

1,211; Penn 1,282; Michigan 1,582; Yale 1,711; and the Beast, Harvard, spaced out to 1,976 pages. Although the lead articles were getting longer, Bok's piece stopped at sixty-nine pages; the major increase came from the publication of student work.

The *Village Voice* says "[a]s character-builders, law reviews rank a cut above high-class bordellos." The Empire disagrees, with Karl Llewellyn expressing the Empire's wisdom that law reviews are "one of the most satisfactory educational tools in existence. The importance of those reviews here lies in the fact that they are themselves also educational machinery with cleanly developed techniques for rapid and amazingly effective training, machinery recognized by faculties as having peculiar value in supplementation of the standard curriculum."

In his vigorous praise, Llewellyn lets the cat out of the bag. People who have not completed basic training in their discipline, do not know how to draft a complaint, and never edited anything other than perhaps a college newspaper are in charge of the primary source of legal scholarship. This embarrassment dogs every law professor. How can one explain this perverse relationship to an economist or even a sociologist? How can a dean rationalize a salary increase on the basis that a journal run by third-year law students published the professor's article? If, as Chief Justice Earl Warren said, "The American law review properly has been called the most remarkable institution of the law school world," we are in deep trouble. Every once in a while someone protests, pointing out the obvious perversions. The protestor gets the requisite fifteen seconds and then goes back to reading the *Times* and sipping brandy. In addition to sloth, there are compelling reasons for uncomfortable acquiescence.

To Outsiders, law reviews were conceived on a plantation in Cambridge. The objective of the *Harvard Law Review* was to serve the interests of the owners. Lamenting the lack of recognition his faculty got, John Henry Wigmore as a student said, "We knew that their pioneer work in legal education was not yet but ought to be appreciated by the profession. We yearned to see the fruits of their scholarship in print." From then on, faulty oppressors and student oppressed would exist in a state of symbiosis: the *Law Review* would use student Notes to advertise the casebook method in exchange for faculty publications. It was a productive synergy; over their careers Ames published twenty-eight articles in the *Review*, Langdell twenty-seven, Williston thirty-four, and Joseph Beale fifty-one.

Even the conspiracy genius of Oliver Stone could not conjure up this drama. The masters of the law school plantation gave the crop to the workers who are responsible for nurturing the product into print. It was a free ride for faculty, and, more important, the opportunity to control legal scholarship. The dominance of the doctrinal scholarship style was ensured. As new reviews appeared, the symbiotic relationship continued, interrupted only by aberrations like McQuire's narrative, Baxter's parable, or Lee (Leon) Pressman's stealth article.

Trained in the classroom to the nuances of doctrinal expression and conditioned by manuscripts to the style of The Article, student editors became doctrinal fanatics. It was more bureaucracy than scholarship; committee editing was used to ensure objectivity and neutrality, and, as Judge Posner observed, "to cultivate a most dismal sameness of style, a lowest-common-denominator style." Flair, humor, and individualism were not tolerated. Through the influence of student editors, the Langdellian influence persisted.

Over the years, knowledgeable law faculty have come to appreciate the advantages of the doctrinal-driven law review system. It is a win–win situation for an author. The almost daily proliferation of journals ensures publication. It is not unusual to get an acceptance within ten days of mailing out manuscripts. From then on, it's a question of strategy. One option is to play Professor Moot's productivity game. Experience has taught him that doctrinal articles are easy to produce: it is simply a matter of organization. The key to the assembly-line approach is an efficient division of labor; Moot writes an outline, while his student assistant does the grunt work of writing rough drafts for Moot to revise. Students are placated with recognition in a footnote. Of people like Moot, Kenneth Lasson says, "They are in greater part, however, competent enough teachers without anything original to write, doomed to scholarly mediocrity by academic imperative—coerced clones who are whipped into a hack's frenzy, urged to jump through hoops held up by the local promotion-and-tenure committee, forced to shimmy down the chutes of the publication process."

Moot and his kind are the good guys; they give the impression to the outside world that law professors are doing something other than writing politically correct op-ed articles and appearing on talk shows. Deans prefer the producers; they can be used to justify high salaries and relative immunity from university meddling in law school affairs. But there is, however, another side to doctrinal writing.

There is a third group, the "shirkers." Exploiting the shield of tenure, they use the law school as a mail drop while they play with computers, visit obscure parts of the world, or dabble in seducing students.

In a footnote, I was describing one of the sorriest embarrassments in legal education. Shirking the scholarship obligation is a fact of life in academe generally and certainly in law. The situation is not as bad as in 1980, when a study found that 44 percent of senior faculty had *never* published. Now everyone has to satisfy the obligatory publish-or-perish tenure barrier. But for many, once over the barrier it's time to enjoy the quiet life. David Gregory describes the reality: "the near-majority of tenured law faculty in the United States ... have utterly eschewed legal scholarship."

When several of my colleagues discovered my footnote, they were furious. The Dean, keenly sensitive to anything that could possibly stir up criticism or inquiry from the alumnae or central administration, accused me of slandering my colleagues' work ethic. The odds were remote that anyone would read my article, much less the footnote, but that was irrelevant; I had touched on a very delicate issue. The footnote was an attack on the shirker's facade, the deception that law faculty are vigorously engaged in research and scholarship.

The doctrinal article is an important component of the facade; it has become the vehicle to semiretirement. A long, heavily footnoted article, which in reprints looks like a monograph, creates the illusion of dedicated research. The protectors of the facade know that it does not take much student assistant time and effort to supply material for the footnote games that we play. Likewise, it is easy to stretch the text to cover additional case analysis, to include more vacuous insights from friends (and thereby generate some reciprocal cites), and to cap it off with a long-winded recommendation for a new restatement of restatements.

The irony of the facade's illusion is that it is perpetuated by the long gestation period for each article. In a bizarre twist, the illusion of hard work and grand scholarship is confirmed by not getting the article published. The experienced shirker can account for years of sloth by simply announcing, "I am working on an article." This humble statement produces reduced teaching loads, subsidized travel to get firsthand research, summer stipends, and sabbatical time. In some cases, this drama can last over a career without any tangible production.

Deans have an affinity for shirking. The time of the scholarship dean, someone who knew the nuances of shirking, is history. Today, deans accept their role as middle-level managers hired to raise funds, satisfy students, and placate faculty. A Stanford dean summed it up: "A dean, at best, is the conductor of the orchestra. He's not a one-man band."

The dean and the shirker share the common aspiration of tranquillity. The dean survives by compromise, a reality that the shirker exploits for survival. The shirker is aware that the dean will be gone in four years and will accept his annual report full of "works in progress" at face value. Even if they are questioned by a new dean after years of sloth, a canny shirker will have a first-draft skeleton manuscript ready for show and tell. Deans have their own compromise ploys. My favorite is the rehabilitation project. The new dean candidly acknowledges that Professor Netkoffee has not published an article in fifteen years but then notes that he is a scholar of great potential, someone who can deliver the big bomb of doctrinals. Then the clincher: "I'm going to rehabilitate him, help him get the recognition he deserves. All he needs is some release time, a lighter schedule." I know someone who has been rehabilitated three times. Of course, there is also the possibility that, as former shirkers, deans are instinctually sympathetic to the problem.

The shirker knows that the best maneuver to support the work-in-progress and rehabilitation scam is to make periodic faculty presentations. The goal is to become a member of Arthur Koestler's "academic call girl" circuit, where fellow shirkers exchange visits. "It becomes a habit, maybe an addiction. You get a long-distance telephone call from some professional busy body at some foundation or university—sincerely hope you can fit it into your schedule—it will be a privilege to have you with us—return fare economy-class and a modest honorarium of. . . ."

Shirkers are an intriguing study in psychology. The common profile starts with an intense burst of energy on the required tenure doctrinal articles. Work like hell to get that union card. Then comes the critical period of post-tenure celebration of revisiting activities that were sacrificed during the past five years. Suddenly four years are gone and the pressure returns with the demand "What have you done for us lately?" It is at this point that the shirker starts the game.

Every new dean is a challenge, someone to play with. Maybe this guy will fall for the "I was preempted" ploy or "except for a few new chapters that I have to add to recognize recent decisions, my book is ready for print." Shirkers expend more energy in playing the game than would be necessary to get an article out every two years. It is this cloud of activity that lulls deans and fools colleagues. It is no accident that shirkers tend to dominate faculty meetings, using long-winded verbal assaults to compensate for blank pages.

The Outsiders Win One

It is overreaching to characterize this group of outsiders as antiestablishment radical outsiders. They were teaching law or economics at the best schools. Some were and others became Nobel prize winners. Despite considerable accomplishments, they worked outside the currents of mainstream intellectual fashion. They are the Law and Economics movement that used interdisciplinary scholarship to generate an attack on conventional legal analysis and in the process challenge the doctrinal method of writing.

The movement traces to the University of Chicago, where some of the brightest economists collected to counter the pervasive influence of John Maynard Keynes over New Deal policy. In the 1950s, when Edward Levi and Aron Director introduced economic analysis to Chicago's law school, Law and Economics became a movement. While serious scholarship started in the early 1960s with Guido Calabresi's *Thoughts on Risk Distribution and the Law of Torts* and Ronald Coase's *The Problem of Social Costs*, the movement blossomed in 1972 with the publication of Richard Posner's *Economic Analysis of Law*. Posner established the definition of Law and Economics as "the application of economics to the legal system across the board: to common law fields . . . to the theory . . . of punishment . . . to procedure . . . to jurisprudence."

Although the Law and Economics people adhere to the doctrinal style of objective analysis, every problem is explored from an economic perspective. Law reviews compete for footnotes stacked with references to economic theory. When I told my economist coauthor we should beef up our notes with some graphics, she obliged. Much to our surprise, the *Pennsylvania Law Review* editors converted each price-and-demand chart to a full page.

The range of Law and Economics has been eclectic. Even sex got a cost-benefit analysis. Posner taught us that the cost of nonmarital sex has fallen due to the increased number of women in the workforce. The economic value of virginity likewise is down: "With women less dependent economically on men, they are less willing to surrender their sexual freedom in exchange for economic support." Gary Becker tormented critics by classifying children as durable goods; once people acquired information on contraception, "the number of children would increase with family income—a reversal of the age-old pattern." Milton Friedman contributed to the shock dialogue when he suggested that the quality of medical care would be better and costs reduced if licensure barriers to practice were eliminated.

In the typical law school faculty lounge, the reaction to Law and Economics was, and often still is, disdain or outright horror. Reducing law and legal scholarship to cost-benefit analysis, efficiency curves, and a celebration of the market system is a rejection of an agenda legal education had supported since the 1930s. There were practical reasons for dismissing the new movement—a repeal of heavy federal regulations that Chicago economists advocated would eliminate the Eastern law schools' influence in Washington. Even closer to the bone, Law and Economics threatens a way of life; it takes direct aim at the Langdellian system of legal analysis. As a colleague once said, "I refuse to defer to those people with their tricky little equations that put the same value on eggs and friends."

Despite the animosity, Law and Economics has successfully carved out a niche in the curriculum. *The Wall Street Journal* called it "the most important thing in legal education since the birth of Harvard Law School." Typically taught by someone with a doctorate, a Law and Economics course is automatic at top-tier law schools and has filtered down to the second level. Success was achieved the old-fashioned way—knock the door down with scholarship. The economist George Stigler describes the repetition strategy: "The new ideas will normally require much repetition, elaboration, and, desirably, controversy, for controversy is an attention-getter and sometimes a thought-getter." As a group Law and Economics people were, and continue to be, talented and prolific writers and a source of irritation to shirkers.

Is there a learning curve in the Law and Economics movement for Outsiders? Unlike the Outsider group, Posner et al. did not try to impose a new scholarship genre on the establishment. They relied on the conventional doctrinal style, improving it with tight analysis. They never got into the victim game, even though they took some nasty hits. The Left considers the efficiency goal the first step toward totalitarianism, while a market economy is instant tyranny. The Stigler strategy was to keep focused on the positive and to avoid petty squabbles. Most important, keep the scholarship flowing.

Law and Economics people are always on the same page. There may be subtle differences at the edges or in emphasis, but Stigler, Bork, and friends had a common theme. The economics movement was sustained by an unusually talented group fortunate enough to gain access to the corridors of power during the Reagan administration. They efficiently exploited their prestige to proselytize and to develop new advocates among young law professors who saw a future and status in merging law with a legitimate discipline.

There is one thing that Outsiders can appreciate from watching the Law and Economics experience play out. No one was aware of it at the time, but the old Liberal establishment was on the edge of serious trouble. It no longer stood as a unified group with a laser focus on teaching the traditional loop of subjects embracing the commercial package of corporations, sales, tax, and so on. While the law schools avoided the full force of the student rebellion of the 1960s, they did not evade the consequences. As reflected in scholarship, political and social pressures created a new and rich menu of new subjects for discussion, including the law of civil disorder, corporate responsibility, minority rights, and tenant equality. Judge Skelly Wright, writing in the *Duke Law Journal* in 1970, anticipated the Outsider resentment by condemning the legal system's Tyranny of Objectivity:

> [T]he aroused Establishment has satisfied itself with half measures heavily larded with rhetoric and patronizing slogans directed at the disenchanted, mostly poor minorities to encourage obedience to law, such as: Respect the law—it respects you and no man is above the law and no man is below it. When confronted with this kind of Babbittry, the poor and the concerned youth of this country have a right to ask: "Does the law really respect those who do not have the political muscle to make the law?"

4

The Greening of Faculty,
Students, and Law Review

"The Chic Conversation Piece of the Fall Cocktail Season"

"That's what you get from Yale; it's no accident that that's where legal realism came from and it was Kingman Brewster, a former law school dean, who capitulated to the radical invasion of the Yale campus." It was May of 1971 and two of my colleagues were in well-behaved debate over Charles Reich's book The Greening of America. *While both were Harvard graduates, they were separated by more than just political generations. Paul Houseman got his LL.B in 1951; Fino finished in 1966. They were good students and after graduation spent obligatory time with white-shoe Wall Street firms. For two months Houseman had been admonishing Fino for tolerating* Greening, *even praising its depth and its "sense of the future."*

"What really disturbs me, Fino, is that you are serious, and, frankly, that is bad for Harvard Law School. That book is a law professor's version of Erich Segal's Love Story. *Didn't that piece of crap get Segal tenure in Yale's English Department? They are both Grub Street trash writers! That's what you get from Yale. Realism breeds slippery slopes."*

"Don't be provincial, old man, you are trapped in what Reich calls the Corporate State." Then, with acquired disdain: "Segal ruined his career at Yale with Love Story *but you should be happy, he made a bundle of money in Hollywood."*

They were at it now, and all appearances of civility disappeared. It was better than a Saturday night brawl at Reggie's Chickenhouse. "Don't preach the Wasteland to me," Houseman said, "I was at Boston Latin while you were dirtying your diapers in some hick town in Idaho. But to the point, I've got some reviews for you. This is what the Atlantic Monthly *said: 'His book is such a tissue of impressions, contradictions and generalizations, not to mention unsubstantiated predictions and prophecies of the most apocalyptic kind, that it is difficult indeed to associate it with an outstanding legal mind.'"*

In 1964, Associate Professor Charles Reich published "The New Property" in the *Yale Law Journal*. Reich made the accepted journey to teaching: editor-in-chief of the *Yale Law Journal*, clerk for Justice Black, then a stint at the prestigious firm Arnold, Fortas and Porter. According to Fino, "The New Property" is a career article. "It's about perceptions," Fino often says with an envious sigh. Reich anticipated the effects of the New Deal control over individual autonomy. Hidden in government largess is the tyranny of granting—or withholding—benefits. Reich recommended the creation of a property right in the government, a type of individual status. Today we call this entitlement.

Reich was a star, expected to track Bill Douglas's route to the Supreme Court. "The New Property" later became the most cited *Yale Law Journal* article. A follow-up article published in 1965 was number ten on the most-cited list. In 1967, Reich spent the summer in Berkeley, walking barefooted on the beach, smoking grass, and listening to rock, while discovering the consciousness of self. He returned to New Haven and started work on *The Greening of America*.

Although it was the chic conversation piece of the year, *Greening* had its critics. "The book is all mush and nuts: sloppy, gooey kiddyspeak euphoria for the broth. . . ." It is packed with infantile comments: "Bell bottoms have to be worn to be understood." "[The] new music has achieved a height of knowledge, understanding, insight, and truth concerning the world, and people's feelings, that is incredibly greater than what other media have been able to express." Reich predicts the coming of *Consciousness III: The New Generation,* a "way of life: energy. It is the energy of enthusiasm, of happiness, of hope."

Now teaching at the University of San Francisco, Reich lives at a lower level than he did during the glory days of a best-seller. He is entitled to recognition for using *The Greening* to stake out what would later become the Outsider's code of principles. *The Greening* identified the enemy as Establishment Liberals. They, with their reactionary friends, cultivated and imposed the Corporate State: "It is the worst of all possible worlds: uncontrolled technology and uncontrolled profiteering, combined into a force that is both immensely powerful and utterly irresponsible."

Like the Outsiders, Reich saw repression in rational reasoning, something *Consciousness III* rejects with "a deep skepticism of both 'linear' and analytic thought." "[T]hought can be 'non-linear,' spontaneous, disconnected." The future is in discovery of self and the recognition of community and altruism. Likewise, the lost self of the Corporate State is the consequence of people, especially students, being forced into a "hierarchy of statuses." For Professor Reich, it starts with academe. "The school is a brutal machine for the destruction of the self, controlling it, heckling it, hassling it into a thousand busy tasks, a thousand noisy groups, never giving it a moment to establish a knowledge within."

The Story of the Tenured Radical

It was Friday, 2 p.m., and time to go home and do some errands. On the other hand, there was no one in the faculty lounge to interrupt his musing on the latest squabble over Evelyn Allegory, who had been voted down for promotion. "Good old Scoff Law School," TR angrily thought, "this place is racist, sexist, homophobic, and redneck. It was the bias against her short stories." Then it hit TR like one of Cathy MacKinnon's atomic bomb sentences. All the portraits in this room are of white males! Old white males with big mustaches. He counted them—fifteen—including the recently retired dean who appeared to be trying to stare him down. Mumbling "I am not called the Tenured Radical for nothing," he jumped up and started his next research project. "It's worth an article."

For the next two days Tenured Radical conducted a careful inventory of Scoff's portrait collection. He searched every corner, including the staff lounge, where it was the same—posters of Elvis, Macho Man Randy Savage, and Sid Vicious. It was disgraceful. As was his typical practice for his projects, he prepared a lecture for his contracts class.

Phallogocentricism and Pagliaism at Scoff

(Contracts Lecture Number Nineteen)

It is a criminal act: the intentional visual race and gender rape of everyone who walks into Scoff Law School. We say we teach diversity, but instead the hegemony imposes a canon of oppressive patriarchal white maleness on Outsiders. And remember, Outsider is capitalized to privilege it over white male. Of the one hundred hanging portraits and photographs sprinkled throughout the Law School, only four do not oppress: Thurgood Marshall, Sandra Day O'Connor, Ruth Ginsberg, and a wife with her donor husband, who no doubt has his heel on her throat. I would like to know who is responsible for a racist representation of the Mayflower landing—an example of exponential oppression, because Native Americans are depicted as stupidly welcoming their eventual murderers. The white male canon dominates legal education. Look at your casebook: everyone is a white male—

the judges, lawyers, parties—everyone is an oppressor. He. All he and no she. As Derrida said in *Of Grammatology*, difference is therefore the formation of form. But it is, on the other hand, the being—imprinted of the imprint.

Tenured Radical was on a roll; he knew that this Lesson Lecture could be expanded to become an article for the Harvard Women's Law Journal *(which, given his anemic publication record, he desperately needed). On the back row, otherwise known as Federalist Alley, he was not on a roll. By now, the Federalist gang was used to Tenured Radical's politically correct proselytizing and automatically gave him the standard law student response—look interested, eyes intent on the prof with an imperceptible smirk of disdain while thinking of beer and sex. Rushman was not playing the game; in fact, he was listening carefully to the Lecture and getting more pissed off with every comment. With a degree in English Lit from Iowa, he knew that Tenured Radical was playing a variation of the canon game.*

Damn it, he yelled to himself, it was a matter of simple logic. The explanation for any canon comes from the objective facts of history. History explains the literary canon, and history is the answer to Tenured Radical's version of a law canon. There never was suppression of female work; how could there be when there weren't any women around until the eighteenth century? As soon as Jane Austen published, she made the list. Later, the key to the door came from social status, wealth, and access to the academic community, which used texts as models for the correct mode of the English language. In other words, you ass, gender has nothing to do with it.

The same history applies to your muddleheaded remarks about the picture canon. Why would there be pictures of women or Blacks on the walls? How many practiced law before 1950? Who gave money to the school? Right, white males. The same thing for casebooks; most of the people involved were—and still are—white males. Do you want the editors to rewrite history? But, of course, that's exactly what you do want.

Tenured Radical was still on his roll when he saw a hand shoot up. Ordinarily he ignored interruptions like this when he was giving one of his Lesson Lectures—but the hand came from a Black student. He nodded to invite a question.

"Professor, why isn't Justice Thomas's picture on the wall beside the other Justices?"

Radical Consciousness Goes to Law School

For law schools, the flush times are over. Applications are dropping, forcing many schools to downsize. Perhaps most ominous, *L.A. Law*, the great television motivator for going to law school, has been discontinued. In the meantime, radicalism gains momentum. Former students from the 1970s and

1980s return to teach Constitutional Law and keep radical ideas alive. More women and minorities are hired to replace retiring white male Liberals.

In the early 1990s, two incidents told me radicalism was now a serious factor in legal education. The first was a mean-spirited outburst from an otherwise imperturbable colleague, a tax specialist who esteems decorum next to the tax code. He was incensed at the deterioration, "almost depravity," in faculty dress, professors wearing jeans, no ties, and, "by God, Nikes . . . next it will be Raiders jackets." In the face of this inferno of indignation, I explained to him that to our colleagues, fashion is politics, and by wearing this style of clothing they were telling the students that they were at war against oppression—mainly people like him. I quoted from Charlie Reich's *Greening*: "Expensive clothes enforce social restraints; a grease spot on an expensive suit is social error, so is a rip in a tailored ladies coat, or a missing button." After that comment, my colleague really blew up. He is still trying to get the faculty to enact a dress code. In response, the dean instituted dress-down Fridays.

The second incident occurred when I attended a student meeting called to coordinate the plans for a national strike in support of various oppression and victim causes with other law schools. Almost immediately, serious haggling erupted: yelling and accusations of elitism, along with "we will not be objectified" and "crits suck." The two oppressive evils of hierarchy and authoritarianism stood in the way of allowing one person to control the meeting as a chair. Even a committee didn't work. All this brain power and education, and they could not conduct a meeting to organize the strike. There was no doubt that Radical Consciousness was here: I knew radical politics when I saw it.

By 1990, the tilt to Outsider ideology was evidenced by numerous reported incidences of classroom radicalization. At the University of Virginia Law School, a professor was investigated because students "sometimes found his classes uncomfortable or his statements insensitive." He was cleared of the charges, but the damage was done, and the professor dropped the course. A visiting professor at Harvard was accused of sexism because he quoted a line from Lord Byron in his Contracts class: "and whispering, 'I will ne'er consent'—consented." It was deemed sexist: "A quote about a sexual 'jockeying' for power, depicting a woman struggling, repenting, and being dominated, has no place in a Contracts textbook . . . such remarks not only reveal inappropriate and sexist attitudes but also pose a more serious problem: the Byron quote exemplifies the attitude that women mean yes when they say no." A moot court problem involving a lesbian mother was withdrawn because it was "hurtful to a group of people and thus hurtful to all of us." Supporting the protest, Patricia Williams said:"There has been a tendency to mix up the ideal of being unbiased and the ideal of a universal right to counsel in a way that makes people believe that every lawyer ought to be able to represent any cause indiscriminately. However, that mentality is useful only for training hired guns." The problem was reinstated after Anthony Amsterdam said: "The declaration that any legal issue is not an open question in law school is a declaration of war upon everything that a law school is."

After diversity, sensitivity is the favorite Radical Newspeak word. Casebooks are scrutinized for lack of sensitivity to women and minorities. Tutorial programs endeavor to sensitize white males to their lack of sensitivity. Students are encouraged to relate experiences of oppression. Workshops flush out the effects of white male privilege and power over women and minorities. I was advised by a student editor of a law review that my use of the phrase "academic call girl" in an article was offensive and insensitive to feminism. The expression was coined by Arthur Koestler to describe the dubious habit of academics who exchange visits and honorariums while boring each other with vacuous presentations.

To avoid hassles and confrontation, administrations use their office to discourage insensitivity. In composing classroom problems, University of Illinois College of Law faculty are encouraged to portray traditionally disfavored groups in a positive light and traditionally favored groups in an inferior light. Tactics can be heavy-handed; Buffalo Law School threatened that "racist, sexist, homophobic and anti-lesbian, ageist and ethnically derogatory statements, as well as other remarks based on prejudice and group stereotype" would result in "appropriate communications to the character and fitness committees of any bar to which such a student applies." Sometimes the efforts at censorship border on self-parody, such as Minnesota Law School's request that each student sign, in front of a witness, a Diversity Pledge. The Pledge obligated the student to reject "acts and expression of bigotry and hatred. I will not endorse such behavior by being silent, but through my actions will demonstrate my support and respect for victims of bigotry and hatred." A group of students calling themselves the Free Speech Movement complained that the Pledge was insulting, threatening, and an inhibition of speech. "We are deeply offended by the implication that anyone who refuses to sign it is a bigot."

Reports of insensitive comments have decreased to a trickle. The Law and Economics people would explain this as risk aversion; everyone in the law school community knows the most effective way to avoid entanglement with the thought police is self-censorship. The standard rule is to avoid risky topics, words, and cases. The common refrain used to rationalize risk aversion for inflammatory topics like rape is: "It's not worth the hassle." Even my colleague the tax specialist avoids insensitive cases involving religion. Proposing a dress code is dangerous enough for him.

Radical Consciousness strategy started with the curriculum. The first maneuver was to subvert the Socratic Method to clear out a landscape for the Compassionate Method. It was "Ho ho, Kingsfields got to go." The attack was conducted according to Radical Newspeak; connect Socratic Method with terms like humiliation, hierarchy, and patriarchy. Duncan Kennedy set the tone for the campaign: it is "humiliating to be frightened and unsure of oneself, especially when what renders one unsure is a classroom arrangement that suggests at once the patriarchal family and a Kafka-like riddle-state. The law school classroom at the beginning of the first year is culturally reactionary."

In describing his Yale Law School experiences, Chris Goodrich accuses the Method of stealing his soul. He singles out Geoffrey Hazard as Yale's version of the malicious Kingsfield, someone who "glorified technical mastery of the law" at the expense of its moral content. Hazard treated students like Marine recruits, forcing them to doubt their self-worth. He used Orwellian techniques to subvert vulnerable students into accepting the evils of the system without qualms.

Even with the increasing number of Outsiders and sympathizers joining in the attack, the Socratic Method would have persevered. It was tradition. But the efficiencies justification (one professor teaching large numbers of students) succumbed to change. Increased enrollment and the addition of new faculty resulted in a significant revision of the curriculum. It was the explosion in the number of upper-class seminars that pushed the anti-Method campaign over the line of success. Large classes were restricted to first-year courses like contracts, property, and torts. As a result, the Method is irrelevant to the last two years of law school.

In 1988, the *New York Times* ran an article titled "What Do Law Schools Teach? Almost Anything." It described the emergence and popularity of what critics call law and a banana courses. Martin Redish of Northwestern Law School was quoted as saying, "Now some people say there will be no law in the law schools." A look at any law school catalogue supports the professor's judgment that banana seminars and courses dominate the schedule. A colleague of mine refuses to give a favorable vote on *any* new course proposal because it diverts students from the canon courses. He, along with

Mary Ann Glendon, contends that flabby seminars entice students into courses that are worthless guts where they are assured of an A grade.

Two groups teach bananas. One group comprises academics who shift careers because of tenure or salary barriers; they go to law school and become law professors. They barter their first career expertise to law schools that compete in offering banana seminars. The second group, the Outsiders, dominates the banana market. The former tend to teach their discipline in a conventional way through rational analysis. In contrast, the Outsiders consciously connect teaching method with ideology.

The Outsider teaching method is politics, absolute politics; the classroom is a vehicle to disseminate the ideology of the cause. Analysis, objectivity, and hierarchy are countered by the Outsiders' method of compassion and caring—the Method of Community. This is, according to Patricia Cain, a method where "the personal is political."

Cain surveyed twenty-four students (including two males) in her Feminist Legal Theory seminar and anguished: "What did they expect? Were they even feminists?" The first class started with the Circle maneuver; Cain drew a circle on the board, noting that it represented all the people in the world. She then cut the circle in half, with one side representing men and the other side women. She drew another line through the men's area, cutting it down to a third. Next, she shaded a "tiny sliver" of this area and told the class, "This is all the educated and privileged white men in the western world. For most of you, this is what you know about the world."

In the course of the sermon, Cain lamented student papers that "were entirely rational, written in the detached voice of a lawyer." Eventually the students were feminized into a recognition that law should be about feelings. After the students thought about oppression and reflected on their feelings, the course concluded with "the telling of personal stories about what it meant to be female or male; what it meant to be black, brown, or white, what it meant to be living in a heterosexist society."

This is the type of lesson plan that shocks and frightens the Liberal system. It subverts efforts to teach students to think like lawyers. The reaction of the traditionalists is the same as that of one of Cain's students: "I couldn't believe that this was a law school class . . . is this real?" There is even more to bug the Liberals of the Empire. Requiring students to compile personal journals of impressions and "personal feelings" is chic. The assumption is that journals record the emergence of the students' understanding of Outsider ideology. The Liberal response: "The common technique of requiring students to keep intimate journals, reflecting personal transformations effected by class discussion, smacks even more of a police state mentality. Of course, honesty is the first casualty."

Outsiders avoid hierarchy and patriarchy by congregating the class in a circle to encourage "connection." The professor is designated as a facilitator or group leader, whose responsibility is to encourage students to say anything at anytime. Writing about a new course, Karl Johnson and Ann Scales say: "We had resolved to renounce our own authority, to try not to lecture, or lead discussion or assign paper topics. We had decided to use emotionally charged materials—from El Salvador to male sexual pathology to nuclear holocaust—knowing classes could end up in recalcitrance instead of growth."

The ideal Outsider seminar is a slice of the Actor's Studio. Stanislavski's Method trumps the Socratic Method. "We start with music and songs: a sonata by Samuel Barber; 'Love Is Just a Four-Letter Word' by Bob Dylan. We play recordings during class. We include poems, essays, cases, letters, slides of paintings and buildings, cartoons, things students bring in, including a bag of dirt from one student's garden." The end justifies the means; if legal education means thought control, so be it. As a feminist partisan bragged: "Malignly, I used my position of power to force them to think about at least one aspect of the feminist critique of patriarchal society."

"Sometimes it's tough to get out of bed when you're wearing silk pajamas." (Quote attributed to former jockey Bill Shoemaker)

My God, it's another Constitutional law course. Another one. Isn't there a limit? It was a faculty meeting to consider a new course, and Professor Peabody Snopes was pissed. He looked sourly at his colleagues. It was a scene from a genetic accident—a room full of rejects from the Clinton cabinet. There was a Warren Christopher prune face, a Donna Shalala look-alike sitting in the corner, and at the podium stood the Dean on a small stool just like Secretary of Labor Robert Reich.

Mary Ann Glendon is right. Constitutional law dominates the curriculum, everyone wants to teach it, students are conditioned to look for a constitutional issue in every corner, and everyone who teaches it puts a biased twist on the message. Now young Marshall wants to put his spin on the First Amendment. I thought better of him— but now he's going to assign crap from Stanley Fish, the English professor who has a scam teaching at Duke Law School, where he provokes with comments like, "On my analysis, the Constitution cannot be drained of meaning, because it is not a repository of meaning . . . ," or calling the First Amendment "the first refuge of scoundrels."

The Dean droned on in that squeaky voice of his about how we needed Marshall's new course. Baloney! Snopes thought about one of his favorites—Allan Bloom, who had infuriated the Modern Language Association radwimps by writing that the 1960s revolution damn near ended higher education. To Snopes, Bloom was too soft. Even worse was the decay that was now doing a job on legal education.

The typical law school is nothing more than a shopping mall of diversionary entertainment 'experiences.' At Harvard, the ultimate shopping mall, "Stevie Wonder," Mr. Steveland Morris, takes care of student boredom with singing lectures. No wonder a Harvard student said, "What do you have to know to go to law school . . . ? You don't have to know anything." Former rock and roller Jackie Fox, now Jacqueline Fuchs and a student at Harvard, says that "law school's easy." At the University of Virginia, students in a criminal procedure class got the special insights of Muhammad Ali. Professor Francis Allen of Michigan got it right fifteen years ago when he said that what we have is the age of "consumerism," where "student demands and dissatisfaction are likely to be given even greater attention." Snopes had memorized what Allen had written about the fun generation:

> "There has developed a widely held conviction in our culture that individuals possess a kind of natural right not to experience pain. When pain is felt, the reactions are often indignation and bewilderment. These assumptions manifest themselves in student reactions to the phenomenon of tension in law school education. Many modern students, having been denied the knowledge that tensions may be normal and inevitable incidents of the educational experience, conclude that the pain they feel is abnormal. Pain creates self-doubts because it is seen as evidence of personal deficiency or of illness. It also produces resentment against the institution and the educational process that engender it."

Law Reviews in Revolt

The profile of the contemporary editorial board sharply contrasts with those of the pre-1970s doctrinally oriented reviews. Students now enter law school with a bias against the establishment. Having served on the admissions committee sporadically for more than twenty-five years, I have noticed a definite change in the applicants' personal statements; the old statements described an interest in the practice of law. As a craft to protect client interests, law was deemed a profession in the classic sense. Competency, dedication to the principles of law, and a work ethic were the code phrases. Now the personal statements speak Radical Newspeak, revealing the desire to become public interest lawyers, to fight corporate greed, and to help capitalism's numerous victims. Statements are packed with victim talk; it is not unusual for applicants to present their own victim status as an added attraction in support of acceptance. Once in law school, they assiduously avoid the nerd courses (commercial-corporate) to specialize in the law and a banana curriculum.

The result is a law review editorial board with little interest in doctrinal analysis and virtually no interest in the traditional curriculum. On the other hand, from the banana courses they learn the legal profession is dedicated to protecting the capitalist apparatus. Banana professors drive home the lesson that practitioners are part of a conspiracy that relies on the ideology of neutrality to cover the antisocial conduct of the Establishment. Most important, it is in the nonlaw offerings that student editors are exposed to a wide menu of nontraditional writing, such as storytelling.

The once close relationship between student editors and faculty has deteriorated into an uneasy coexistence. The break started with the shift of the editors' interest to new forms of scholarship. The separation widened with the emerging student rejection of the Liberal white male values of the Establishment. *The Wall Street Journal* noted in 1986 that the "campus turmoil of the 1960s produced a new crop of assertive student editors unwilling to bow to faculty meddling." From that point on, doctrinal scholars and student editors no longer spoke the same language.

An increase in the volume of faculty criticism of law review performance put the students on the defensive. When the Harvard Law faculty voted to publish its own journal ("It is incongruous to have students sounding off on the state of law in a self-important way"), a student, noting the bitter faculty politics prevailing at the time, joked that they could not agree on a typeface, much less content. "We predict a real barroom brawl." The students won this one; the Harvard faculty journal never saw the light of day.

The affiliation between authors and editors exists on a spectrum of tense to adversarial. On the student side, a sense of power has emerged. When publication became a nonnegotiable requirement for promotion and tenure, it was obvious that the editors would become players with leverage. Egos escalated as stories circulated about authors pleading for acceptance or early publication to satisfy a promotion vote. The students demonstrated their leverage with petty demands: "It was a ghastly experience, easily one of the more horrible of my professional life. Every time the phone rang, my stomach sank. They always wanted more footnotes, more rewriting, more, more, more." To writers, obnoxious editors rudely convert riveting and carefully crafted syntax into see-Jane-run sentences.

Authors see an unbearable situation of student hubris and incompetence. The inmate revolution occurs every year as new editors appear to harass authors. Authors retaliate with multiple submissions (is eighty a record?) and leapfrogging. "I have an offer from *Michigan Law Review*; can you make me an offer?" They can also be nasty. "Student-edited journals are the scandal of legal publishing. . . . You get these kids who check for all the commas but not for the substance." James Lindgren, who qualifies as an expert on law reviews, cuts to the gut: "Law-review editors are the most aggressive and ignorant editors that you will ever encounter." Editors are more than willing to rebut Lindgren with examples of poorly written and research-defective manuscripts. The awful experience of editing pretentious prose signifying nothing is the common bond among student editors.

> "We are interested in increasing diversity without sacrificing standards." (Editor-in-chief of the George Washington Law Review announcing the adoption of new law review selection standards)

> "There is no evidence of discrimination here." (George Washington law professor Banzhof arguing against the legality of the plan)

To some critics, Harvard terminated whatever credibility student journals could muster when the editors revised the criteria for selection to the law review to include the diversity factor. Until then, grades had been the sole criterion. The assumption was that grades accurately reflect the intellectual qualities necessary for editorial responsibilities. It was an objective method; take the students with the top grades and make them editors.

By the 1980s, the grades criterion was deemed vulnerable for several reasons. First, the grading system had succumbed to the egalitarian mood of the radical movement. Grade inflation, now a fact of life at every level of academe, renders the entire system suspect. At any law school, a shrewd student can control grades by judicious selection of the banana courses. The second factor was an even more serious problem: image. By relying exclusively on grades, editorial boards were indictable for violating the politically correct code of elitism. The editor-in-chief of the *George Washington Law Review* is quoted as saying that without diversity, "the elitism would be overbearing."

At *Columbia Law Review*, applicants submit a two-page statement explaining how their race, ethnicity, socioeconomic background, sex, physical handicap, or sexual orientation would enhance the diversity perspective of the *Review*. A student editor explained the reason for the new criteria: "The *Review* does not have a great image here. There is a view among minorities that they have been underrepresented." *Cornell Law Review* goes beyond Columbia in defining diversity. It considers an applicant's "unique life experiences," which include "prejudices faced and perspectives offered as members of racial groups or as economically disadvantaged persons. The committee may also consider character strengths shown in overcoming particular personal tragedies or hardships."

The consequence of diversity selection criteria is to replace one image problem of doubtful importance and relevance—elitism—with an image issue of substantial impact—caving in on quality control. The actual effect on quality may be modest; the number of set-aside slots is small. Many law reviews do not use diversity criteria. But when the top law schools offer slots on tenuous factors such as sexual orientation and economic hardship, doubts of overall quality and competence are inevitable. It is another thing for authors to complain about.

Alternative Law Journals

Alternative journals are a phenomenon of the 1980s. Deans endorse them for the public relations value of listing additional journals in the catalogue. The PR spin is that they provide writing experience to more students while serving as a new source of information for lawyers. For students who could not satisfy law review criteria, they provide a second-best avenue for getting a journal on their résumés. The narrow focus of the alternatives offers the opportunity for specialization. The most influential alternatives have been composed of political activists, people with agendas who need a forum.

Alternatives cover a broad range of topics, from gay rights to sports law. Larger schools subsidize as many as six publications. Columbia publishes journals on business law, human rights, environmental law, gender issues, transactional law, and law and the arts. While mainstream reviews are published quarterly or more, most alternatives are semiannual. Some alternatives adhere to the mainstream standard of publishing doctrinal articles, while a few rely on active faculty participation in article selection. The distinctive characteristic of the alternative movement is unrestrained advocacy and politics. There are a few conservative publications like Harvard's *Journal of Law and Public Policy*, published by the Federalist Society, but the majority of ideological alternatives reject the white male Liberal doctrinal line to engage in aggressive support of Outsider race and gender causes.

The radical alternative's vision is often a declaration of 1960s rhetoric. Yale's *Journal of Law and Liberation*'s statement of purpose begins with the premise that this nation's "basic legal framework" was designed "to secure the power and prerogatives of a group of white male elites" and to deny "the personhood of a large segment of the population." The material in *Law and Liberation* has been an eclectic collection of attack journalism, testimonials, and stories authored by lawyers, "political prisoners," Black Panthers, and a poet serving sixty-eight years for revolutionary activities in Puerto Rico.

The bulk of alternatives get modest attention, even from those with an interest in a journal's field of specialization. One reason for this apathy is that most faculty are too lazy to keep up with the top-tier journals, much less the bland production from the remainder of mainstream reviews and certainly not the alternatives. The other reason is the perception that alternatives have serious quality problems. The suspicion is that they are edited by law review rejects who do just enough work to get résumé credit. They have marginal status with Empire promotion and tenure committees and thus do not attract the best work from the most productive source—the young people under the gun to publish. In effect, they publish the overflow from the over-populated mainstream market. Because of understaffing, footnote verification is likely to be casual.

As a subgenre, radical alternatives get attention and criticism. While the neutral centralist journals get praise for providing students with writing experience, advocacy journals are accused of conducting a counterscholarship campaign by, as *Law and Liberation* enthuses, "not editing some of the pieces according to traditional academic guidelines of style and footnoting." To Empire people, the most damaging counterscholarship consequence is in content: articles and student commentary bristle with radical babble about marginalization and victimization. To make matters worse to the critics, the alternatives reject the doctrinal model favored by the Empire. As is often the case, criticism signifies success; advocacy alternatives have had significant influence on the editing process, on style, and on substance.

It is amusing to catch the looks of amazement and distress when a white Liberal male discovers the in-your-face *National Enquirer* type of articles published by radical alternatives. Here is a short representative sample: from "The 'F' Word: Mainstreaming and Marginalizing Feminism": "Feminism is widely perceived as a 'dirty' word, reduced to its first initial rather than spelled out." From "Toilets as a Feminist Issue: A True Story": "Comparing notes with a male contemporary, I was surprised to learn that there were pay stalls in the men's bathroom but the urinals were free. Thus, women were penalized because no one had created the 'feminine' equivalent of a urinal." From an article titled "Untitled": "I found myself choking on the purely capitalist values in contracts and how they were not even acknowledged, never mind questioned." From "Using Literature in Law School: The Importance of Reading and Telling Stories": "But what was remarkable was how they took over the class (with my encouragement): 'What should we do first? Who are we? Why did we take this class? What do we hope to get out of it?'"

The Politicization of Footnotes

Footnoting is a serious activity in the sciences. Citations identify sources, act as hedges against plagiarism, and leave a track record of research. They have been likened to a summons to a witness in a court of law. Failure to cite a relevant source is tantamount to a breach of ethics, resulting in peer condemnation for failing to acknowledge a debt to a colleague. It is a serious breach that can harm a colleague by adversely affecting the source's citation index, which counts the frequency with which an article is cited and identifies the source. Since citations are viewed as a reliable proxy for determining the reputation of scholarship, index scores are used to help decide who gets promotion, grants, and other benefits.

When scholarship became a tenure requirement, footnote strategy entered legal education as a fact of life. Promotion and tenure committees, along with deans confronting salary decisions, use the cite index to evaluate a scholar's work. It is considered an objective criterion. Hence the adage: "To footnote an author is to cast a vote for his tenure or grant." Indexing has become a cottage industry for librarians; we now have index counts on the most frequently cited law reviews, the most frequently cited authors, and the fifty most frequently cited articles.

Footnote strategy involves the use of *The Bluebook: A Uniform System of Citation*. No discipline has been harassed by an imperative like *The Bluebook*, a regime dedicated to the uniformity of the mundane and to rejoicing in minutiae. *The Bluebook* is packed with inflation-producing steroids like "supra," "cf.," and "infra," which can be used to cross-reference a single source into infinity. *Id.* is the ultimate steroid, seducing one author into using 474 ids. out of a total of 574 notes. Instead of trying to cope with substantive material in the text, student editors spend countless hours playing mental games over the proper cite form. "*The Bluebook*," according to Judge Richard Posner, "creates an atmosphere of formality and redundancy in which the drab, Latinate, plethoric, euphemistic style of law reviews and judicial opinions flourishes."

Footnote research recognizes a spectrum of motivations, from pure reference to ignoble objectives such as citing a friend who is expected to return the favor. It's called conspiratorial cross-referencing, the academic equivalent of "I'm OK, You're OK." Self-citation is another ploy—it gets through the computer to become another credit in the cite index; the computer can't tell whether it's you or someone else with the same name citing you. Richard Delgado introduced the victimization motivation to legal scholarship in 1984. It was footnote oppression, consisting "of white scholars' systematic occupation of, and exclusion of minority scholars from, the central areas of civil rights scholarship. The mainstream writers tend to acknowledge only each other's work." It was, according to Delgado, an academic power play; white males wanted to control the race game: "The desire to shape events is a powerful human motive and could easily account for much of the exclusionary scholarship I have noted."

When it came to footnotes, the advocacy alternative journals followed the 1960s radical Jerry Rubin's advice in his book *Do It!*: "Break the rules" was the slogan. In the *Harvard Women's Law Journal*, Mari Matsuda urged the Outsider movement to politicize footnotes. The "affirmative action scholar" should counter the overpopulation of white male authors "by making a deliberate effort to buy, order, read, cite, discuss, and teach outsider's scholarship" and by making it a political duty to cite Outsider scholarship. When Professor Martha Minow of Harvard cites Andre Lorde, she is saying to women, to people of color, and to lesbians, "I am talking to you. I am learning from you." In radical alternative journals, footnotes are ideological statements:

> At the time I gave these remarks, I was proudly and painfully wearing a decade-old button that says, 'Defeat the Fetus Fetishist,' which was given to me by my dear friend Rhonda Copelon. . . . Although relatively old, the button has new vitality in the age of so-called Operation Rescue, which I prefer to call by any of its street name equivalents, including Operation Bully, Operation Harass-You, or, simply, Operation Screw.

Outsider scholars realized *The Bluebook* was a barrier to their vision of enlightened footnoting and scholarship. As long as the student brigade was under the control of the aphrodisiac of *Bluebook* detail, it would be hostile to Outsider work. Sitting in their dollhouse cubicles, drooling over a copy of *The Bluebook* that will follow them to the grave, student editors checked manuscripts for footnote orthodoxy. Stonewalled by *Harvard Law Review Bluebook* addiction, Katherine Bartlett complained:

> I had wanted to humanize and particularize the authors whose ideas I used in this article by giving their first as well as last names. Unfortunately, the editors

of the Harvard Law Review. . . insisted upon adhering to the "time-honored" Bluebook convention of using last name only. . . . In these rules, I see hierarchy, rigidity, and depersonalization of the not altogether neutral variety. First names have been one dignified way in which women could distinguish themselves from their fathers and husbands. I apologize to the authors whose identities have been obscured in the apparently higher goals of Bluebook orthodoxy.

The guerrilla war against *Bluebook* patriarchy and marginalization eventually reached the mainstream reviews, where it produced ideological chainsaw shock. *Hastings Law Journal* published this footnote: "Our practice of masturbation as moral terrorism must seek not to commodify women, but to demonstrate the dialectical potentialities inherent in the practice of orgasmic delight for its own value, a value which blatantly ignores and openly denies phallocentric economies of sexuality." Then, like the *Village Voice* personals section, there is footnote catharsis:

> The author is an open lesbian, in a monogamous and committed relationship; she likes sex, and she loathes violence; she finds vibrators, winks, teddy bears, and kitty cats sexy; she feels disturbed by sadomasochism, in part because of childhood and adolescent physical, emotional and sexual abuse of which she is a recovering survivor, in therapy; she believes in the Bill of Rights as a wild but still-too-elitist experiment in which women, in and among other oppressed groups, are struggling for inclusion; she is generally optimistic, as opposed to cynical, about legal process, even as she is very exasperated and disgusted with the repression of people by law in this society.

When the fifteenth edition of *The Bluebook* capitulated to Outsider pressure by requiring the use of the author's first name, footnote terrorism became a fact of life. Clever writers learned to exploit footnote techniques to create a unique package distinguishable from the conventional format. To the protectors of footnote orthodoxy of the Empire, Outsiders had joined the conspiracy of student editors who hide their ignorance behind footnote games.

Outsiders practice affirmative-action footnoting in which race and gender determine who gets cited. Cross-referencing political friends is de rigueur. *The Bluebook* now tolerates gossip. "I owe this insightful observation to my former students Sharon and Bernard, who shared their thoughts with me." The University of Chicago, the home of Milton Friedman and Richard Posner, let Robin West sneak this juicy tidbit into her article on sexism in law: "Conversations with Marcy Wilder and Toni Fitzpatrick (Stanford Law School '88) have helped me see the gender bias in Gabel's work."

There are the automatic cites, the people who must be indexed. Derrick Bell is number one; ignore him and it's exile. Matsuda warned "I have noticed in myself, for example, an immediate reaction of rage when someone tells me they did not like [Bell's] *Civil Rights Chronicles*." Marx, Nietzsche, and Ludwig Wittgenstein get thrown together in a boilerplate cite. But there is a problem: "I hate to rely on a dead white man [Wittgenstein] to illustrate this, but I like his weird clarity."

> Happiness is a long footnote. Happiness for whom? For him who writes it? "In my early days on Law Review," notes footnote opponent former Judge Abner Mikva, "I was told that footnotes are the real measure of worth in legal writing."

To my knowledge, law is the only discipline to measure the quality of scholarship by footnote numbers and density. Watch the eyes of a colleague when you present a reprint of one of your articles; the gaze *always* goes to the last page to check out the number of footnotes, and then comes a leisurely perusal of the density, that is, the ratio of text to the barking of the footnotes at the bottom of the page. The assumption: the more the barking, the higher the quality of the article. Who is the Hank Aaron of footnotes? Probably someone named Jacobs, with 4,824 notes.

It is a game of titillation. The Woodstock generation favors cartoons, poetry, and rock. To support the statement: "Otherwise, outsiders who become insiders simply define new groups as 'other.'" Martha Minow, daughter of the man who described television as a vast wasteland, attached this cite: "See Holly Near and Adrian Torf, 'Unity,' a song recorded on 'Speed of Light' (Redwood Records, 1982) (One man fights the KKK/But he hates the queers/One woman works for ecology/It's equal rights she fears/Some folks know that war is hell/But they put down the blind/I think there must be a common ground/But it's mighty hard to find.)"

Citation to exotic fugitive sources separates the footnote artist from the poseur. Dr. Hunter Thompson is chic, while only scoundrels cite Oliver Wendell Holmes Jr. or Jacques Derrida. And when it comes to scoundrel time and bad habits, no one can compete with that scandal known as the Author's Note. It starts innocently with an expression of appreciation to people who read or vetted the manuscript: "I am indebted to. . . ." Then comes a history of presentations before various groups, seminars, and, ideally, a few stops on the Call Girl circuit, trailed by a list of students who helped with the manuscript. Finally comes the side show of genuflections of acknowledgments to mother, father, grandfather, friends, beautiful wife, sons, bicentennial baby, sister, community, and women in the audience. There are sex attributions: The Author "would like to express appreciation to her lover, Lisa Bloom, for her many invaluable contributions."

The Author's Note is a thinly disguised effort to create a back door form of peer review. In effect the Note constitutes a tombstone advertisement of the endorsement of peers, minus the critical notes that typically accompany serious vetting. Listing a presentation does not tell us whether the audience read the paper in preparation for discussion or went to the presentation in exchange for free lunch and sherry. Student editors, who get no advice on the Author's Note from *The Bluebook*, buy into the pseudo peer review ploy without checking references. Footnote addicts should remember Noel Coward's wisdom: "Encountering [a footnote] is like going downstairs to answer the doorbell while making love."

The End of the Doctrinal Article

Alternative journals played an important role in helping feminists and minorities pad their résumés while gaining credibility. The first indication that feminists had reached the influential mainstream audience came with the publication of the *Women in Legal Education* symposium in the *Journal of Legal Education* in 1988. Recognition from the official publication of the American Association of Law Schools provided the impetus for crossing over from alternative outlets to the law reviews. Whether they read it or throw it away, every law professor gets a copy of the journal. Apparently the special edition was a success; I am told that all the back copies have been sold, making it a collector's item.

For many white male Liberals, this issue was the first exposure to the feminist's oppression thesis and the charge that the Empire "rests on an ethnocentric, audiocentric, racist, Christian, and class-based vision of reality and human nature, all of which makes it inherently flawed." The symposium acknowledged feminist ideology as mainstream and warned that things would never be the same.

By the early 1990s, it was obvious that the volume of nontraditional writing was increasing. All one had to do was look at the monthly law review index of articles to be amused, puzzled, or flustered by the bizarre titles. Symposia on various law and banana topics came out in the top-tier law reviews on a regular basis. The success of the Law and Economics movement attracted criticism for its nonlaw techniques, criticism that increased with the judicial appointments of Chicago School people like Richard Posner, Frank Easterbrook, and Antonin Scalia. Most of academia came to work with a vague sense of change, a sense that something was out there, but the assumption persisted that when it came time to fish or cut bait, the good old doctrinal article would still be around. In 1981, Richard Posner, then a professor at the University of Chicago, said doctrinal analysis is the "traditional and still the dominant mode of legal scholarship."

Four years after the Women in Legal Education symposium, the future arrived with the publication of "The Growing Disjunction between Legal Education and the Legal Profession," by Judge Harry Edwards. Edwards was the ideal messenger; after practice he taught at Michigan and was then appointed to the D.C. Circuit Court of Appeals. He has been a prolific scholar. His conclusion: "There has been a clear decline in the volume of 'practical' scholarship published by law professors."

The judge's article was like hitting a donkey over the head with a baseball bat; it got the community's attention. His essay was enough grist for a symposium a year later in the *Michigan Law Review*. Edwards had accurately caught the pulse of a growing frustration with theoretical scholarship. The Dean of Yale Law School was on record for complaining that "law professors today are more concerned with intellectual currents among their colleagues in the arts and sciences and less concerned about law practice and the output of the bench."

Edwards's article captured attention because he wrote like a lawyer; he collected his facts and described the consequences of "ivory tower dilettantes" writing for other dilettantes. When a law and a banana professor writes about his banana discipline, the result is mediocre scholarship. Leave literary criticism to the English department. To Edwards, nontraditional scholarship undermines the prestige of doctrinal work: "The problem is not simply the *number* of 'practical' scholars, but their waning *prestige* within the academy." The advocacy and bias of the impractical scholars "makes for aggressive intolerance, occasionally turning classroom and common rooms into battle fields." Impractical scholars scorn practitioners, giving students "the impression that law practice is necessarily grubby, materialistic, and self-interested." Students are dumbed down by banana lessons in irrelevant topics like deconstruction. One of Edwards' former clerks wrote that "It makes no sense to me that, in the first year of law school, I was expected to *deconstruct* a body of law before I understood it." The long-range projection from dilettantes writing for dilettantes is a conversion of the law school into a department of arts and sciences.

5

"CLS Is Dead As a Doornail"

A Short Introduction to the Movement

When he left to visit a southern law school, Fino was ensconced in the accepted career groove. He published several long and dense articles with a high footnote density ratio while becoming an irritating bore at faculty meetings. More important, Fino had overcome a pronounced and obviously affected Harvard Stutter as he developed student support by giving high grades. Although the students did not have a clue about what he said in class, they appreciated his fashion—an ascot, crimson blazer with Harvard crest, and a cane.

What a difference a year can make. The students were the first to pick it up: "He was always out to lunch, but now it is pure countertalk; everything involves 'indeterminacy,' 'oppression,' and 'opposition.' He says that he deconstructs the cases, whatever that means. I liked him better when he was just your typical faculty phony." We got it at the first fall faculty meeting when Fino unloaded a new vocabulary of praxis, deification, intersubjective zap, purposinist, altruism—all in a brief thirty-minute spirited attack on "Liberal hegemony." From then on, everything was a "mask." Fino said: "Legal reasoning is a texture of openness, indeterminacy, and contradiction." "The law is a major vehicle for the maintenance of existing social and power relations." "I suggest that the demonstration of indeterminacy and the linkage between indeterminacy and the fundamental problem of knowledge and power can clear the way for some new inquiries into how and why cases get decided the way they do." "The law is a denial, at the level of social interpretation, of our collective experience of illegitimacy." "Legal reasoning is an inherently repressive form of interpretive thought that limits our comprehension of the social world and its possibilities." "Modern legal doctrine, however, works in a social context in which society has increasingly been forced open to transformative conflict."

Then Fino started complaining to any unfortunate soul he could corner about being "alone." He said he needed someone to rap with, someone who could uncover "the indeterminacies of life, the key to intersubjective zapism. If I want to discuss a new mask that I have uncovered, I have to call Duncan, the Tush, or someone at Miami." Then, with no warning, the show stopped. Fino dropped the mask talk and went on to Bud-dhism. He even changed his name to Ganku. He also stopped writing and hasn't published a word since his Crit days (except for Buddhist recipes).

Fino's story is the story of the Life of Critical Legal Studies. As Duncan Kennedy said, CLS is "dead as a doornail. There isn't at Harvard Law School or nationally any CLS movement left. The movement completely collapsed several years ago."

CLS was the most ambitious challenge to the Empire since the Realist movement. To some, CLS was a rejuvenation of Realism, perhaps a more definitive rejection of the neutrality of law and objectivity. There were other similarities; the Crits started their careers as members of the Liberal establishment and followed the accepted path of top-tier elitism. As was the case for the Realists, the timing was right; the Liberals were fat, smug, and lethargic, enjoying the fruits of the post–World War II boom and relieved at having avoided the damage from the student insurrection of the Vietnam era. The Crits, like the Realists, were the beneficiaries of Liberal tolerance.

The rebellion shocked the Liberal mentality. Instead of Brahmin reformers, the Crits came on as uncivilized thugs. With frequent references to terms like moral terrorism and guerrilla warfare, Crit rhetoric conjured up images of 1960s violence. Comparing Crits to Huns, Dean Robert Clark of Harvard accused them of carrying out a program of "a ritual slaying of the elders." Accustomed to a civilized community where differences are resolved through dialogue and compromise, the Liberals were outflanked by the politicization of everything from admission to law school to admission to practice, with free restrooms thrown in. The Crit motto, "office politics is real politics," was not the accepted Liberal style.

It was not only the rhetoric that offended the Empire, it was the substance and the ambition of the challenge. The CLS goal was the termination of the Empire's system—from legal education to practice. The Realists had tried tinkering with reforms and failed. The Crits demanded a new playing field, with new rules and new values skewed to favor a new agenda.

In 1983, Roberto Mangabeira Unger wrote: "The critical legal studies movement has undermined the central ideas of modern legal thought and put another conception of law in their place." The movement started with the benefit of membership in the academic palace. Crits were effective recruiters. Duncan Kennedy, as Nickey Morris, received praise from Scott Turow in *One L*: "In Morris's class I found myself launched once again on that kind of scrutiny of the most fundamental assumptions regarding the way we lived each day—the manner in which we treated each other—which had seemed so important when I had come to school."

They were the only radical Left game in town; in 1977 the feminist and the Critical Race movements had not generated the momentum that would explode in the 1980s. It was chic to talk Crit. Even tax and corporate law types were picking up CLS buzzwords and talking about trashing a rival's article. It was the ideal story for national media coverage—young, arrogant radicals running around in army fatigues biting the hands of the Liberal elitists who fed them. Crits got the opportunity to unload on the legal education hegemony in *The New Republic, The National Law Journal,* and the *New York Times.*

Trashing is a Critspeak term used to ridicule the Empire's dedication to rational and analytical criticism. At one level, trashing is a tactic to sabotage objectivity by uncovering indeterminacy. According to Mark Kelman: "Take specific arguments very *seriously* in their own terms; discover they are actually *foolish* ([tragi]—*comic*); and then look for some (external observer's) *order* (*not* the germ of truth) in the internally contradictory, incoherent chaos we've exposed." This is a pretentious way of saying the objective of CLS scholarship is the demystification and the unmasking of the delusion of the Liberal system of law. In a broader sense, trashing implies a license to heap scorn on the Empire.

Trashing can be ad hominem, such as Mark Tushnet's calling Tribe's constitutional law treatise corrupt. It can also get silly: David Fraser encouraged Crit colleagues "to engage in acts of 'macho self-immolation,' to become moral terrorists, to 'whack-off' in faculty meetings, to construct a praxis which is meaningful, public, and dangerous." Trashers take pleasure in heaping contempt on their Liberal foes: "America is wobbling, torn by a callous court, a bitter and self-indulgent electorate, special interest groups dominance, class and racial conflict, a superficial but seemingly impregnable Congress, and an isolated, frequently arrogant Presidency."

Duncan Kennedy is the master of trash and taunt. A self- described "existential-Marxist anarcho-syndicalist modernist," he both titillates and infuriates. Alumni were indignant when he used the *Harvard Law School Bulletin* to advise law students on how to radicalize their future law firms. They were told not to laugh at partner's jokes but to respond with blank expressions when the oppressor expects a compliant smile. His strategy "involves fighting with your elders and scaring them, maybe; undermining them, maybe; hurting their feelings, certainly." The response from the alumni was not generous: "the vocabulary of the late 1960s—early 1970s radical chic—splendidly preserved without any contamination by the events of a decade." "Sententious drivel." "The ramblings of a narcissistic."

Duncan piqued his colleagues by recommending that the best way to solve the politics of hierarchy was to pay everyone in law—lawyers, law professors, paralegals, secretaries, and janitors—the same salary. This irritated the Harvard janitors; as one said: "The only thing worse than scrubbing a toilet would be to have to pretend to be some fancy-pants, egghead college professor, usually some dweeby guy who could never do anything but read books."

Once trashing was unleashed, it became fashionable to compete over who could compose the most vicious taunts or the most outlandish attack on a legal institution. My vote on both counts goes to Mark Tushnet. Tushnet once complained that the term "Crits" was marginalizing "and when used by adherents of critical legal studies an internalization of that marginalization." A prolific writer and a cofounder of CLS, Tushnet produced shock waves with his review of *Strange Justice: The Selling of Clarence Thomas,* by Jane Mayer and Jill Abramson. Justice Thomas lied "beyond a reasonable doubt" about his relationship with Anita Hill. This raises the question: What do we do about it? One possibility is impeachment, but Tushnet rules this out as unlikely to happen. Congress "is concerned solely with the politics of the case and not with the directive the Constitution might give about whether Thomas can or should be impeached." Nevertheless, there is a way of penalizing Thomas for his perjury: when the Court hands down a 5-4 decision with Justice Thomas part of the majority, citizens should simply ignore the decision "as law at all." "Although the prospect of widespread disregard is slight, at least it is a remedy in the hands of citizens themselves, rather than their representatives."

Tushnet got what Crits crave, media attention, including a photograph in the *National Law Journal.* It didn't make any difference that the Mayer and Abramson book did not conclude that Thomas lied. When questioned about the article, Ms. Abramson replied with "poppycock." "It's inflammatory," she said, and called the notion Thomas should be impeached "silly."

Professor Tushnet was as happy as a fox in a chickenhouse, explaining that his article was an academic exercise. "Academic in the sense of academic freedom, and academic also in the sense that no one is ever going to do it." It was the last gasp by a relic of a failed movement, a confession that when all the Critbabble is carved away, CLS is basically antipragmatic, little more than a blend of elitism and narcissism. While the Crits were accusing the Liberals of playing games with the Socratic Method, they were playing games with radical trash talk.

Trashing had a dissipating effect on the credibility of the message and the messengers. One consequence was the loss of student support. At Harvard, Kennedy became the symbol for a backlash; students saw his proletariat pose as hypocrisy, his wearing work boots to classes an affectation, and his Crit-babble in class incomprehensible. His courses are considered sociology projects. Students "just want to see what make this lunatic tick. The whole thing is passé. It's like watching a bad movie."

The Demise: External Criticism and Internal Self-Destruction

CLS was a short-lived movement, officially starting with a conference in 1977 at Madison, Wisconsin, then beginning to implode in 1984 with two publications: a symposium in the *Stanford Law Review* devoted to CLS, and Dean Paul Carrington's article "Of Law and the River."

Mark Twain's *Life on the Mississippi*, the story of a young man's spiritual growth as he learns to manage the twists, turns, and tides of the Mississippi River, provides a frame of reference for Carrington's blistering analysis of CLS. The river is a metaphor for law; it is never constant, and its currents are always changing, compelling the pilot to rely on judgment, courage, and acquired experience. Twain's instructor was the Mississippi River version of Kingsfield, constantly asking tough questions and making harsh assessments of his pupil's performance. There were no "no-hassle passes." (Duncan Kennedy once proposed that students be allowed to pass on questions without penalty. His colleagues passed.) Like the river, law is power; but unlike the river, law is an aspiration, and a lawyer who does not believe in the aspiration, or believes it is a deception designed to oppress, has succumbed to nihilism. The same applies to law professors who, as nihilists, "are more likely to train crooks than radicals. If this risk is correctly appraised, the nihilist who must profess that legal principle does not matter has an ethical duty to depart the law school, perhaps to seek a place elsewhere in the academy."

The river metaphor gave Carrington's advice to the Crits a subtle but powerful resonance. It generated angry correspondence. There were charges of a purge of Leftist ideology. Paul Brest wrote: "To be more blunt, I thought that the sort of Red-baiting that Carrington is engaging in had disappeared once and for all after the 1950s." Some conceded, as did Yale's Owen Fiss, that although the Crits denied the existence of law—so what? "But I believe that they too have an important role to play in legal education, and thus take some exception to your recent invitation for them to leave." The real signif-icance of the imbroglio was that people who had only a vague idea of CLS got a lesson in what it was all about. For many, it was a revelation; what was posing as an important movement in law and legal education was accused of openly advocating the rejection of law.

If there was any doubt that CLS was walking in the corridors of power naked, it was dispelled in the Stanford Law Review CLS Symposium. "Roll Over Beethoven," the lead article by Peter Gabel and Duncan Kennedy, proved beyond dispute that when Crits proudly 'fess' up to obfuscation and obscurism, they are telling the truth. A few basic Critspeak definitions pref-ace a synopsis of Beethoven being rolled.

> "Intersubjective Zap" is a sudden, intuitive moment of connectedness. It is a vitalizing moment of energy (hence "zap") when the barriers between the self and the other are in some sense suddenly dissolved.
>
> "Body snatchers" and "cluster of pods" are references to the film *Invasion of the Body Snatchers*. . . . [P]ods sent into space by an alien civilization find their way to earth. When a pod comes into contact with a sleeping human, it de-velops into a duplicate body, killing the original, and effectively taking over the human form for alien purposes. The reference illustrates the manner in which one's ideas and expressions can be appropriated by others for their own pur-poses. [A]n appropriated phrase loses some of its original meaning and sense of historical contingency.

The story: Peter accuses Duncan of going beyond indeterminacy to com-pose practical philosophical formulations. Duncan replies that Peter is talk-ing rationalist, formulaic, positivist yuk. He goes on to say Peter is guilty of explicitness and the body snatchers are always lurking, ready to turn explic-itness into a cluster of pods. The two then debate intersubjective zap and un-alienated relatedness. Peter connects janitors teaching at law schools with in-tersubjective zap. Peter agrees with Duncan that unalienated relatedness is not a phenomenological thing. Duncan delivers a short lecture praising the interspace of artifacts, gestures, histrionics, soap opera, pop culture, and "all that kind of stuff." Peter complains that intersubjective zap is falsified when it falls into the hands of body snatchers. Duncan posits that jokes can be used to protect the reality of the community. Peter disagrees. When Peter criticizes him for evading explicitness, Duncan wants to know how to reconcile that criticism with his proposal that janitors receive equal pay and his no-hassle pass proposal. At this point, Peter unloads on the fundamental contradiction, arguing that it is being appropriated by the body-snatching rights theorists who use it as a pod for self-serving objectives. Duncan goes ballistic, saying he renounces the fundamental contradiction. "I recant it, and I also recant the whole idea of individualism and altruism.... I mean these things are absolutely classic examples of 'philosophical' abstraction which you can manipulate into little structures." Duncan threatens to recant his critique of rights theory. On and on it goes for more than fifty pages. Finally, Peter concludes: "that I think is indeterminate."

"Roll Over" is an indeterminate read; the reaction depends on mood. On the first reading, I found it a postmodern version of a gangsta rap session wherein Kennedy and Gabel hammer the Liberal body snatchers and rap on tactics for destroying the pods. After a second reading it seemed to be performance art: two professors acting out an outlaw role by metaphorically rubbing feces on the faces of the readers. After reflection, I concluded that "Roll Over" anticipated Live Painting, an art in which artists cover themselves with car paint and hang for hours on hooks, talking or staring at onlookers. The idea is to challenge the traditional view of art, which assumes the viewer can read any type of criticism into the work. Live Painting permits the artist to look critically at the (reader) viewer, even to harass him. "Words drifted out unconnected" [from a Live Painting at a New York exhibit]. "If you hooked them all together, they made their kind of sense. 'It's all part of the piece . . . it's funny, and it's threatening.'" As an example of Outsider writing, "Roll Over" was classic; it defied and violated every principle of doctrinal writing. It was not analytical, neutral, or coherent. Carried to the ultimate, "Roll Over" was trashing into a mirror to reflect self-caricature.

Anyone who reads the Kennedy and Gabel introduction to CLS would be inclined to be receptive to the critical articles in the symposium that followed. The authors were in agreement that the Crits produced incoherent, dense, and impenetrable scholarship. This is not the result of a lack of composition skills but a function of CLS strategy. The objective is the calculated use of a private Critspeak "in" jargon to intimidate the Liberal community. They compound the problem for Liberals by giving code words like "praxis" double meanings. It was fun mocking the establishment while playing the role of the political revolutionary, bragging at the yearly conferences that "when they find out what we've done, they're going to come after us with guns."

The critics were also in agreement that CLS did not have a message to deliver—a deficiency they sought to hide under the murky syntax of Critbabble. Flushing out indeterminacy is an exercise that relies on anti tactics: anticapitalism, hierarchy, Liberalism, patriarchy, and the rest of Critspeak target words. Anti screeds on topics such as contracts, property, and torts exposed instances of indeterminacy in Empire law but then stopped. Practical solutions or political strategy were never mentioned. When it came to the trench warfare where rights activists live, the Crits were AWOL, playing wonk games at conferences. Phillip Johnson identified the consequence of indeterminacy and trash scholarship: "In fact, Critical writing has practically nothing to suggest in the way of a positive political program. For a movement that claims to be political, this is truly an astonishing vacuum."

Louis Schwartz likened CLS to surrealism, Dali, and Picasso: "We do not deal here with reason but with volcanic sub-rational emotion; we are in the domain of id, not ego." Schwartz traced the roots of CLS to the radicalism of the Vietnam era and to "that famous and sentimental piece of utopianism that emanated from the Yale Law School in 1970, Reich's *Greening of America*." The criminal law professor was on target. While Professor Kennedy accuses Liberals of snatching CLS idea bodies, it is Kennedy who did the snatching; he and his followers were pods from *Greening Consciousness III*.

Crit Body Snatching

Kennedy may recant the individualism and altruism pods as frequently and vehemently as he wants, but the two pods remain an accepted wisdom within the CLS cult. His 1976 article, "Form and Substance in Private Law Adjudication," is an obvious heist of individualism and altruism from *Greening of America*. Without Reich's murky bell-bottom-pants syntax and without the use of heavyhanded Critspeak, Kennedy sets up a face-off between individualism, a form of Consciousness II, and altruism, which is his version of Consciousness III. Individualism relies on self-reliance to protect one's interests; the principal theme is that not sharing with others is an affirmative moral right. Individualism rationalizes noninterference by government (always worse than the problem it seeks to cure), justifies basic legal institutions like contract, property, criminal law, and tort, and legitimizes the invisible hand that ensures unimpeded selfishness interacting for the public benefit.

In Reich's Consciousness II, individualism was a process of natural selection governed by meritocracy. While people in the II era may start at the same level, only the best, as determined by neutral and rational criteria, make it to the top. "Consciousness II sees life in terms of a fiercely competitive struggle for success." This merely restates rugged individualism. Reich took this to another level with the charge that Consciousness II institutionalized individualism into the Corporate State, an unholy joint venture between individual individualism and corporate individualism. "It is" according to Reich, "the worst of all possible worlds: uncontrolled technology and uncontrolled profiteering, combined into a force that is both immensely powerful and utterly irresponsible." Reich was an early Crit, using Consciousness II to provide a legacy for Critspeak to exploit. He anticipated Critbabble by defining key terms: hierarchy, which "results in automatic, clearly defined inequality," and false neutrality, which holds that "the law has lost any pretense of neutrality." He also anticipated the widely held Crit view that "law can teach that what is wrong is right, that what is false is true," and does so.

In "Form and Substance" Professor Kennedy assures the reader that individualism is so dominant, it is "difficult even to identify a counterethic." Nevertheless, he uses the remaining sixty pages to endorse altruism as a viable alternative. Altruism is sacrifice, sharing, and mercy. One does not prefer self over the interest of others. Sharing involves the rearrangement of losses and gains at the expense of self. Altruism is inspired by "communal involvement, solidarity, and intimacy" and the interaction of "moral fault or moral virtue." It is "Love thy neighbor as thyself."

The Greening of America says: "The world is a Community. People all belong to the same family, whether they have met each other or not." Again Reich anticipated CLS; this is the altruism of Consciousness III. Like Kennedy's version, it rejects meritocracy and linear or analytical thought and is suspicious of logic. Kennedy's intimacy is Reich's sensitivity, communal involvement is Consciousness III's togetherness, and solidarity is a "genuine relationship with others."

The critics had been highly critical of the spongy content of Consciousness III, perhaps prompting Kennedy to remind the reader that the usefulness of the altruism alternative is highly problematic and that "law is unequivocally the domain of individualism." This concession is followed by a vigorous self-rebuttal through the use of indeterminacy strategy. It begins with the intuitive belief in the existence of two modes of thought. Like Romanticism vs. Classicism, individualism and altruism exist as two rhetorical arguments, creating indeterminacy in every decision. "Given that individualism and altruism are sets of stereotyped pro and con arguments, it is hard to see how either of them can ever be 'responsible' for a decision." Once altruistic skepticism subverted the presumption of the dominance of individualism, legal institutions such as contract, tort, and property became indeterminate. The individualist still believes in neutrality and judicial nonintervention. The altruist argues for the enforcement of communitarian, paternalist, and regulatory standards.

"Form and Substance" helps explain the demise of the CLS movement. On the theoretical level, it is a challenging read. The argument of a connection between rules and individualism and a connection between standards and altruism deserves, and has received, a serious audience. The Patchwork argument (the inability to develop a general legal doctrine from incompatible ethical concepts like individualism and altruism) has generated debate among scholars. These and other Crit arguments have created a dialogue lawyers should be exposed to in law school. On the practical level of institutional change, "Form and Substance" proved to be as ineffectual as Reich's Consciousness III.

The Crits Lose Their Constituency

When it came time to attract a constituency and to translate theory to practice, CLS stumbled. Disdain for real politics ultimately led to the movement's being viewed as elitist. The Crits never congealed into a unified self; instead, they faded into a loose alliance of Left-Liberal activists and academic Marxist sympathizers from the Liberal camp, plus splinter cells with idiosyncratic biases. They bickered about everything from intersubjective zap to the nature of the linkage between standards and altruism. The goal was revolution by revision: altruism over individualism. It was a grandiose aspiration that ignored the practical remedies sought by feminists and Critical Race rights activists.

Using narrative, Patricia Williams draws on a series of personal experiences to illuminate her concern with the CLS disdain for the rights activists. She starts with a short impressionistic allegory about renegade high priests (Crits) rebelling against other priest-keepers of the celestial city (the Liberal establishment) to strike out on their own, eventually finding a home in the Deep Blue Sea. At the bottom of the Sea a group of people (Blacks) were living a battered life of oppression. Williams then takes the reader through three personal experiences, beginning with her memories of working in a Los Angeles Criminal Courtroom where the bulk of defendants were minorities. (What have high priest Crits ever done for them?) Next is the rental allegory. When a white colleague (Peter Gabel, before his "Roll Over" fame) leases an apartment, he seeks to diminish his status as a lawyer authority figure in dealing with the landlord. Williams, as a Black female, formalized her status as a lawyer: "I am still engaged in a struggle to set up transactions at arm's length . . . and to portray myself as a bargainer of separate worth, distinct power, sufficient *rights* to manipulate commerce, rather than to be manipulated as the object of commerce." The third experience was the story of her great-great-grandmother, who was, as private property, sold into slavery. Williams analyzes the sale as an issue of formation of contract and concludes that the best solution is the "consciousability and humanitarianism" argument—"that she, poor thing, had no rights." This is the point that CLS overlooked: the need for *more* rights. "Give them to trees. Give them to cows. Give them to history. Give them to rivers and rocks." Williams concludes: "[W]hat is too often missing from CLS works is the acknowledgment that our experiences of the same circumstances may be very different; the same symbol may mean different things to each of us."

The Waste Land: Deconstruction

Transcendental Deconstruction, Transcendent Justice. Oral Sex in the Age of Deconstruction. The Deconstruction of the Fourth Amendment. Deconstruction and Marxism: Implications for Law and Society. The Karl and Smith Appeals: Deconstruction of Tax Shelters. A Deconstruction of Motherhood and a Reconstruction of Parenthood. Aspects of Deconstruction: The Failure of the Word Bird. The Deconstruction of the Marital Privilege. Deconstruction, Structuralism. Anti-Semitism and the Law. Towards the Deconstruction of Legal Relativism. Epiphanies of Darkness: Deconstruction in Theology. Good Bye to Deconstruction.

This collection of titles suggests that deconstruction is popular in legal scholarship. The Crits started the fashion with references to decon in support of indeterminacy and used it as a compass in their articles. The threshold impression is that decon is a fundamental CLS principle, a method of analysis and interpretation that defines the Crit perspective. While Crits profess to practice decon, few do, and most seemingly do not have the foggiest notion of what it is or how it works. When Posner said: "Deconstruction is at once the most skeptical of critical methods and the one least well understood by lawyers," he could have included Crits.

Deconstruction is a derivative of literary criticism. The role of the critic is to act as a missionary by educating the reader rather than executing the author's reputation. Professors as critics gain reputation and power by operating in schools such as Realism, Humanism, Aestheticism, or Regionalism. A school defines the rules for evaluating literature. The selection of a school determines the success or failure of one's career.

In the hierarchy of the literary world, critics are second class. They could not cut it in the real world of writing and thus opt to sit on the sidelines, condemning real writers while playing word games. They eavesdrop on what the writers already know. This is the source of the critics' antagonism; they are derivative to the text and are dependent on the writers for a living. As long as the text and the author control, critics are intellectual parasites feeding off the work of others. No matter how imaginative the critics' insights, no one disputes the author's control over the text. Deconstruction reverses this hierarchy. Joel Schwartz describes the reversal: "[D]econstruction elevates the interpreter or critic above the literary or philosophical figure that he studies. His (or her) Shakespeare has nothing to learn from Shakespeare himself. The thrill of being Shakespeare's superior is not to be understated."

Jacques Derrida is the acknowledged master of decon. A French philosopher, he dazzles American academic audiences with his sermons lambasting the established view that the spoken word is superior to the written one. His interpretation of culture and history is that knowledge comes from the writing on paper. The meaning of the written word is both "differential" and "deferred": "the product of a restless play within language that cannot be fixed or pinned down for purposes of conceptual definition." Derrida rejects the notion of conceptual closure, that is, the reduction of text to ultimate meaning.

Deconstruction is best understood by reference to differentiation under the structuralist approach. Language simplifies meaning by differentiating categories. We refer to the words "cold," "warm," "hot," and "scalding" to describe the temperature of water. As an arbitrary point on the spectrum, the word "warm" is differentiated from "cold" or "hot." The meaning of "warm" is determined by reference to the difference with other categories. The letters w–a–r–m compose a "signifier" that evokes the "signified" warm in the reader's mind. John Ellis explains: "It is the system of differentiation, therefore, that is the source of meaning: the way in which a language simplifies an infinitely complex set of phenomena to make up a finite set of categories, to one or other of which all phenomena will be assigned." This is structuralism; deconstruction is poststructuralism.

Derrida and his followers exploit the principle of differentiation to conclude that meaning is never final but is instead an evolving process without a final resolution. Meaning is constantly deferred, postponed indefinitely, and thus *never* final. Frank Lentricchia calls it "the very process of linguistic de-

ferral, an illusion continuously undercut by the cunning movement of signi-
fication as the structure of difference." Meaning is suspended through trace;
each word has a trace of meaning from previous words, while simultaneously
holding itself open to the traces of subsequent words. It is similar to the flight
of an arrow; the word as arrow is in motion but at any instant it is not, and,
according to Jonathan Culler, "every instant is already marked with the traces
of the past and future." Hence there is *never* a privileged meaning, never a
final, ultimate meaning for any word, document, or screed. It allows Sanford
Levinson to say there "are as many plausible readings of the United States
Constitution as there are versions of *Hamlet*."

Deconstructionists use textuality to subvert the influence of the author.
Textuality is a restatement of the trace-arrow concept; texts are not controlled by the author's intention but have a textuality of their own. According to the deconer Terry Eagleton: "All literary texts are woven out of other
literary texts, not in the conventional sense that they hear the traces of 'influence' but in the more radical sense that every word, phrase, or segment is
a reworking of other writings which precede or surround the individual
work." To the hard-core deconer, the text is no longer subject to any convention or rule of interpretation. The final wisdom comes from Derrida:
"*There is no outside-text* [there is no outside-text; il n'y a pas dehors texte]."

"There are no truths, only rival interpretations" best describes the process.
Deconstruction is a performance where the reader identifies a *privileged* interpretation of the text. The doctrine of individualism was Duncan
Kennedy's privileged interpretation of contracts. Privileged meaning is a political term that serves as a symbol for the establishment view. The performance continues by "undermining, subverting, exposing, undoing, trans-
gressing, or demystifying" the privileged meaning. A counter or conflicting
interpretation, such as Kennedy's altruism, is identified to challenge individualism, thereby creating indeterminacy and doubt about the legitimacy of
the privileged reading. The clash between the two conflicting interpretations
is called *aporia*, a Greek word meaning "full of doubts and objections."

The counterinterpretation, the repressed writing, comes from the margins
of the text, underground sources such as minor passages, historical references,
footnotes, or even surmises by the reader. Without the presence of an author,
the deconer can argue that his interpretation is just as correct as the privileged view. Kennedy could decree that altruism is the new paradigm, the
new privileged meaning, and that it should dictate legal policy and resolution of cases. But in the world of deconstruction, altruism would have a short
life.

Deconstruction never stops; as Derrida says, not to continue the deconstruction performance is to "confirm the established equilibrium." The marginalized view replaces the privileged reading, which disappears into oblivion, having served its purpose as a target. The reader then uncovers a new marginal view to create an *aporia* to oust the new privileged interpretation, and thus it continues. Culler says: "If deconstruction criticism is a pursuit of differences—differences whose suppression is the condition of any particular entity or position—then it can never reach final conclusion but stops when it can no longer identify and dismantle the differences that work to dismantle other differences."

A Deconstruction Striptease

In the excitement of the CLS revolution, the Crit deconers disregarded the consequences of deconstruction as a critical literary exercise. Laws, regulations, and decisions involve commands that produce tangible consequences. The real world has a vital interest in how these commands are formulated and processed. Changes occur in doctrine and commands only after reflection and analysis. There is no place in this system "for arguments that mean nothing and say nothing" or for Derrida's denial of the author's authority over the text. Lawyers and judges cannot function if any interpretation or command they offer is subjected to deconstruction and a permanent state of indeterminacy. When pseudodeconstruction is mainlined into legal scholarship, the result is an immature product, a hodgepodge of trashing, office politics, and irrelevant games. Fino, our colleague who flirted with deconstruction during his Crit days, spent a summer deconning the Second Amendment. Here is what Fino wrote but never submitted to a law review.

Fino's Deconstruction

A well-regulated militia being necessary to the security of a free state, the right of the people to keep and bear arms shall not be infringed. (U.S. Const. amend. II)

Everyone assumes the Second Amendment is a weapons (guns, tanks, and other combat instruments of death) issue, i.e., what type of weapon is covered and the limits of the restraints. This is what the democrats, the republicans, and the N.R.A. squabble over. [Notice that Fino privileged the N.R.A. over the two political parties. He wanted to force the reader into a minor *aporia*.] The weapons characterization argument is more than a waste of time, it is a sordid example of the "politics of politics," a mask for what the Second Amendment really says. The Second Amendment refers to the Right to a Coat of Arms and not to the privileged politicized interpretation of weapons.

This Nation does not have titles of nobility; when the Second Amendment was enacted, titles were deemed symbols of tyranny and were not recognized by the framers of the Constitution. The framers resolved that merit and achievement would determine status and function to encourage social and economic upward mobility. Remember, it was a time of Individualism. Whatever one's origin, the Constitution ensured the opportunity for success and status. Here the first shadow of a reading from the margin appears in opposition to the privileged weapons interpretation. In a democracy, status comes from the glare of recognition of being a gentleman. The framers, as gentlemen, replaced the titles of nobility with the Gentleman as the ideal of the new country. Having opened the way for a new class system, the Gentleman Class, the framers had to devise a way to protect it. That is exactly why they included the Second Amendment in the Constitution. Here is how the meaning emerges.

We can discern stress in the amendment's use of the words "keep," "bear," and "arms." The next step is to extricate these stress words from the ordinary relationship of the adjoining words. In its deconstructed context "arms" refers to heralding, i.e., coats of arms. Eugene Zieber, in Hereditary in America, says: "There is no reason why any American should not bear arms, if entitled to them: in fact, there is every reason why he should bear them." The use of the word "bear" certifies the right that people have to publicly display the design of the coat of arms. Reference to "keep" supplies further protection; to keep a coat of arms means all hereditary rights are protected from political interference. Zieber notes that "a man's son would feel a natural pride in preserving the memorial of his father's reputation, by assuming, and also by transmitting his device." Now the amendment's reference to militia makes sense. Militias fight wars, and war is the origin for the use of coats of arms. In battle, the design of the coat of arms identified comrades. "Arms let us know, if the Bearers are Noblemen or Gentlemen and what their dignity is: that appearing by their Helmets."

The result is that the Coat of Arms reading from the margin trumps the privileged weapons interpretation. But as Earl Weaver (or was it Kate Smith) said: "It ain't over until the Fat Lady sings and in deconstruction she never sings." It is not that there are no right answers, but that there is never a correct interpretation. Hence I can identify a meaning in the margins to challenge the new privileged coat-of-arms meaning. Notice that the framers were all male, that the status they sought to protect was Gentleman. In other words, the Second Amendment is derived from patriarchy and implies the oppression of women. The word "arms," for example, symbolizes the male ethic of individualism, power, and aggression. [Fino's manuscript ends at this point.]

Fino candidly admitted to himself that deconning was great fun and gave him an immense sense of power. The reference to "arms" in his manuscript was a lead into a feminist decon to expose the patriarchal warrior culture where women are reified as possessions. He played the role of word terrorist, metaphorically subverting the canons of conventional interpretation while sowing seeds of discontent. And no one could dispute his correctness. When he circulated a draft among his colleagues, it created a mild stir. Another power surge—he had never received that amount of attention from people who viewed him as an annoyance. The senior faculty were negative, most agreeing it didn't have anything to do with law. "A puzzle without a solution." "Fino is yelling into an abyss; I wish he would fall into it." Younger colleagues were complimentary. Tenured Radical said it was a technique that could be used against the oppressions of patriarchy and phallogocentricism.

Quite by accident, Fino got hold of a paperback edition of David Lodge's *Small World: An Academic Romance*, a satirical account of Professor Morris Zapp, an academic con artist and ace deconstructionist. *Small World* is a tale of life on the literary call girl circuit where reputations come and go, depending on the latest fashion. Fino was jolted by Zapp's now famous striptease lecture on deconstruction: "The reader plays with himself as the text plays upon him, plays upon his curiosity, desire, as a striptease dancer plays upon her audience's curiosity and desire." Then it hit him like a George Foreman right cross; decon was all con, vacuous, a waste of time, and a ploy to create a level playing field of popular legal culture scholarship, a form of academic populism where all thoughts and interpretations are equal, which means all law professors are equal. Baloney! Fino acknowledged that only a vain academic would suggest that the Second Amendment protects the right to a coat of arms or that an eighteen-year-old is eligible to be President. Zapp's striptease lecture changed Fino to Ganku.

The publication of attempts at deconstruction without serious objection (the dissenting articles in the Stanford CLS symposium are a notable exception) confirms that the Empire has lost control over the law reviews. In fact, the reviews were actively competing for decon pieces. In accepting my article criticizing the application of deconstruction to law, an editor remarked that they had been looking for a decon piece. They appreciated my article because, as written in the introduction, "in a fit of '*aporia*' the author deconstructs himself."

Even before that incident, I learned that pseudodeconstruction was the fashion among the new generation of editors. *Cardozo Law Review* published my version of a deconstruction graphic. (Cardozo was the first law review to publish the words of Derrida.) A deconstruction graphic is an extension of what Derrida calls Double Session. In *Glas*, Derrida created a face-off between the philosopher Hegel and the writer Genet by using Hegel's quotes on the left side of the page and quotes from the thief, homosexual, and writer Genet on the right side of the same page. Christopher Norris writes that it is Derrida's "most graphic demonstration of how texts can invade each other's space. . . . Hegel and Genet are brought face to face in a kind of perverse interlinear gloss which exposes philosophic reason to the lures and obsessions of the homosexual thief-turned-writer." The objective is to glean knowledge from the encounter by experiencing alienation, confusion, and passion. My graphics were crammed full of quotes from various sources to create a series of encounters over such topics as storytelling, antitrust, and chaos. As Norris said, each sentence was "wrenched out of context and transformed into a mindbending parody of itself."

Deconstruction is, as Professor Morris Zapp advised Fulvia Morgan, "kind of exciting—the last intellectual thrill left. Like sawing through the branch you're sitting on." It is the exercise and the performance that attracts. The performance is all thrill and challenge, working to achieve *Glas*—maybe alienation, maybe tension, maybe boredom, but making no commands and giving no directions.

More Striptease

The training in deconstruction starts at the undergraduate level, where it is still the fashion. I asked a writer in residence at the University of Virginia about the influence of Derrida and the French invasion. He exploded: "I am the only S.O.B. around here who tells the truth, and I write fiction. They talk in tongues of nonsense. Nothing is nothing." He stalked away, mumbling something about "where do these people come from?" My most memorable encounter with the tongues of deconstruction came in a faculty workshop conducted by an English Lit professor accompanied by a copyright expert. They selected the optimum target—a copyright decision by Judge Richard Posner. Posner, with his dedication to efficiency and individualism, is anathema to the Crits. Deconers like to go after copyright. It is a basic Marxist principle that property is shared by the masses; hence, no individual is entitled to carve out a monopoly in copyright. As academic Marxists like to say, private property is theft. More to the point, Derrida textuality teaches that words and text never have a fixed meaning and therefore can never become a property right in a fixed form, a requirement for getting copyright protection.

The case involved the copyright of a derivative work. The plaintiff sued M.G.M. for infringement, alleging she had a valid copyright on a painting of Dorothy from the motion picture *The Wizard of Oz*. Much to the chagrin of the decon professors, Posner held that the plaintiff's image of Dorothy lacked originality and therefore was not copyrightable. After stating that as an ardent feminist she saw pervasive evidence of patriarchy, the English professor detected numerous references that validated this oppression. The first example was Judge Posner's use of Miss, rather than Ms., to describe the plaintiff. Then she was singled out by Posner as an "employee," a hierarchial put-down. When she refused an offer by her employer to do the painting, Posner wrote that "she did not like the contract terms," a suggestion to the professor that she was being marginalized as an irrational female. The fact that a male finally got the contract from M.G.M. to paint Dorothy was conclusive evidence of patriarchy marginalizing the female plaintiff as victim. The law professor confused everyone with the contradictions and privileging clichés of the law on authorship. The incident that sticks in my memory is that near the end someone posed the question: "With all this indeterminacy, where does it end?" No answer.

Every popular culture has its cult heroes. For CLS it is Duncan Kennedy, while for Crit-decon it is Stanley Fish, the model for Morris Zapp. Fish fashions himself as "a new breed of superstar as much concerned with professional notoriety as with the humdrum of scholarship." An article by Fish is automatic success for law review editors who have encountered his book *Is There a Text in This Class?* in undergraduate courses and know that he is the Derrida of legal education. His text is *not* indeterminate; it commands like a Supreme Court decision that students accept without reservation the ukase that the "objectivity of the text is an illusion and moreover, a dangerous illusion, because it is so physically convincing." The *Yale Law Journal* published his deconstruction of baseball heroes such as the pitcher Dennis Martinez and the manager Earl Weaver. When his ratings dip, he comes up with essays with provocative titles like "There's No Such Thing as Free Speech and It's a Good Thing, Too." Quoted as saying the First Amendment is "the first refuge of scoundrels," Fish explains, "its foundations have been shown to be built on sand." With typical Zapp insouciance, Fish claims deconstruction "relieves me of the obligation to be right . . . and demands only that I be interesting."

Fish is the master of sleight-of-hand, skillfully avoiding the abyss of indeterminacy. He argues that interpretation is governed by the presence of interpretive communities, "groups composed of those who share interpretive
strategies not for reading (in the conventional sense) but for writing texts, for
constituting their properties and assigning their intentions." That deals with
my colleagues who question the two copyright deconers on indeterminacy;
if we can get someone to agree with our interpretation, we have a community of agreement. Fish's answer does not change the process; interpretation
is still fluid. Communities appear and then disappear, "providing just enough
stability for the interpretative battles to go on, and just enough shift and slip-
page to assume that they will be settled."

How Much Did Deconstruction Hurt CLS?

Deconstruction is, in part, a catastrophe theory, for behind it there is the assumption that the whole western metaphysical tradition can be put in reverse.
(Frank Kermode, *The Art of Telling: Essays on Fiction* 7 [1983]).

Unquestionably, the indeterminacy thesis of deconstruction served as a mag-
net to many CLS scholars, especially that group Andrew Altman calls the radical wing. We know CLS assimilated deconstruction theory, and it had *some*
influence, including Crit vocabulary, which absorbed decon buzzwords such
as foregrounding, privilege, problematize, valorize, contextualize, and phallogocentricism. Like the deconers, Crits avoid transparent language and comprehensible syntax to show disdain for fixed meaning. While the exact nature and extent of its effect on CLS defies accurate judgment, several observations are tenable.

Very little, if any, scholarship incorporates the Derridaian deconstruction
performance method. CLS people restrict their efforts to a two-step process:
First, identify the dominant privileged interpretation and flush out the marginalized counter meaning, then rationalize the social and political benefits
and superiority of the marginal position while trashing the oppressive effects
of the privileged meaning. This is an abridged application of deconstruction
that adds nothing other than a rationalization for advocacy scholarship. There
is a more sinister mask. CLS revised deconstruction to match its office politics agenda and then popularized it as a legitimate legal process to be used in
evaluating institutions, laws, and decisions. It was a process that always uncovered the indeterminacy of an evil privileged side and a good counter
marginal position.

"Deconstruction" was the buzzword of the 1980s, beating "paradigm." Spreading like a virus, everything was deconstructed. A West Virginia State supreme court judge advertised for clerks who could apply "deconstructionist textual theory to workers compensation statutes and Article 9 of the U.C.C." Young professors thirsting for publication used the word "deconstruction" in their titles to lure impressionable student editors who assumed there was deconstruction in the text. "Deconstructing Reconstructive Poverty: Practice-Based Critique of the Storytelling Aspects of the Theoretics of Practice Movement" has an impressive Derridaian flourish, but no deconstruction. (The article discusses client-lawyer dialogue as stories.) Another ploy is to get a buzzword edge from using the word in section headings, for example, "Deconstructing the Differences in Approaches, Reliance Deconstructed." These are relatively harmless tactics, the excesses of the ambitious seeking shortcuts to tenure. Where many Crits got into trouble was in attempting to actually engage in deconstruction or to give the impression that they were deconning.

In copyright, authorship is central to the allocation of property rights and various financial rewards. Peter Jaszi used an historical approach to describe the different constructs in which authorship has occurred, focusing on the struggle between author and publisher over control of the work. To Jaszi, the key to understanding the authorship construct springs from the Romantic view of the author as an inspired individual who has a preferred status over everyone, including those who make derivative works. Emerging and then receding, the Romantic model of authorship reflects copyright's continuing recognition of the author's "creative autonomy."

It is an interesting analysis with a fresh perspective, but with one disconcerting problem. Jaszi says that his article will adhere to "modern literary theory" and "[b]roadly speaking my attack on 'authorship' aspires to deconstruct." Reference to this word, and all it connotes, introduces confusion. In a footnote, he acknowledges that the application of deconstruction "inherently calls all notions of 'authorship' into question." Jaszi is correct; how can Shakespeare claim authorship of *Hamlet* when all literature is intertextual, and there is no such thing as a first or original work? This is more than a footnote issue; confronted with the trace and intertextuality process that deconstruction imposes on the text, I assumed Jaszi wanted to explain how to rationalize writing about authorship, a concept denied by deconstruction.

Perhaps the author sought to avoid this contradiction by stating that his objectives "may be less than completely true to the aims of deconstruction." In fact, in the next sentence he indicates that his methodology of acquiring meaning and knowledge is "characteristic of structuralism itself." So what the reader finally gets for guidance is a blend of structuralism (which assumes that systematic knowledge of meaning is possible) and deconstruction (which claims to know only the impossibility of this knowledge). An interesting contradiction: the author is deconstructing his own article.

Crit deconstruction politics eventually devolved into meaningless chatter, a device to inject a sharp bite into trashing. With one known exception, the targets were predictable: Liberals, capitalists, the Chicago school of economics, Eurocentrists, and other Liberal forms of oppression. The exception is the irrepressible Robin West, who, in *Deconstructing the CLS-Fem Split*, decons the equally irrepressible Duncan Kennedy into being a sexist. In the process, she demonstrates that the Crit-Feminist version of deconstruction is word manipulation, a hodgepodge of trashing, verbal gamesmanship, and value judgment. It is barking from the abyss. West says deconstruction, in its most broadly conceived agenda, is simply a way "to examine the verbal masks constructed by groups of powerful people." This is a Crit way of acknowledging the use of decon for political statement. West likewise ignores the consequences of deconstruction performance, which demonstrates that the text never has a permanent privileged reading. West says: "Deconstruction commits the theorist to at least the coherency of the claim that what a culture or institution has defined as natural is in fact a social, cultural or institutional imperative." This comment is in direct defiance of what deconstruction does. In the process of deconning, the theorist is *never* committed to any meaning because there is never a fixed meaning. West cannot verify that what *she wrote* is correct. As Morris Zapp said: "[Y]ou, are not the *you* that you started with. Time has moved on since you opened your mouth to speak, the molecules in your body have changed. What you intended to say has been superseded by what you did say and that has already become part of your personal history."

In spite of these problems, the West piece is an underground classic in humor and in ideological victimology. It starts when she identifies CLS as privileged and empowered, while feminist faculty are "relatively powerless." Duncan Kennedy and the male Crits, who consider themselves oppressed by the Liberal faculty, vilified by the media, and purged at Harvard and Yale, are informed by West that they are the oppressors. Duncan made the mistake of noting a "feminist taboo" as inhibiting sexual contact with male Crits, and then described three critical aspects of CLS sexual politics:

First, there is desire—between men and women and also between men and between women.

Second, there is the historical fact of the oppression of women by men.

Oppression on the basis of gender is the actual context within which CLS came into being—"it's no accident that the mentors are men"—and CLS has never been a counter-sphere within which it was absent.

[Three], [t]he internal structure of the conference is unmistakably reflective of the larger patriarchy. Men have much more power than women.

Looking at word choice and grammar, West concludes that the conjunction of the first and second Kennedy claims of sexual politics deconstruct to mean that powerful and empowered male Crits desire oppressed feminists while disempowered women desire empowered men. It is a natural desire, not the result of a socially imposed construct. This leads to the Kennedy vision: gender oppression is bad, while natural heterosexual desire between oppressor Crit males and oppressed feminists is good. "The fruit is treasured even though the vine is rotten," West says. Kennedy's mistake, revealed by West's deconstruction, is assuming that heterosexual desire is natural. This is simply wrong; instead, heterosexual desire is a *social* construct that functions to marginalize women and assumes that rape victims ask for it, pornography is benign, marital rape is merely bad sex, and so on.

The irony of West's deconstructing Kennedy to reveal the CLS sexual marginalization of Crit-Fems is worth plowing through indefatigably obscure and convoluted syntax. As a strawman Kennedy symbolizes the CLS practice of fighting patriarchy in the outside world, while practicing it with Crit-Fems. It is also worth the price of admission to follow West's effort to deconstruct feminist claims into determinacy and coherency. She concludes: "The core radical-feminist claim that 'heterosexuality is compulsory'—socially rather than naturally imposed imperative—badly needs the deconstructionist's commitment for its minimal coherency." West perpetuates the Crit contradiction that deconstruction, which rejects coherency and fixed meanings, can nevertheless be used to define the coherency and meaning of Liberal oppression.

To an Empire professor of contracts like Kingsfield, it was over after the first three paragraphs. No wonder Professor Clare Dalton chose the popular legal culture pages of the *Yale Law Journal* to publish her tenure article. Even the title, "An Essay in the Deconstruction of Contract Doctrine," was offensive to Kingsfield. Essays belong in publications like *Harper's* or *Atlantic Monthly*, and the use of the word "deconstruction" in a title conjured up Yeat's warning: "Cast a cold eye on life, on death, horseman, pass by!"

"Law, like every other cultural institution, is a place where we tell one another stories about our relationships with ourselves, one another, and authority." The first sentence is designed to grab the reader's attention. Dalton was speaking in the voice of the Fem-Crit agenda, a voice derived from the research of Carol Gilligan. A boilerplate citation, Gilligan's research argues that women are dominated by male values of rights and individualism. *In a Different Voice* is used by the feminists to rationalize a new feminist legal paradigm. Citing Gilligan, Dalton argues that feminist stories are needed to critique the dominant male voice of contract doctrine.

Describing one's work as a story is a claim that resonated in feminist circles in the 1980s. To make sure that the reader got her point, Dalton compared law stories to *Mother Jones*, the *Boston Globe*, the CBS evening news, and the events of a faculty meeting. "[O]ur stories also limit who we can be." The "stories told by contract doctrine are preoccupied with what must be central issues in any human endeavor of our time and place." This is a fancy Fem-Crit way of saying a feminist is speaking, telling a story, and the message is unique, countermale, and important. Dalton attaches an epilogue that ensures indeterminacy: "I do not believe that my story is the only one that can be told about contract doctrine. I insist only that it is *an* important story to tell." Dalton next indicated that her story relies on deconstruction to critique Liberalism. Specifically, Jacques Derrida enables her to expose Liberal sleight-of-hand tactics "to perpetuate a world view that imposes itself upon constituencies that it simultaneously leaves essentially without power or resources."

Dalton's reference to Derrida and to deconstruction epitomize CLS's misguided reliance on a literary theory that is incapable of supplying useful insights on law or legal doctrine. Dalton was warned of the barrier by Derrida's translator, whom she cites. Gayatri Spivak says deconstruction is an abyss, with the critic intoxicated over the prospect of never hitting the bottom.

> To locate the promising marginal text, to disclose the undecidable moment, to pry it loose with the positive lever of the signifier; to reverse the resident hierarchy, only to displace it; to dismantle in order to reconstitute what is always already inscribed. Deconstruction in a nutshell. But take away the assurance of the text's authority, the critic's control, and the primacy of meaning, and the possession of this formula does not guarantee much.

Calling an article a story does not make it a story, but it does distract the reader. How can the reader handle comments like: "By presenting doctrine as a human effort at world-making, my story focuses fresh attention on those to whom we give the power to shape our world"? What follows is not a story but an effort at doctrinal analysis. Even more distracting and perplexing is Dalton's promise to attack contract doctrine with Derridaian poststructuralism, followed by the absence of the application of Derridaian deconstruction. Four pages into the article, Dalton laments that the privileged assumption that contract doctrine can resolve the various polarities is in reality "empty." "The doctrinal scheme provides us with no way to fill these empty vessels," leaving contract doctrine in a Derridaian abyss. Then comes a lengthy discussion of tensions and contradictions in doctrine and the admission that the abyss has a floor and is stocked with competing interpretations. As every first-year law student learns, the bargain concept of consideration defined in Section 71 of the Second Restatement competes with detrimental reliance from Section 90 of the Second Restatement. Like the traditional Empire law professor, Dalton posits guidelines for courts to follow in determining whether to apply the bargain theory or reliance. This type of analysis is hardly the stuff to trigger an *aporia*.

Dean Robert Clark, then a professor, is quoted as saying that "Deconstructing Contracts" was a "very bad piece of work, full of jargon. It didn't make any original points." This comment raises an intriguing question: Would Dalton have received tenure if she had avoided the use of story and deconstruction jargon?

Paul de Man: The Final Blow

> Continental criticism . . . represents a methodologically motivated attack on the notion that a literary or poetic consciousness is in any way a privileged consciousness, whose use of language can pretend to escape . . . from the duplicity, the confusion, the untruth we take for granted in the everyday use of language. (Paul de Man [1983])

Unexpected events thwart or frustrate a movement: occurrences like a war, a death, or a Watergate. What happened to deconstruction was an academic version of Watergate, except more devastating and invidious. CLS, with its close association with deconstruction, took a hit from the scandal. Crits professed to publish decon scholarship, while many young professors used it in class to show the privilege and oppression of the Liberal establishment. Much of the criticism of CLS in the *Stanford Law Review Symposium* was directed at its use of deconstruction. Stanley Fish, as law professor, popularized his version of decon with pithy Morris Zapp sound bytes and gained fame for his disdain for the First Amendment. (To which Calvin Woodward observed: "[T]hough Mr. Fish's learning is wonderfully instructive, readers may find his insights of limited practical value.")

In the 1980s, the Yale School of Criticism was the leading reservoir and training ground for deconstruction in the United States. Its faculty was known as the decon Mafia and its Godfather was Paul de Man, second in the hierarchy only to Derrida. Immigrating to this country following World War II with no money and no position, he quickly made a reputation at Yale for advocating the total subversion of meaning. He took delight in flushing out endless traces in texts, while demanding that the critic was obligated to demonstrate that the traces had no end and no beginning. Admiring critics bragged that de Man was "the only man who ever looked into the abyss [of deconstruction] and came away smiling." In 1984, Paul de Man died; according to the New York Times, he was honored as "the originator of a controversial theory of language that some say may place him among the great thinkers of his age."

On December 1, 1987, a *New York Times* headline read, "Yale Scholar's Articles Found in Nazi Paper." While researching a doctoral dissertation, a student unearthed evidence that during the span of at least two years during the early 1940s, de Man published 170 articles in *Le Soir*, a Belgian pro-Nazi newspaper. The articles unquestionably showed he was a Nazi collaborationist and propagandist. The evidence was overwhelming; de Man speculated that Jews had "polluted" modern literature, then said: "What's more, one can thus see that a solution to the Jewish problem that would lead to the creation of a Jewish colony isolated from Europe would not have, for the literary life of the West, regrettable consequences."

There was more: de Man was a common scoundrel, a cheater, and swindler at business. The reason he came to America was to avoid angry creditors and the threats of lawsuits. Adhering to the duplicity of language lesson he later embraced, he lied to U.S. immigration officials to get in and lied to stay. Paul de Man was a bigamist, leaving behind a wife and son, whom he completely ignored, and marrying a graduate student in the hope of improving his chances of naturalization. The novelist Mary McCarthy got de Man his first job at Bard. Her opinion of him: "[He was] given to lying, evasion, fantasy, greed, possibly even theft—in short, plastic and formless, with an intelligence that's outdistanced his morals."

Efforts at comprehending the scandal proceeded through three stages. First were the shock effects from the enormity of what had happened. This was not the fall of an ordinary or even exceptional professor; it involved the number two scholar in the world in his field. At the time, his field dominated literature and philosophy. Likewise, it was not the ordinary academic scam, like embezzling university funds or doctoring research. Paul de Man stood accused of a most serious moral violation—participating in the Holocaust. David Hirsch states the indictment: "In this world, Paul de Man . . . permitted himself to become an accessory to the Nazi crimes, not by 'transmitting orders,' but by helping to circulate the poison that infected the entire society."

The second stage shifted the focus to the credibility and morality of deconstruction. Detractors argued that the objective of deconstruction was the denial of the author and the rejection of text, and, by implication, the repudiation of history. If textuality and trace can be used to destroy literary history, why not history itself? His critics argued that de Man invested his career in developing the abyss view of deconstruction *because it was the ideal system to obliterate his past.* His pro-Nazi articles had no tangible existence; they were floating around in the abyss with all the other traces.

There was another unsavory ramification from the de Man affair. Critics pointed to de Man's own words in *Allegories of Reading*: "It is always possible to face up to any experience (to excuse any guilt), because the experience always exists simultaneously as fictional discourse and or empirical events and it is never possible to decide which of the two possibilities is the right one. The indecision makes it possible to excuse the bleakest of crimes because, as fiction, it escapes from the constraints of guilt and innocence." Without history and without meaning there is no good or evil. By nullifying the moral system, deconstruction does more than tolerate Nazism; it encourages it. De Man's defenders, including Derrida, turned the last battle in the controversy into a circus of bizarre arguments. When the conflict receded, so did deconstruction's credibility.

Until the de Man troubles, deconers could counter dissenters by pointing out that whatever the criticism, it was subject to trace and textuality and therefore had no fixed meaning. It may be correct in the eyes of the critics, but in a world of trace that did not carry the day. Now, the roles were reversed; *they* were on the attack, seeking to deflect if not subvert the allegations against de Man. If they chose to cling to the argument of uncertainty they pressed against their critics, they would have to concede the allegations, which, in the eyes of the opposition or the interpretative communities among the public, were "correct." To quote Stanley Fish: "There are no truths, only rival interpretations." The other prong of the dilemma is that if they defended on the facts by arguing that de Man was *in fact* innocent of pro-Nazi writing, they would have to embrace the fixed meaning of the text. Some take the latter position. J. Hillis Miller, in complaining of "errors" by the accusers, said that "All these propositions are false . . . the *facts* are otherwise" (emphasis supplied).

Derrida resolved the dilemma by doing what he does best; he and other defenders deconstructed de Man's pro-Nazi articles to exonerate him. Deconstructing one of the more notorious articles, Derrida, in what James Atlas called "an astonishing 30,000-word cry of pain," found that de Man had composed a code message in defense of Jews. Charles Lehman summarizes: "Making a deconstructive move you demote the center and elevate the marginal; you repeat yourself, add an emphasis, drop a qualifier, insert a few parenthetical digressions—and in the end you get just what you expected to find: [O]ne of those undecidable aporias that not only let de Man off the hook, just a little, but also let you salute de Man's theory of reading in the process."

The Closure of an Episode

CLS was an episode, not a movement—a mild hangover from the Consciousness III of the 1970s. Maybe it was a question of character; the perception among students and colleagues was that after deconning in class and encouraging students to take to the streets in revolution, Crits got in their BMWs and Jaguars and drove home to their wine cellars to continue the fight against hierarchy and privilege. They openly eschewed the trenches of real politics, lawyering, or lobbying, instead preferring the easy life of the lecture circuit. That was a major tactical blunder; as Felix Frankfurter and his Happy Hot Dogs demonstrated during the New Deal, there is no revolution without active participation. The second mistake was the style and tone of CLS scholarship. Trashing, an Animal House frat tactic, got the censure it deserved. The creation of an intersubjective zap vocabulary served to emphasize the immaturity of the CLS episode. Manufacturing a vocabulary from the movie *Body Snatchers* does not inspire confidence. "It is true," said a Crit, "that our utopian 'work' has been strictly anti- or nonintellectual." In retrospect the Stanford CLS symposium anticipated the end of the episode. The end started on the first page, when Gabel and Kennedy went into an embarrassing vaudeville act of show and tell.

The de Man revelation was the coup de grace for deconstruction and CLS. Rather than repudiating de Man as a Nazi sympathizer, Derrida tried to sanitize him with deconstruction. His cry of pain for de Man failed, graphically exposing deconstruction as a house-of-mirrors game. It was impossible to evade the reality of de Man's articles; the words had meaning, meaning with reprehensible implications. The CLS message of indeterminacy went down with the unmasking of Paul de Man.

Numerous factors contributed to a high deficit count on CLS's credibility. Actual instances of indeterminacy are not as prevalent as the Crits would have us believe. As Andrew Altman observes: "Even when the convention that prescribes a (principle of) decision having maximum coherence with the settled law completely breaks down, there is still a convention operating that demands that the (principle of) decision fit with a substantial portion of the settled law." Playing games with deconstruction, giving silly advice to young associates, and preaching insurgency while sitting on the sidelines is not the stuff of revolution. These are symptoms of a more profound problem; the CLS revolution was an abstraction, an intellectual utopia that its designers never connected in a meaningful way to reality. Designers like Roberto Unger, the theoretical guru of the movement, sketched out a utopia composed of institutions perpetually open to revision and reconstitution. The interaction of concepts like counterprinciples, subversive implications, disharmonies, plasticity, and deconstructionist doctrine would lead to the "systematic remaking of all direct personal connections—like those between superiors and subordinates or between men and women—through their progressive emancipation from a background plan of social division and hierarchy." Unger's theme is a continuous transformation of institutions accompanied by a form of rolling participatory democracy, altering itself to resolve new problems while assuring egalitarianism.

First, the utopia engineers, the people who would like to lead the revolution, would have to understand what he was talking about. Reviewing one of his books, Peter Holmes of *The New Republic* notes its "obscurities, contradictions and unanswered questions," calling it a "riot of inconsistency" and "overdose of rhetoric." Next, even if they could comprehend what Unger had in mind, the implementation would entail the most far-reaching revolution in the history of civilization. It is no wonder that Duncan and the gang chose to argue over what they had said and then go home to a glass of good wine.

It was, by no means, a victory for the Empire. The Crits enjoyed open access to the law journals whose editors willingly published whatever came their way. At least for a while, they had a student constituency. They got support from Fem-Crits like Clare Dalton. They were, as David Halberstam would say, "the best and the brightest," working at the top law schools in the country. Yet they lost.

6

Critical Race Scholarship

The Outsider in Legal Scholarship

Years ago it was de rigueur for students in London to make sure that everyone could see that they were carrying a copy of Colin Wilson's *The Outsider*. All the students had to read was the first sentence to know that it captured their ethos: "At first sight, the Outsider is a social problem. He is the hole-in-corner man." While others compromised with the cold intolerant authority of the bourgeois, the student remained outside. "He is an Outsider," Wilson wrote, "because he stands for Truth."

Wilson focused on literature because he knew writers are outsiders in how they live and do their work. The universal theme of the outsider is alienation from the mainstream. The modern paradigm for outsider psychology is the Lost Generation of Ernest Hemingway, F. Scott Fitzgerald, and John Dos Passos, who, alienated by the war, dropped out to become expatriates in deed and residence. For them, it was alienation by choice. Alienation may be the result of external factors, such as race, religion, or class. With the Beats of the 1950s (Ginsberg, Kerouac, and Holmes), it was class. At Columbia, they were outcasts. David Halberstam wrote, "Everything about them was wrong: their clothes, their manner, their background."

Both the Lost Generation and the Beats eventually achieved status as influential outsiders. Hemingway and his Lost Generation became mainstream, dominating U.S. fiction from the 1930s through the 1950s. They achieved success by playing alienation politics. The accepted political strategy was to create a mystique around outsider status while denigrating the dominant group as insiders who shield obsolete dogma for personal gain. Meg Greenfield calls this "the pose of outsiderness." In politics, everyone hates insiders; therefore, candidates, even if they are billionaires, identify themselves as outsiders and automatically become esteemed as reformers. "Only the person," according to Charles Reich, "who feels himself to be an outsider is genuinely free of the lures and temptations of the Corporate State."

It is generally assumed that the Outsider movement consists of CLS, Critical Race Theorists, and Feminists. They share the common aspiration of subverting the Empire. Their mutual bond is the rejection of law as objective and neutral. Blacks and women share the experiences of a history of exclusion from the law academy. As a coalition, they seek recognition and identity through nontraditional scholarship and genres designed to offend and subvert the Empire. Numerically they are a small group; even combined, they are outnumbered by the populous white male Establishment.

Each group has its own unique outsider credentials. CLS justifies its status on alienation from mainstream law, the purge of Crits at Yale, and a Leftist–Marxist pedigree (some are what Mark Tushnet calls "red-diaper babies"). Crit credentials also include participation in the Vietnam antiwar Consciousness III movement, the publication of revolutionary articles advocating the overthrow of the Liberal establishment, and the boycotting of the practice of law as a protest over oppressive policies. A closer look at these credentials indicates that a CLS outsider characterization is inappropriate.

At the present time the Crits are content to live a soft life of accommodation with their former enemies. From time to time there is an outburst of lingering rage, but for the most part it is a docile group. Dean Robert Clark observed: "I just think that the movement entered another phase of its life cycle. You might say it retired or changed." Even in the glory days, CLS played the pose of outsiderness game. Like political candidates, they identified themselves as outsiders while positioning the Liberals as insiders who used devious tactics to retain power. The message of the pose was that Crits were victims, suffering from Empire discrimination. The victimology pose doesn't wash. They had jobs at top-tier law schools: "Not only is the group thus given on occasion to the common Liberal vice of putting institutions first and individuals second," confessed one of the founders, "but it also suffers from more than a dose of Liberal elitism." Avoiding the mundane experiences in real law or working for a congressional committee while attending trendy conferences (called summer camps by the Crits) is not exactly a demonstration of revolutionary zeal. As wannabe victims, they exploited hyperbole to convince each other they suffered; hence the denial of tenure becomes a "ritual slaughter of innocents." Ignored was the fact that the victims quickly found residences at top schools. The Crits have another identity problem; as Robin West demonstrated, they spoke in the voice of patriarchy, hardly a home for outsiders. A Harvard student summed up CLS victimization: "[T]hat's Critical Legal Studies—playing squash in cutoffs; teaching at the great prestigious law school and thinking of oneself as the vanguard of the proletariat; trying to be radical but only in the most traditional sense."

The Critical Race Theory movement also appears to be engaging in the pose of outsiderness. As law professors, its followers are solidly in the elitist category. They made a conscious decision to become activists, thereby distancing themselves from other minorities who adhere to the Liberal culture. The wages and perquisites they get from their profession puts them in a high income bracket. There is the psychic gratification from having made it in an alien environment. If they are alienated, it can be argued that the alienation is self-generated, motivated by the benefits that can be derived from alienation politics. What defines Critical Race Theorists (CRT) as Outsiders is race; it comprises a people of color movement encompassing Blacks, Asians, Hispanics, and any other nonwhite racial group.

For CRT, Outsider status is predicated on history and politics. Since the majority of CRT are Blacks, their history is the voice of the movement. The underlying motif for CRT is slavery; whatever the context, the effects of slavery are express and patent, marginalizing Blacks as permanent outcasts and invisible in a white world. Derrick Bell, the godfather of CRT, and Patricia Williams, its storytelling laureate, use slavery as the definitive factor in the Black experience. Bell refers to the Declaration of Independence's toleration of slavery as the source of racism and exclusion. Thomas Jefferson authored the white man's manifesto by demanding proof "that nature has given to our black brethren talents equal to those of the other colors of men." Williams sees slavery as robbing Blacks of a sense of self. "The black slave experience was that of lost languages, cultures, tribal ties, kinship bonds, even of the power to procreate in the image of oneself and not that of an alien master."

To CRT, slavery never ended but extended through the Black Codes, Jim Crow, and separate-but-equal laws. Ironically, slavery became more subtle and insidious under the Civil Rights Act and affirmative action programs. Affirmative action has been a massive campaign to create a class of outcasts. Entitlements based explicitly on race have the unintended effect of triggering bitter divisions and a two-world society. Well-intentioned efforts result in angry charges and countercharges. All surveys reveal growing disaffection among successful Blacks and an increasing belief in resegregation. At the *Washington Post*, Black reporters justified hiring Blacks to cover Black events and political figures on the basis of experience. "I'm a black man," said one reporter, "The black experience is part of who I am. And I try to incorporate that in my coverage."

Integration was an ephemeral incident in higher education, more goal than reality. Separateness, or resegregation, became the official policy in the 1970s with the appearance of Black studies programs at major institutions. Presently every school has minority programs specializing in race consciousness. The primary role is to question the accepted wisdom. In doing so, the instructors by necessity must focus on unique cultural distinctions between races and ethnic groups. Some of the instruction is extremist—misinformation and distortions are used to build group self-esteem—while some is consistent with orthodox teaching techniques. But whatever the context or environment, the inevitable teaching, either expressly or implicitly, endorses racial separateness in a nation in which Blacks are typecast as outcasts. It is, for Blacks, a mental and physical state of isolation exacerbated by a communitywide pervasive feeling that minority programs are concessions by weak-willed administrators seeking to avoid confrontation and willing to tolerate academically inferior curriculums.

The politically correct movement has institutionalized Black separateness to satisfy the rubric of diversity and multiculturalism. Diversity in theory demands that all races and ethnic groups share in access to knowledge under an all-encompassing academic big-tent doctrine. In practice, it adheres to the Orwellian principle "All animals are equal but some animals are more equal than others," that is, people of color as the challenged race are more equal than the whites. Accordingly, the number of nonacademic minority support programs increases daily, while a number of schools separate races in ethnic dorms. Speech codes mandate politically correct language, an express deference to the sensitivity of minorities as Outsiders.

Derrick Bell argues that white society uses laws to ensure its perpetual dominance, leaving Blacks as permanent Outsiders. Bell's use of narrative techniques to describe the dynamics of the Black as Outsider galvanized the CRT movement. He used shock to overcome the tendency of white audiences to tune out his message. In his popular parable about the space invaders, a fleet of spaceships suddenly appears to trade with an economically besieged United States. The space traders make a nonnegotiable offer: they offer gold, critically needed chemicals, and safe nuclear power to replace the existing obsolete and dangerous systems. In exchange, they demand all African Americans. The initial reaction is one of consternation, then indignation—it is, after all, slave trading. After the United States government reflects on the serious state of affairs confronting the nation, however, the offer becomes an "irresistible temptation," prompting the quick passage of a constitutional amendment to legalize the trade. "And just as the forced importation of those African ancestors had made the nation's wealth and productivity possible, so their forced exodus saved the country from the need to pay the price of its greed-based excess."

Black Storytelling as an Exclusive Voice

Outsider status subsumes a distinct culture that counters the dominant white male culture. Black Outsider culture is reflected in a strong church movement, oppression music, and, in the words of William Faulkner's Dilsey, perseverance. Over the years, white society's influence has been displaced in Black culture. CRT imitates the broader Black culture by using a form of counterscholarship to displace, or moderate, the white male Liberal influence in legal education and in law. Scholarship is assumed to be the bridge to power, and the Empire uses it to impose its majoritarian code to subordinate Blacks and minorities. CRT counterscholarship cancels and subverts objective and neutral scholarship by introducing the congeries of Black experience through autobiography, narrative, and parable. The context is shifted from objective analysis to the subjective, empathetic, and emotional. This presents the law academic with a sharp contrast and a choice. Derek Bok writes about corporate mergers by using quantitative data on markets, prices, and barriers to entry to analyze the economic effects on competition. Factors like the number of firms in the market, their size, and their pricing strategy, are relevant to Bok's analysis. In the CRT writer's story about mergers, the theme would be the impact of the merger on the lives of the minority workers, taking into consideration possible discriminatory layoffs, effects of the loss of medical coverage, family displacement, and the damage to dignity. The CRT version of a merger brings a new and different perspective to the reader's consideration.

One of the political implications of CRT counterscholarship is exclusivity, the assumption that the experiences of those who produce the work gives them and other similarly situated Outsiders control over meaning and evaluation. While majoritarian insiders can be affected by the message and perhaps ultimately transformed, they can never fully comprehend the experiences that guide the author. Insiders do not have standing to question the authority of the Black voice, a voice that comes from the life traces extending from slavery. Alex Johnson Jr. summarizes: "The voice of color is identified and synonymous with marginalized groups in our society whose marginal outsider status enables them to relate important stories—stories that cannot be sincerely told by their privileged majoritarian peers."

Exclusivity can also be defined as an expression of the authenticity principle, which says that being Black does not, in and of itself, mean the person is authentic. Taking a cue from Lani Guinier's vision of the authentic Black political representative, the authentic Black scholar has psychological and cultural ties to the Black community and a commitment to represent its interests. When Jerome McCristal Culp Jr. says that "all scholars of color have a voice of color," he means that a Black person may be speaking as a Black but not necessarily in an authentic voice. A Black law professor could write a doctrinal law review article in the dominant language of the white male that would not be authentic. According to Culp, perspective determines authenticity; Black perspective is scholarship in opposition to the racial oppression of the white culture. Culp uses Justice Clarence Thomas to demonstrate the distinction; while Thomas obviously speaks in a Black voice, his support of measures inconsistent with the Black perspective (such as his rejection of affirmative action) renders his voice unauthentic. CRT's aggressive oppositionalist scholarship renders their voice authentic by definition.

The assumption of exclusivity in legal scholarship cuts directly against the prevailing code. Legal scholarship assumes that the professorate community uses universally recognized criteria to pass judgment on quality and that participation is inclusive. Criticism determines quality by separating quality work from the chaff. Exclusivity rejects the role of criticism. Instead, it rationalizes a closed intellectual universe that deflects criticism from colleagues deemed nonauthentic.

The code of inclusion and criticism is universal; those who defy it risk ostracism and condemnation. Exclusivity vs. inclusion defines the Outsider-vs.-Empire conflict. There is the anomaly of Black scholars having the option of publishing articles adhering to the majoritarian norm or writing Black-perspective work while whites are denied the privilege of engaging in Black-voice scholarship. In response to these concerns, some CRT have made a concession; it is possible for white scholars to speak in a Black-perspective voice. Johnson uses the Forrest Carter story to explain the concession.

The Education of Little Tree by Forrest Carter is the autobiography of a Cherokee orphan, Little Tree, who was raised by his grandparents in the hills of Tennessee after being orphaned at the age of ten. Published by the University of New Mexico Press in paperback, the book became an instant hit, selling more than 350,000 copies. Critics saw it as a masterpiece that high-lighted the unique experiences and culture of the Native American. How-ever, it was a hoax, the product of one Asa Earl Carter, a Ku Klux Klan ter-rorist, a "gun-toting racist," and the author of Governor George Wallace's most virulent white supremacist speeches.

Johnson says of *Little Tree* that "it is only logical that someone other than a person of color should be able to speak in the Voice of Color given the right experience, learning, and aptitude." It is a bait-and-switch concession. Having conceded that a Euro-American scholar can speak in the Voice of Color as bait, Johnson pulls the switch. Asa Earl Carter was not *really* speak-ing in the voice of color: "His speaking in the Native-American voice was the equivalent of an affectation that he used when it was to his advantage and discarded when it was not." Asa Earl "ostensibly portrayed" the Native Amer-ican voice, but in fact it was "counterfeit." Asa Earl was an impostor who wrote what the majority group wanted to hear.

Johnson's vaporized concession on exclusivity was preceded by Jerome Culp's version of bait-and-switch. Culp said that while a white can theoret-ically speak with a Black perspective, it is highly unlikely, if not virtually im-possible. There is the history of the white professorate's disdain for the au-thentic voice, which Outsiders consider a form of white supremacy in legal scholarship. Culp voices another problem: "the white voice using a black perspective may not be heard by blacks in the way intended, and not all those who wish to speak with a black perspective will adopt conclusions that re-ally oppose white supremacy."

In literary criticism, Johnson's efforts to marginalize Asa Earl as an impos-tor speaking in a counterfeit Native American voice is a result of what Henry Louis Gates Jr. calls the ideology of authenticity. "There is an assumption that we could fill a room with the world's great literature, train a Martian to an-alyze those books, and then expect that Martian to categorize each by the citizenship or ethnicity or gender of its author." Gates rejects authenticity, pointing out that all authors are cultural impersonators, drawing from mul-tiple experiences, including real experiences, along with experiences from friends, books, the pool room, TV, and so on. The sheer volume of cultural impersonation in literature subverts the credibility of authenticity. In addi-tion to *Little Tree*, Gates cites *Famous All Over Town*, a book about a fourteen-year-old Chicano boy who dukes it out with the primitive elements in an East Los Angeles barrio. Presenting a literary award to its author, Danny San-tiago, who was absent at the ceremony, John Kenneth Galbraith said: "*Famous All Over Town* adds luster to the enlarging literary genre of immigrant experience, of social, cultural and psychological threshold crossing. . . . The durable young narrator spins across a multicolored scene of crime, racial violence, and extremes of dislocation, seeking and perhaps finding his own space."

Danny Santiago is Dan James, a seventy-three-year-old Anglo, a Yale graduate with a major in Greek. When asked about producing a hoax, James "shrugged and said the book itself was the only answer." The list of impersonators is endless, including James Baldwin, who cross-raced with all white characters in *Giovanni's Room*. When asked by Julius Lester how best to resolve the barriers facing black writers, Baldwin said: "This may sound strange, but I would say to make the question of color obsolete." For CRT the question is: If an Anglican vicar can cross-race as an Asian woman or a white Australian man can write as an aborigine, which they have, how can we be sure a conservative law professor has not cross-raced by authoring a Black perspective narrative?

The Politics of Authenticity

Race dominates the dialogue on authenticity. Even in the best of times, authenticity is a volatile issue, but more so in an era of a strong separatist movement. Controversy is inevitable; inherent in the Black perspective claim is the accusation that majoritarian scholarship is consciously racist and consciously utilized to exclude Blacks from rising to the upper levels of the academy.

The acceptable criteria for reviewing and evaluating research and scholarship in the university community are well known. Allowing for variations in specific fields, standards should be objective and neutral. The model relies on individual performance without reference to one's religion, race, or other group status. Class is irrelevant. For legal scholarship the terms of the model are, with community consensus, subject to change to accommodate new trends in information and knowledge. When legal education was practice focused, vocational scholarship was esteemed. As law schools became academic, the doctrinal article became fashionable. Regardless of new accommodations, for the Liberal scholar the ideals of merit, objectivity, and neutrality remain intact.

What makes this racist to CRT? History tells them those who benefit from the merit model are Liberal white males. On this point CRT can rely on an echo from the Crit thesis; the Empire favors the objective-neutral style of scholarship as part of its dominance strategy to convince the masses that the policies of patriarchal oppression are fair, objective, and based on merit. The merit model's self-serving accommodating capacity hypocritically embraces the doctrinal and interdisciplinary techniques, yet rejects Outsider storytelling. Having cut through the facade, CRT reaches the inevitable conclusion that the dominant merit model is a social construct that uses code words to protect the white male hegemony. "Merit is defined by white men to reward what white men become."

By now, there are as many articles on the authenticity issue in print as there are voice narratives. Criticizing criticism has become a popular submarket. The distance between the critics of voice writing and its advocates has not lessened; if anything, hostile static has intensified. Professor Culp accused Judge Posner of being "no different than the white slaveowners in the ante-bellum South who were kind to their slaves." In response to a cutting criticism of his work, Richard Delgado countered by suggesting that the author is "Coming close to replicating the sin of the slavemaster . . . in her mistaken analysis" of CRT scholarship. The ongoing hot debate, the growing submarket of critical scholarship, and the acknowledgment of the authenticity issue as worthy of a dialogue is the resonance from Randall Kennedy's "Racial Critiques of Legal Academia," published in 1989.

Derrick Bell published "The Civil Rights Chronicles" in 1985. Contemporaneously, Williams and others were perfecting their storytelling skills, mostly in alternative journals. In 1988 the *Baltimore Sun* announced that Robin West's work reflected a "new genre of legal scholarship." Yet CRT was on the academic fringes, unknown to the mainstream and not taken seriously by those who were aware of their work. To some, they were a splinter group from CLS. Then came "Racial Critiques," a thorough rebuttal and rejection of core CRT assumptions. "Stated bluntly," Kennedy said, "they failed to support persuasively their claims of racial exclusion or their claims that legal academic scholars of color produce a racially distinctive brand of valuable scholarship."

The article was a cause célèbre. Much of the uproar occurred because Professor Kennedy, as a Black, had violated the no-internal-criticism code; brothers and sisters do not publicize their squabbles. He was called a traitor to his race and an academic minstrel carrying out the white man's agenda. A false rumor circulated that he had bartered integrity for tenure. The real reason for Outsider fury was Kennedy's success in accurately diagramming the relevant arguments and the points of contention and, in the process, defining future debate. "Racial Critiques" served another function; it was the catalyst that got CRT recognition among the mainstream people as a movement to be taken seriously. Whatever they may think about his views, CRT owes Randall Kennedy a sizable debt.

Authenticity assumes that a Liberal white male Empire conspiratorially excludes Blacks and minorities from the opportunity to participate in scholarship. The conspiracy is conducted through hiring and promotion criteria that are socially constructed to disfavor Outsiders. Bell argues that white-constructed standards ignore talents Blacks and minorities possess, such as practical experience as lawyers along with voice insights of an oppressed group. Under Bell's tipping-point doctrine, even if the traditional merit standards are relevant to teaching and writing, the schools will retain their white image by putting a cap on hiring qualified Outsiders. To Bell and CRT, it is a matter of statistics: the presence of a few token Blacks means the conspiracy is working.

The academy invariably responds with the argument that the pool of qualified candidates is too small to accommodate demand. Bell's tokens are all the market can supply. Kennedy divides the pool response into two issues. First is the factual issue of whether the pool of qualified Black candidates is limited. He answers yes. Blacks are confronted with substantial structural barriers, poor schools, poverty, discrimination, and other restraints that function to keep them out of the educational system. Young law graduates with a choice of going into academe are lured by high salaries into the business sector. The real issue is the correctness of the criteria used to define the pool. If the traditional hiring standards are not reliable, that is, have no nexus with job requirements, the dimensions of the pool change, significantly increasing the number of qualified Blacks and minorities under Bell's criteria.

Kennedy challenges Bell on a decisive point: the debate over the appropriate criteria for employment in the law academy and the criteria for scholarship. Kennedy acknowledges that the descriptions of standards come from a social construct and "embrace the biases of sectors of society that possess the power to impose such standards" and to benefit from the standards. If CRT makes a demand for the abolition of the prevailing majoritarian standards, they have the burden of demonstrating their irrelevancy and of presenting a persuasive justification for new criteria. Bell does not meet this burden; instead, he quits after delivering "mere assertion." "It is self-defeating, however, to leave unexplored why it is that criteria that seem innocuous and relevant on their face have such disastrous consequences for minority candidates."

The other component of exclusion is the marginalization of Black scholarship. Delgado has accused majoritarian civil rights scholars of maintaining a closed intellectual universe by not discussing or citing the work of Black scholars. The objective is to monopolize the field and deflect criticism of the status quo. To Kennedy, it is a question of meeting the burden of persuasion, which he says Delgado cannot satisfy. Other than assumption, Delgado fails to offer proof that the excluded scholarship deserves more recognition than it receives. Kennedy flatly rejects Delgado's assertion that minority status carries a presumption of expertise. "One's racial (gender, religious, regional) identity is no substitute for the disciplined study essential to achieving expertise."

Delgado is correct in his assertion that white civil rights scholars ignored minority work. He is wrong in attributing this exclusion to racial bias. Instead, Liberals were adhering to prevailing citation customs. During the years of Delgado's survey—1959 to 1979—citation motivation gave first and almost exclusive priority to legal sources. When authors went to other disciplines, they were careful to rely on the best-known scholars. In his 1960 article on mergers, for example, Bok cited the scholarship of the best economists in the discipline. It was not until the 1980s that footnote skulduggery blossomed and authors started citing everything that had an odor or could breathe. (In 1976 *The Bluebook* had 190 pages; in 1996 the count was 365.)

There is the cross-referencing factor. Members of the same specialty typically cross-cite each other. It is a matter of academic courtesy, and, more important, it obligates the cited scholar to return the citation. A small group of Liberal white male elitist professors engaged in the old custom of conspiratorial cross-referencing, rather than race-conscious citing. Nevertheless, the effect was the same.

As a Japanese-American, Mari Matsuda expands the distinctive voice assumption to embrace all people of color, that is, everyone except white males. To her, distinctiveness is derived from experiences of racial victimization. As victims, people of color have peculiar and original narrative insights. Like her ideological colleagues, she is reluctant to be cornered. After denying having ever made the "determinist arguments from race" attributed to her by critics, Matsuda said:

> I believe there is a complex, vibrant and at times contradictory intellectual tradition of subordinated people in the United States. I know this because I was raised in that tradition and it has made my life rich. In spite of the forces of assimilation and internal colonization, there lives on a progressive strand in America that is characterized by a recognition of conditions of domination and a distrust of elite claims of objectivity and necessity. Within this body of separate knowledge lies the key to the liberation of all of us.

Assigning unique and exclusive insights to people purely on the basis of race is, to Kennedy, classic stereotyping. It ignores the vast array of conflicts within all races—different reactions among Blacks or Asians to racial discrimination, strong intellectual disputes (such as Conservative vs. Liberal), the cultural differences between people of color, between law professors and people living in poverty, and the philosophical split between CLS and CRT. Kennedy accuses Matsuda and CRT of substituting a traditional negative stereotype of people of color with a positive superstereotype. This is still stereotyping, with all its destructive implications.

Whether CRT will go the way of CLS to expire into sullen irrelevance depends on what Randall Kennedy calls the politics of argumentation. His influential guide in discussing the flash points of the CRT rationalization of a race-conscious movement is Robert K. Merton's analysis of privileged access. According to Merton's *Insider Doctrine*, "Some groups [insiders] have *privileged access* [to particular kinds of knowledge], with other groups also being able to acquire that knowledge for themselves at great risk and cost." White males are the outsiders, while people of color have the advantage of privileged access. No matter how talented, the white outsiders are "excluded in principle from gaining access to the social and cultural truth" of Outsider experience. In the academic community, it is a rationalization for the redistribution of power. Holding themselves out as insiders to an agenda of ambitious radical reforms, CLS tried and failed to achieve a privileged status. Now CRT and feminists make the privileged-access argument. As Merton acknowledges, it is payback time for minorities:

> And just as the social system has for centuries operated on the tacit or explicit premise that in cases of conflict between whites and blacks, the whites are presumptively right, so there now develops the counterpremise, finding easy confirmation in the long history of injustice visited upon American Negroes, that in cases of such conflict today, the blacks are presumptively right.

Merton, with Kennedy in agreement, concludes that privileged access ignores the critical role of individual variability in research and scholarship. The individual differences within a discipline's community generate the friction and criticism for the advancement of knowledge. The value of criticism is that it is an invitation to colleagues to counter, subvert, and correct scholars' judgments. Moreover, the Insider/Outsider division is a double-edged sword that inevitably leads to chaos and division. If Blacks have privileged access in the civil rights area, do white males have privileged access to antitrust and tax law? More significant, Outsider privileged status forces a disempowering identity on Black scholars. As Vince Passaro observes: "[T]he black artist, writer, scholar, or politician cannot define himself freely but must work with a complex role that already has been established for him—that of the outsider, the outlaw, someone heroically disadvantaged and separate."

Privileged-access assumptions misperceive the function of experience in the production of scholarship. To CRT, the defining Black experience is shared oppression, the legacy of slavery. This indigenous experience creates privileged access and exclusive rights to Black scholarship. It is an explanation that leaves out some critical gaps. There is a linear trace from experience to perception to scholarship that is consumed with static. Experience is determined by a multitude of factors: intelligence, economic status, race, luck, opportunity for acquired experience, among others. Perception is equally elusive, shaped by the blending of experiences into the individual's perception of the environment. Every person has privileged access to his or her perceptions but does not have privileged access to his or her culture, race, gender, and so on, which compose a cluster of experiences available to everyone. Black perspective advocates cover this gap with a presumption of privileged access. It does not, however, meet the legal definition of a presumption: "high probability that if the basic facts exist, the presumed fact also exists. . . ." The major problem for CRT is their inability to satisfy the first step in the presumption process: defining blackness with more specificity than general references to oppression.

Parables and Allegories

The Preacher

I first encountered Derrick Bell around 1984 when he visited the Law School to give a reading from the manuscript of "The Civil Rights Chronicles." Twenty of us were sitting in the faculty lounge when he introduced Geneva Crenshaw. A civil rights lawyer in the South during the 1960s, Geneva survived a murder attempt in the Mississippi Delta, only to remain in a catatonic state for twenty years. She recovered and wrote Bell, inviting him to visit so that she could share "strange and allegorical visions that came to me while I was away" for them to interpret jointly. For an hour Bell patiently, and with subdued passion, read excerpts from the *Chronicles* to us.

When it was over and I was walking back to my office, my only thought was: What the hell is going on? Whatever that was, it was not a law review article. My colleagues were equally perplexed; with blank expressions they exited the lounge, shaking their heads. Some of those people are no doubt still puzzled when they encounter stories.

The next time I saw Bell, I knew what he had done and where he was headed. When he returned to the Law School in April 1992, he was the symbol of the storytelling movement. "Chronicles" had broken new ground when it was published in the *Harvard Law Review* in 1985. He was no longer at Harvard; a two-year absence in protest over the Law School's failure to hire Black women faculty was deemed a resignation. I knew enough about Bell's activities to conduct an interview for our alumni bulletin.

Bell explained that his allegories were natural extensions of class hypotheticals and fictional exams. He lamented the inability of doctrinal analysis to fathom the subtleties of race conflict. Allegory avoids this deadend barrier to understanding with a "broader perspective." The two world experience—going in and out of the Black and white cultures—is an important theme in Bell's work. Bell was influential in emphasizing the virtue of oppression. "It's simply true," he explained, "that we gain more insight about life from pain than pleasure. From being left out than from being included. The excluded in our society have a view of that society that most of those who are in it don't know."

Derrick Bell's personality explains and defines his use of allegory. He is a contentious advocate with experience in front-line civil rights litigation groups during the 1960s, including six years with the NAACP Legal Defense Fund. Bell is remembered for his confrontation tactics at Harvard: sit-ins, fiery rhetoric, and press conferences. After one of his sit-ins, Robert Clark, not yet dean, purportedly said: "This is a university, not a lunch counter in the Deep South." With this background, it is not surprising that Bell abhors the abstract: "I am not theoretical, I am a proselytizer." Anyone who has encountered him can verify his skills as a preacherman. And, as any preacher knows, the most effective way to reach the souls of sinners is by reference to the lessons of allegories and parables. "Therefore," says Bell, "I think you can use illustrations that are fantastical to illustrate, and I think illustrate more effectively, that which you believe is real but not much accepted."

[P]arable, a brief tale intended to be understood as an allegory illustrating some lesson or moral.

[A]llegory, a story or visual image with a second distinct meaning partially hidden behind its literal or visual meaning.

Bell's allegory "The Final Report" is considered a must-read for story-tellers. To those outside the CRT loop, the question is whether it is legal scholarship or a sermon on hellfire and damnation. The "Report" is an allegory that starts in the real world. In 1988, Bell coauthored a report on the state of affirmative action at Harvard University. It was not the typical academic report, stuffed with boring statistics, long-winded syntax, and self-serving conclusions. It was a shock allegory; in the first paragraph, we learn that an "earth-shaking explosion" has killed the President of Harvard University and every one of the 198 Black professors and administrators employed by the school. After grabbing the reader's attention, Bell describes the events leading up to the explosion. The President has convened a meeting to discuss complaints about Harvard's affirmative action policy. Documents and tapes discovered after the explosion reveal concern by Blacks over hiring tokenism and the rejection of nontraditional scholarship for promotion and tenure. "As a result, the selection process favors blacks who reject or minimize their blackness, exhibit little empathy for an interest in black students, and express views on racial issues that are far removed from positions held by most blacks." The allegory pauses for a "triumph." A proposal for a massive minority program the president intended to present at the meeting is discovered and read at the memorial service. "With seldom-seen unanimity," it is quickly implemented.

When I was growing up in the Shenandoah Valley in Virginia, every summer our town was visited by an assortment of revivalist groups. Arriving in the middle of the week, they would set up a big tent and conduct nightly meetings through Sunday, then disappear before dawn on Monday. It was like the opera season; the same aficionados made it a summer of visiting revivals. Like Pavarotti, the preacher was the star. Every summer my father, with me along for company, would go to some of the Sunday night finales. During the finales the preachers would turn it on—went after Satan, as they used to say. This was what my father wanted to see. He was a small-town lawyer who did a lot of litigation before God-fearing local juries, and to him the best instructors in persuasion, rhetoric, and ability to read an audience were God's litigators. With this background, I can spot a sermon when I see one, and Bell's "Final Report" is a classic sermon.

The one thing that sticks in my memory of God's litigators is they always got your attention early in the message. Note the fire and brimstone imagery in Bell's introduction describing the explosion: "None who heard or saw it ever forgot the earth-shaking explosion and the huge, nuclear-like fireball." Then came the message of misery and oppression: in Bell's article, the white administration sitting on the status quo, hiding behind the hypocrisy of objective hiring and promotion standards. The rational academic system imposed by Harvard's white male administration emerges as Bell's Satan. On a tape recovered after the explosion, a tenured Black professor tracks Randall Kennedy with the rational argument that "there are very few blacks out there qualified for professional teaching." Caught in the clutches of the evils of rationality and thinking white, the professor pompously says to a colleague: "Romona, protests are not appropriate for persons in an academic setting." The rational Kennedy mentality thus misses the point of the allegory-sermon: without an explosion and a body count, nothing will change!

In one of his books, Bell quotes an older civil rights worker in Mississippi who was asked what kept her going in dangerous times. She responded: "I loves to harass white folks." And this is what Bell did in "Final Report," harassing Harvard President Derek Bok and the white male law academy with a good old-fashioned revivalist sermon. Any pretense at analysis would have undercut the allegory's message while constituting a concession to Satan's main weapon—rationality.

Sermons do not tolerate dissent; they show the audience what the evil is and how to fight it. So it is with Bell. The dominant message in his sermon is: "Black people will never gain full equality in this country." Each allegory is a variation on the crisis theme—nothing will change without an explosion. Even with a crisis, any gain will be minimal. While the white system may make a concession, it will invariably turn out to be a trick to cover up some new form of oppression. The ostensible victory in *Brown v. Board of Education* lulled Blacks into complacency as whites perfected covert and more subtle forms of discrimination. In one of his more popular allegories from "The Civil Rights Chronicles," Bell shows the inevitability of the Empire's suppression of Black achievement.

Geneva Crenshaw was a law professor at a prestigious law school when the owner of a successful Black business promised to use his company's facilities and contacts to recruit qualified minority faculty candidates for the law school. The campaign was successful; in little over a year the school recruited six outstanding young people. Then came the seventh candidate, an exceptional recruit with the traditional elitist credentials: law review editor, Supreme Court clerk, and highly successful lawyer. As this latest recruit was being processed, Geneva received a visit from the dean, who explained that the addition of the seventh recruit would push the minority level to 25 percent—an unacceptable level. "[W]e want to retain our image as a white school. We do appreciate your recruitment efforts, Geneva, but a law school of our caliber and tradition simply cannot look like a professional basketball team." Geneva immediately recognized the devil's trick. She had been suckered into recruiting top talent subject to the white man's implicit condition that the number of Black faculty would not exceed the tipping point that would threaten the school's white male image.

The mixture of allegory-sermon separates Bell's writing from Williams's autobiographical narrative. She describes a personal encounter and encourages the reader to reflect on the experience as it relates to the legal system. Bell uses each chronicle as a law exam hypothetical. The Dean's response to Geneva's suggestion that the seventh candidate would probably sue is a red flag: "We think, however, that there are favorable precedents on the issues that such a suit will raise." This is an invitation to Bell and Geneva to debate the 1984 Supreme Court term along with other precedent and commentary. It is a conversation between lawyers— processing decisions and engaging in legal analysis. Like any rational and analytical lawyer, Bell suggests that the Supreme Court "might draw an analogy to housing cases in which courts have recognized that whites usually prefer to live in predominantly white housing developments." This is the source of Professor Bell's tipping point thesis, which he persistently uses to demonstrate the permanence of racism.

In his early law review articles, Bell used a consistent allegory formula, the allegorical encounter—Geneva states a thesis, Bell responds with analysis. Throughout the allegory, Bell adhered to a doctrinal theme; relevant decisions and commentary are on the table for the reader to assess the quality of research and arguments. Nevertheless, Bell has never been dedicated to the analysis of substantive legal issues. His priority, as he readily admits, is preaching. "I have," he concedes, "managed a metamorphosis into one of the 'new, black, public intellectuals.' It may be intended as a compliment, but it is used by those who find in our writings and statements what they want to read and hear." With his recent book *Gospel Choirs*, Bell has moved from law allegory to a blend of storytelling and allegory. Bell has created a style, doctrinal allegory, that, when done with substantive thoroughness, will satisfy the most rigid traditionalist.

Rodrigo's Chronicles

"The debate is about voice . . . about making everybody speak one language. The whole idea of the dominant legal discourse is to limit the range of what you can express." So says Richard Delgado, who has joined Bell as one of the new Outsider public intellectuals. Delgado is a tireless promoter.

One of his most successful ventures was convincing the *Michigan Law Review* to publish a symposium on storytelling in 1989. In a Foreword by Kim Lane Scheppele, a political scientist, we learn that the justification for storytelling is derived from the "we-they" explanation for legal discourse. "'We,' the insiders, are those whose versions count as 'facts'; 'they,' the outsiders, are those whose versions are discredited and disbelieved." As an objective test, the judgment of a neutral observer of the event is privileged and presumed to be the best method of ascertaining truth. It is a false presumption. "Observers," Scheppele says, "even those not directly involved in a dispute, bring with them a conceptual scheme already formed, a set of presuppositions and expectations, that influences what they see and report." Scheppele is describing a version of the Crit's indeterminacy principle, which requires the presence of oppositionist stories to counter the privileged view of truth.

The Foreword's view is not the storyteller's accepted thesis that assumes the truthfulness of experience in Black voice writing. It is, instead, a relativist solution. Everything—trials, testimony, lawyer's argumentation—in legal discourse is a form of storytelling, and each story is conditioned by various contexting factors. There are the stories of "we" and the oppositional stories of "they." When it comes to truth, indeterminacy exists. Witnesses see the same thing differently, but, according to Scheppele, that "does not automatically mean that someone is lying and that a deviant version needs to be discredited." The goal of the Foreword's indeterminacy analysis is to open the door and create a level playing field for marginalized stories.

What accounts for the description of storytelling as a function of indeterminacy strategy? A demand for a level playing field is modest when contrasted with the contemporary demands for exclusivity over voice stories. The *Michigan Law Review* editors sought to present legal storytelling as an inclusive field for all legal discourse. They projected the legal system as a collection of stories. Hence the symposium focused on the conventional Crit analysis of the privileged stories suppressing the stories of the oppressed. The selection of symposium articles supports this theme: the American Indians' story of subordination, the political narratives of Dr. Martin Luther King Jr., the account of workers trying to cope with plant closings, differences in lawyer and client perceptions, a piece on choosing between competing stories, and an article on hate speech.

The indeterminacy thesis has lost its attractiveness with the demise of CLS. While the indeterminacy justification has faded, the Michigan symposium served as the catalyst for the emergence of the voice storytelling movement. Prior to 1989, storytelling as autobiography or allegory was an emerging genre. Williams had several narratives in print but was awaiting the fame and glory *The Alchemy of Race and Rights* would produce upon publication in 1991. Delgado's reputation also was yet to come from the *Rodrigo's Chronicles* series. To most observers, Bell was the movement. The symposium, with stories by all three authors, changed that. Williams introduced her now famous sausage-making metaphor, Bell's "Final Report" allegory appeared, and Delgado concluded the trilogy with a series of parables on race in faculty appointments. In a plea in support of narrative he said: "Legal storytelling is an engine built to hurl rocks over walls of social complacency that obscure the view out from the citadel."

"Excuse me, Professor, I'm Rodrigo Crenshaw. I believe we have an appointment." If the Crenshaw name is familiar, it should be. Rodrigo is the brother of the formidable Geneva Crenshaw and the main character in a series of parables appropriately called *Rodrigo's Chronicles*. His father is Black, his mother is Italian, and he is a graduate of a top foreign law school. The reader cannot suppress the obvious suspicion that he is Delgado's alter ego. They even look alike: indeterminate age, somewhere between twenty and forty, "tightly curled hair and olive complexion." Each *Chronicle* follows the same structure: Rodrigo presents a problem on a race or gender topic to a wise Black law professor in the later stages of a career at a prestigious school. The wise professor bears a striking resemblance to Bell.

The series received top-tier law review exposure at Yale, Michigan, California, N.Y.U., U.C.L.A., Penn, Virginia, Georgetown, Southern California, and Stanford. In addition to the appeal of a topical issue like race, it intrigued student editors with its parable structure. Since the parable style cuts against the conventional doctrinal article, it is a welcome relief. At the same time, each chronicle comes across as variation of the standard doctrinal technique: there is a problem, a discussion by Rodrigo and the Professor (similar to a seminar analysis), and a conclusion, all supported by copious footnotes.

The first chronicle is a review essay of Dinesh D'Souza's *Illiberal Education: The Politics of Race and Sex on Campus.* D'Souza condemned the politically correct movement's attack on Western culture and the deterioration of academic standards, which he attributed to affirmative action. Rodrigo offers a counterthesis: the decline of Euro-civilization. "Saxon-Teuton culture has arrived at a terminus, demonstrating its own absurdity." "It is a ruthless, restless culture" that has relied on linear thought to enslave, ravage, and oppress. Rodrigo even blames the Saxons for developing "the hundred-page linear, densely footnoted, impeccably crafted article—saying, in most cases, very little." What it takes D'Souza a book to say, Rodrigo can counter in a few sentences. This is the advantage of parable—it is fiction, thereby acquiring a license for provocative, even outrageous remarks not subject to verification or analytical support. The only possible source of counterargument is the Professor, who is a mild-mannered old lion who is mostly concerned with Rodrigo's getting in trouble with the dominant white male Liberal group for his outspokenness, especially when he suggests that sabotage and terrorism may be necessary to "speed things up."

Delgado's parables convey the impression that he is playing with the reader and having fun doing it. In the first chronicle, he acknowledges the help of Lash LaRue, my favorite boyhood B-movie cowboy hero. With so many impertinent, sly, and partisan comments from the Professor and Rodrigo, it is often difficult to know whether Delgado is serious or funning us. It does keep the reader intrigued. A more serious distraction is Rodrigo's habit of generalization: "It is not just happenstance that Western democracies pioneered the slave trade, plantation system, coolie labor, Native American relocation, and Bracero programs." I suspect Delgado is dead serious on this point, but it is an assertion that he never could—or should—get away with in a conventional doctrinal article without a thick layer of support.

The existence of footnote sourcing for the parable story is an important factor in achieving status as acceptable scholarship. Delgado makes the point that, unlike unadorned narratives, the Bell parable model that he "instinctively" follows is structured to include source references for the textual arguments. Not exactly; he is certainly a generous footnoter, but the dog barking from the bottom of the page does not bark in the conventional doctrinal voice.

In 1992, Delgado revisited the scene of his 1984 description of the Imperial Scholar as a group of elite Liberal white male scholars who dominated civil rights scholarship by ignoring the work of minorities and feminists. Things were a little better; minorities and feminists were getting their work published regularly in the top reviews, but the unconverted among the elders still continued to marginalize the new voices. A new generation had moved in, the "neo-imperialist scholars" who employ "an almost baroque variety of ways to minimize, marginalize, co-opt, soften, miss the point of, selectively ignore, or generally devalue the new insurgent writers." It was a form of citation tokenism, a case of citation victimology. When I first read the revisit article, I was mystified, then amused; here was one of the geniuses at footnote politicization accusing others of ideological skulduggery.

In the first *Chronicle* on D'Souza's book, we encounter in footnote 2 the first of many self-cites. In note 3, a brief description of Geneva gives Professor Bell a cite (next to Delgado, Bell is the most frequently cited author, with fourteen notches for his cite index), and then comes note 4 celebrating Geneva's prowess: "Like the child who declares the emperor naked, she punctures myth after comforting myth about progress toward racial justice." Delgado is imaginative at using seemingly innocuous text material to advertise the work of friends. Rodrigo says that he just got his law degree last June, which is referenced to footnote 5: "So that accounts for his stylish Benetton clothes," the Professor says to himself, then goes on to call attention to Professor Williams's *Benetton* story (see chapter 7). "After Professor Williams wrote of this incident, many minority law students and professors initiated an informal boycott of Benetton." His search for self-citation is irrepressible, a lesson to young professors; the text has the Professor "reaching for a much-thumbed reprint," which according to footnote 12 is a Delgado article.

With the third *Chronicle*, Delgado introduced a boilerplate self-cite for each new story: a citation listing each previous *Chronicle* with a short refresher course on the topic. In the tenth *Chronicle*, he broke the boilerplate cite into five separate notes: an introduction to Rodrigo, a description of his graduate law education, his undergraduate and law school history, background on Giannina, "Rodrigo's friend and soulmate," and a list of all previous *Chronicles*. Counting only footnotes and discounting multiple citations of his articles within a single footnote, Delgado's self-cites came to fifty of 121 citations. In the first *Chronicle*, the self-cite percentage was around twenty-four; by number ten, it was forty-one; by *Rodrigo's Final Chronicle* it was at forty-five, 35 percent above the average.

Delgado is correct on one point; footnoting has been politicized, but politicized in a much more diverse way than he suggests. Much of the CRT and feminist literature is imperialistic under Delgado's standards; authors have networks of friends they cite while ignoring or barely acknowledging oppositionalist writing. This is the inevitable result of the increase in advocacy scholarship, which is itself highly slanted and politicized. Younger legal authors, regardless of perspective, purposely ignore the conventional doctrinal standards of balance and the obligatory consideration of opposing arguments. One could call Delgado the "Imperial Scholar of CRT." His *Chronicles* have become a primary source for his citations. When Rodrigo makes a statement about white assumptions on affirmative action, the reader is directed to an article by Richard Delgado, rather than to original sources. He follows another Imperialist practice by using footnotes to advocate. After self-cites, Delgado relies heavily on CRT sources, with Bell a favorite. Reference to oppositionalist writing is rare; in the tenth *Chronicle*, I counted only eight references to politically incorrect people like Allan Bloom and Roger Kimball.

Delgado disputes the notion that "outsider scholars cite each other more often than they cite Whites." In a survey of Outsider scholarship he counted 767 citations to white authors and 741 for authors of color (Blacks, 576; Latinos, 95; Asian-Americans, 47). His own figures refute Delgado's conclusion that CRT scholars do not rely "unduly on scholars of like color." The paucity of Black law faculty—something that Bell and Delgado often point out—results in a very small pool of sources yet cites to CRT people almost equal white cites.

7

Can Voice and Truth Coexist?

Experience Drama

Kingsfield, Williston, and Bok do not write in the first person. It connotes subjectivity, the antithesis of the impersonal style. Resort to the first person blurs the distinction between analysis and whimsy. Kingsfield's worst nightmare is narrative, the ultimate in first-person perversion. To Kingsfield, narrative includes the parables of Derrick Bell and the autobiographical stories of Patricia Williams. In addition, there are experience dramas.

> Eleven years ago, a man held a an ice pick to my throat and said: "Push over, shut up, or I'll kill you." I did what he said, but I couldn't stop crying. A hundred years later, I jumped out of the car as he drove away.

This is the first sentence in Susan Estrich's *Yale Law Review* article "Rape." A firsthand experience with a violent crime forced Estrich to face the reality that "the law was against me." When she was unable to identify the assailant from mug shots, the investigation ceased. To the police, rape was not a high-priority crime; it did not involve the violence of armed assault, robbery, or murder. Then came the psychological trauma and the unacceptable contradiction: "If it isn't my fault, why am I supposed to be ashamed?"

Kingsfield would disapprove; he would see the reference as a tactic by Estrich to gain sympathy for her arguments and analysis. It is personal, and the proper place for the disclosure of a personal interest is in a footnote. Kingsfield is wrong. It is an extremely effective use of an experience as an introduction. In the first two of ninety-seven pages, she uses a personal drama to anticipate the implications of the points she covers in her article.

"Experiencing" an article with a brief description of a personal drama does not always work. Sanford Levinson writes that the Second Amendment allows citizens to arm themselves in order to repel the illegitimate authority and activities of the state. The ramifications of Levinson's republicanism disturb Wendy Brown, who considers it similar to a big tent, covering groups with little in common—nature lovers like her along with evil NRA types. She also sees the lurking menace of patriarchy and, to dramatize her point, concludes her doctrinal rebuttal with an experience. After a week of hiking in the Sierra Nevada, she and her friends discovered their car would not start. There was help: "a California sportsman making his way through a case of beer, flipping through the pages of a porn magazine, preparing to survey the area for his hunting club in anticipation for the opening of deer season." He fixed the car, and she drove away. Then it occurred to her that under different circumstances—for example, had she encountered him in the woods without her friends—her "one great and appropriate fear" would have been rape. Given her prowess at self-defense, his gun could have made the difference. The vision from her encounter with the NRA crystallizes: putting her and other females under the same big encompassing tent leaves them at risk to patriarchy. "Is his right [to guns] my violation, and might his be precisely the illegitimate authority I am out to resist?"

Outsiders circulate the refrain that everyone is writing stories. This has nourished the chic subgenre of using descriptions of experiences to introduce and furnish context for analysis. It worked for Estrich because her encounter verified specific defects in the administration of rape laws and validated her analysis. The experience of an implied threat from a NRA type fails to say anything about the Second Amendment. It subverts the energy of the text. Good editing would have encouraged Brown to spin her anger against the NRA as symbol for patriarchy into a separate article.

The encounter is too contrived. The ring of truth gave Estrich's story power; we know it happened. The ice pick threatening her throat gets the reader's attention. Maybe Brown did have her experience, but a good ol' boy sitting by his trusty Winnibago guzzling "a case" (twenty-four is a case, six is a six-pack) of beer while ravishing a porn magazine is sufficiently stereotypical to make the reader pause. This pause exposes a serious problem with the use of the experience genre; by going autobiographical, the author makes veracity an issue.

Credibility is critical when reference to an experience is used to embellish substantive arguments. If Estrich is lying, it is over on page one. Her account of the police response, their lack of focus, and her trauma cannot be separated from her substantive analysis. On the other hand, if the reader concludes Brown's encounter never occurred, the effect on the credibility of the legal analysis is devastating. The author's personal experience should convert what is otherwise an abstraction into a shared experience, thereby enhancing the credibility of the analysis. Instead of context and a sense of validation, Brown's story instills doubt, virtually forcing the reader to question its relevance.

> I want to know my hair again, to own it, to delight in it again, to recall my earliest mirrored reflection when there was no beginning and I first knew that the person who laughed at me and cried with me and stuck out her tongue at me was me. I want to know my hair again, the way I knew it before I knew that my hair is me, before I lost the right to me, before I knew that the burden of beauty—or lack of it—for an entire race of people could be tied up with my hair and me.

This is Paulette Caldwell's introduction to "A Hair Piece: Perspectives on the Intersection of Race and Gender." The next four paragraphs play on the same theme: "When will I cherish my hair again?" Caldwell then switches to conventional autobiographical narrative to discuss her reaction to an article about a cashier who was fired by the Hyatt Hotel for violating a company policy that prohibited extreme and unusual hairstyles. The article described a court case, *Rogers v. American Airlines,* in which the employer's right to prohibit employees from wearing braided hairstyles was upheld. Caldwell was "outraged"; it was as if the Hyatt Hotel management had reached out to intrude into the privacy of her grooming. When a student asked her to discuss *Rogers* in her Employment Discrimination Law class, she hesitated, putting the student off. As one who wore a neatly braided pageboy, Caldwell resented becoming a law school hypothetical. *Rogers* affected her personally: "by legitimizing the notion that the wearing of any and all braided hairstyles in the workplace is unbusinesslike, *Rogers* delegitimized me and my professionalism." She nevertheless eventually covered the decision in class and wrote the story-article to relate "some of what we have learned and what we need to know."

The key to the plaintiff's argument in *American Airlines* was the factual assertion that "the completely braided hair style, sometimes referred to as corn rows, has been and continues to be part of the cultural and historical essence of Black American women." It was an easy case for Judge Sofaer. In little over three pages, he ruled that American Airlines applied the grooming policy evenly to all races and to men and women alike. Furthermore, the policy did not regulate employees on the basis of an immutable gender or racial characteristic. The Court noted that braids are an artifice, easily changeable, and, "even if socioculturally associated with a particular race or nationality, [are] not an impermissible basis for distinction in the application of employment practices by an employer." It was this comment that angered Caldwell. By ignoring the effects of the unique intersection of race (Black) and gender (female), the Court left Black females unprotected against discrimination based on negative myths and stereotyping. Caldwell's story of resentment alerts the audience to her frustration over having to justify to the dominant group something so incidental as a particular hairstyle. An effective preface for legal analysis, her rage and frustration come across as genuine, thereby gaining the interest of the reader. Like Estrich, she forces the reader to acknowledge a new level of implication. Unlike Estrich, Caldwell continues to forcefeed the reader with experience drama, ultimately subverting analysis.

One of the subtle consequences of mixing narrative with analysis is a disconcerting mélange—a hybrid mongrel of misdirection that leaves the reader confused over what the author is trying to say. In Caldwell's case, the second half of her article is a sociological/historical story of hair and stereotyping. We learn in one section that hairstyle choice is a search for a survival mechanism and that hair has its own history. Hair texture, rather than skin color, determines race, and choice of a hairstyle "represents an assertion of self." Another section is a story about the history of malevolent gender discrimination in the airline industry, while a third section discusses the sociology of braids, citing the writings of the Black writers Maya Angelou, Alice Walker, and Toni Morrison. Caldwell concludes with a plea for resistance to hair stereotyping by resorting to various tactics such as protests. "Sometimes it can come from nothing more than a refusal to leave a grandmother behind."

Her agony experiences involve other people, such as the white female student who pestered Caldwell about discussing the *Rogers* case. She perceived racial overtones in white colleagues' commentary on her new hairstyle, while a male colleague's significant other addressed her in "that chastising, condescending tone of voice reserved for slaves and women in domestic service: 'Every time I see you, you've done something else to your hair.'" These experiences are critical to the personalizing effect Caldwell seeks to generate. The objective is to convey the victim's story: the damage to the spirit, the frustration, and the outrage that are never exposed in the sterilized language of a court opinion. There is, however, a risk in personalizing reactions with descriptions of experiences and encounters. It forces the reader to confront the issue of truthfulness. How do we know that the narratives actually occurred? Where is the validation mechanism? Does truthfulness make any difference?

Autobiography: Verification and Truth

> Autobiography: "Retrospective prose narrative written by a real person concerning his own existence, where the focus is his individual life, in particular the story of his personality."

Pentimento is the playwright Lillian Hellman's autobiographical account of various encounters. It is remembered for the highly acclaimed derivative film *Julia*, starring Jane Fonda and Vanessa Redgrave, that was based on one of these encounters. Hellman's childhood friend Julia studied at Oxford and went on to medical school in Vienna, where she became involved in the pre–World War II anti-Nazi resistance movement. Julia asked Hellman to act as a courier to deliver fifty thousand dollars for use as bribe money to help Jews and other persecuted people get out of Austria. After the successful mission Hellman never saw Julia alive, for, after being severely beaten by Nazis, Julia escaped to England, where she died. Hellman retrieved her body, returned to the United States, and, when Julia's family refused to handle the burial, had the body cremated. The movie version followed the Hellman autobiographical script; Jane Fonda played Hellman, Redgrave was Julia, and Jason Robards was Dashiell Hammett.

The unraveling started in January 1980 when Dick Cavett interviewed the writer and literary critic Mary McCarthy on his TV show and asked her about overrated writers. McCarthy identified Hellman as "a bad writer, overrated, a dishonest writer." When Cavett pursued to get an explanation of the "dishonest" characterization, McCarthy replied: "Every word she writes is a lie, including 'and' and 'the.'" Ignoring the advice of friends, Hellman sued for libel, thereby issuing an invitation for others to closely scrutinize her writings. She had plenty of enemies who were more than willing to oblige.

In *Julia*, Hellman wrote: "I think I have always known about my memory: I know when it is to be trusted and when some dream of fantasy entered on the life, and the dream . . . led to distortion of what happened. But I trusted absolutely what I remembered about Julia." Her trust in her memory was misplaced; proof came from numerous sources that Hellman had lied. There was a Julia, but Hellman had never met her. The real Julia was Muriel Gardiner Buttinger, well known for her resistance work, so her experiences were a perfect fit to the *Julia* plot. There was a connection between Buttinger and Hellman. A lawyer named Wolf Schwabacher lived in one half of a double house while Buttinger and her husband lived in the other half after they returned from Austria in 1939. Schwabacher knew of her background and told friends, including Lillian Hellman, a client for whom he did legal work. In copyright infringement cases this is called access, an important element in proving infringement.

Samuel Johnson warned that definitions of autobiography are hazardous. There is the conflict between self as the author and the actual events being described, existing, and occurring independent of the narrator. "The self," Lindon Barrett says, "as it turns out, is always a questionable fiction, whether that fiction is exposed in terms of relations to a community, or in terms of narrative complexities that betray a self performing the narration over and against a self being narrated." Jerome Brunner notes the "cunning of diegesis," a process by which the narrator creates the facts to fit the narrator's need. When people write about themselves, any attempt to uncover their motivation is like bungee diving—snap, crackle, and pop. In 1798, Friedrich Schlegel observed that autobiographies are written by neurotics, by people with "adventuresome self-love," by born historians, by women who "coquette with posterity," by people with pedantic minds, and by self-worshipers. Hellman might fall into the self-worshiper category; William Wright suggests she had acquired the belief that Muriel Buttinger actually was a close friend. The more plausible explanation is that Hellman broke the contract with the audience by consciously lying.

When Caldwell describes her reactions to her colleagues' comments and gestures of disdain, it is the self exposing emotions and alienation. On the other hand, Caldwell's various encounters and conversations with colleagues and students are external to the self: they exist as referential facts. The coming together of the author's self, referential facts, and the reader as audience and chorus constitutes the autobiographical contract. The author and the reader engage in a joint effort to discover the narrator's self; the reader accepts the author as author, narrator, and protagonist, while the author makes a commitment to make a sincere effort to understand the reality of self and experience. An additional term of the contract further separates autobiography from fiction by assuming the truthfulness of referential facts. The essence of the autobiographical contract is truth. Roy Pascal says: "Not only does the reader expect truth from autobiography, but autobiographers themselves all made more or less successful efforts to get at the truth."

Lillian Hellman's story about Julia was a material breach of the autobiographical contract. Her egregious misrepresentation of the referential facts rendered the self at best irrelevant and at worst a fraud. She gives a lesson in the dilemma of the autobiographical contract: the reader is forced to assume the risk of untruthfulness and the burden of verification. The risk is elevated for readers of Outsider-perspective autobiographical narrative, where detection of a breach of the contract is extremely difficult. In this genre, the self dominates to generate the unique Black voice. Referential facts are present but exist in the background as anonymous vehicles, like the students in Caldwell's narrative who serve as props. Unlike the Hellman autobiography, where there was a long trail of referential facts, including Julia/Muriel as protagonist and a record of dates and events, in voice narrative, the reference facts are shadows, virtually impossible to verify.

There are three responses when a possible breach of the autobiographical contract cannot be determined by reference to objective criteria. Daniel Farber and Suzanna Sherry have adopted the honesty test, based on the question: "Is the author's account what it purports to be?" To answer this, they identify three different statements about the perceptions of an event: this is what you would have seen if you had been watching; this is how it felt to me, even though it might have looked different to you if you had seen it; although this is how I feel about the event now, I had a different feeling when I first saw it.

The first statement is the "customary test" of truth, whereas the latter two are voice or perspective descriptions. When the narrator describes events that are covered by the second or third statements, it is dishonest unless the reader is given an "explicit disclaimer." Saying "he slapped me" when the narrator means that "although if you had been present you would not have seen violence, it felt as if I had been slapped" is a form of "intellectual deception."

Farber and Sherry acknowledge the impossibility of conclusive verification, thereby putting the burden on the reader to assume the risk that the narrator has not breached the contractual term of truthfulness. But, in the final analysis, verification is an irrelevant issue to them, washed away with a question and answer: "In other words, can an unadorned account of personal experience, standing alone, constitute good scholarship? Unlike many current legal storytellers, we can conclude that it cannot."

The second response comes from the autobiographical storyteller voice purist, who rejects the relevance of truthfulness and verification. As an expression of the self, the Black-perspective narrative possesses independent integrity that, because it is perspective, constitutes the truth of the author's feelings. As an oppressed self, the author speaks for the entire community of the oppressed, functioning as a communal self. This constitutes a revision of the autobiographical contract; it shifts the primary concern from truth of the story to the impact of the narrative on the reader. Truth and verification are of peripheral concern when the objective is to transform the reader or to expose the discriminatory effects of social practices and the tyranny of laws and governmental policy.

This revision of the contract gets support from Williams's communal interpretation of the Tawana Brawley incident. On Thanksgiving 1987, Tawana Brawley, a Black teenager, was discovered in a plastic garbage bag, dazed, her arms and legs covered with feces and slurs. "KKK," "nigger," and "bitch" were written on her back. Brawley told authorities she had been abducted by three white men, one with a police badge, and taken to a field where she was urinated on and beaten senseless. It exploded into what could have been a model for Tom Wolfe's *The Bonfire of the Vanities*. The impresarios of race, rage, and riot, the Reverend Al Sharpton, Alton Maddox, and C. Vernon Mason, verbally beat up on New York Governor Mario Cuomo and his befuddled officials to feed the yellow pages of the *New York Post* and the *Daily News*. A police officer accused by Sharpton et al. of the assault committed suicide, while careers were ruined. Yet the episode was a hoax, according to the grand jury that investigated the allegations. Brawley had staged the incident to cover her absence from home and to avoid a beating from her stepfather.

Williams was at a conference, half tuned in to the ongoing verbal warfare while musing over raciality (which is socially constructed) when she was asked to comment on the rape of Black women and the death of Black children. After finessing the question, her thoughts turned to the case of Tawana Brawley, who "has been the victim of some unspeakable crime. No matter how she got there. No matter who did it to her—and even if she did it to herself." At no point in the ensuing discussion of Brawley did Williams acknowledge the hoax and its devastating consequences. Troubled by this oversight, Richard Posner calls it an "evasion" that to him "further illustrates Williams's habit of blurring the line between fiction and truth."

Judge Posner misses the reason for Williams's use of the Brawley incident. The assault and rape did happen to Brawley, beginning with slavery, proceeding through Jim Crow and on to the present. To Williams, Brawley is the communal "wild black girl who loves to lie, who is no innocent . . . and whose wiles are the downfall of innocence, jaded, desperate white men." When Williams says, "Tawana Brawley herself remains absent from all this," she means more than Brawley's literal absence (she was in hiding). Tawana is also figuratively absent, replaced by the communal self of all Black women, subjected to a history of oppression. As one of her storytelling colleagues observes: "Professor Williams requires us to see the world through her eyes; her words will not permit us the freedom to ignore her reality."

Good lawyers know the best way to revise the fine print of a contract is through self-serving interpretation. Kathryn Abrams seeks to deflect the truthfulness problem by redefining truth to mean "some quality or qualities that, if present, incline the reader to credit the account of reality being advanced through narrative." This definition explicitly circumvents reliance on objective proof of truthfulness. Agony experiences involve personal anguish and revelations that may stigmatize the narrator. According to Abrams, this deep sense of agony encourages readers to accept the account. What other motive than truth could the narrator have? In the *Art of Self*, William Gass answers:

> Are there any motives for the enterprise that aren't tainted with conceit or a desire for revenge or a wish for justification? To halo a sinner's head? To puff an ego already inflated past safety? Who is smug enough to find amusement or an important human lesson in former follies? Or aspire to be an emblem for some benighted youngster to follow like the foolish follow the standard borne forward in a fight. To have written an autobiography is already to have made yourself a monster. Some, like Rousseau and St. Augustine, capitalize on this fact and endeavor to hide deceit behind confession. Of course, as Freud has told us, they always confess to what their soul is convinced is the lesser crime.

Professor Abrams adds that when an author speaks with the authority of an expert witness by telling "what it must be like," acceptance of the account is justified. Likewise, when the narration triggers a flash of recollection in the reader's mind of a similar experience, assent can be expected. When the author describes agony, it is validated when the reader "feels" pain. In effect, Abrams has adopted a deconstruction strategy by elevating the authority over the truthfulness of the text to the reader. Paul de Man said: "Autobiography, then, is not a genre or a mode, but a figure of reading or of understanding that occurs, to some degree, in all texts."

"A Sense of Disquiet"

"Buzzers are big in New York City." To storytellers, this line is a more powerful signal than "Play it again, Sam," or "April is the cruelest month." Mention this quote and Outsiders at the annual Association of American Law Schools meeting will gush: "She is a genius!" She is Patricia Williams, the quintessential law storyteller. Her career was not made by publishing a doctrinal article on the Federal Communications Act in the *Harvard Law Review* (which she did) but by publishing narratives in the *Harvard Civil Rights-Civil*

Liberties Review, in the *Maryland Law Review*, and in "Fetal Fictions: An Exploration of Property Archetypes in Racial and Gendered Contexts" in the *Florida Law Review*.

> *Selected quotes from "Fetal Fictions":* The article "reframes the historic struggle of Blacks to involve the explicit interests of all people of color, of women, of gays and lesbians, and of physically and economically disadvantaged people." "The original vehicle for this interest . . . was my family history. I write frequently about the extraordinary emotional significance of my sister finding vestigial documentation of my great-great-grandmother's existence in Bolivar, Tennessee, as the property of a wealthy white lawyer who fathered and owned her children." "A student was angry at me because, she said, my class was 'out of control.'" "I think, in an odd moment of connection, of my great-aunt Mary who, back in the 1920s, decided that her lot in life would be made better if she pretended to be a white woman." "If you are disenfranchised either racially or monetarily, you cannot be happy because you're the object of revulsion and ridicule." "I missed the street I lived on in New York. I could always see, just by stepping outside my apartment, the dimension of meaning in my great-great-grandmother being a chattel: the life-or-death contrasts of lifestyles." "I am reminded of a cartoon my colleague, Professor Alta Charo, mentioned seeing in a German magazine." "It must be understood in the context of the continuing genocide of indigenous people around the globe. . . ." "[L]et me set the scene a bit, to frame better what I think is the essential craziness of these cases, even at the risk of revealing what may be my own insanity." "I had a headache and was sure I was going crazy." "Have I yet given birth to myself as the 'Black Pat Williams?' I wondered about children, how I, as an insane, black female, commercial law professor, shall have to be split in order to give life. . . ." "Hearing about this case made my head throb harder than before, and my craziness advanced several notches. . . ." "What a cycle of absurdity, I thought as the melting ice dribbled down my nose. . . ." "These are insane times."

This sample of quotes defines the Williams style: literary, extremely personal, and liberally supplemented with instances of shock and flashing rage. Somewhere in the middle of this catharsis—and all of her narratives are cathartic—is a legal decision that upheld a company policy of barring women of childbearing age from working in a plant that manufactured batteries. Williams gave the opinion a one and one-half page discussion (in a thirteen-page article), accompanied by some interesting commentary: "[T]he analysis in *Johnson* invites the sort of prostitutive self-partialization that occurred in Brazil where similar demands by employers have contributed to Brazil's having one of the highest sterilization rates in the world." Court decisions are latchkeys to Williams's storytelling; borrowing from newspapers, television, and numerous experiences and musing over self, she writes about "boundary." "The complexity of role identification, the politics of sexuality, the inflections of professionalized discourse—all describe boundary in my life, even as they confound one another in unfolding spirals of confrontation, deflection, and dreams."

Door buzzers are crowd-screening devices used by retail stores to control entry and to filter out people who fit a crime profile. While Christmas shopping on a Saturday to buy her mother a sweater, Williams pressed the buzzer at a Benetton store. (Benetton is a chain of stores that sell trendy men and women's fashions.) "A narrow-eyed, white teenager wearing running shoes and feasting on bubble gum glared out, evaluating me for signs that would pit me against the limits of his social understanding. After about five seconds, he mouthed 'We're closed,' and blew pink rubber at me." Williams was "enraged. . . . I literally wanted to break all the windows of the store and take lots of sweaters for my mother." By participating in the buzzer system, she accepted self-hatred. She was frustrated at her impotence when confronted by a faceless, indifferent Benetton store. "I was willing to boycott Benettons' random white-owned businesses, and anyone who ever blew bubble gum in my face again." Williams returned home to post an account of the event and her feelings in her journal. Still fuming the next day, she typed her "story," made a big poster, and "stuck it to their big sweater-filled window."

Williams's book *The Alchemy of Race and Rights: Diary of a Law Professor* is the storytelling movement's flagship, assigned in law and undergraduate courses. Robin West speaks for storytellers: "This is a book that we should celebrate: it reminds us that books are occasionally very, very important, that reading can be transformative, and that writing sometimes can be and should always strive to be a moral act of the highest order." Richard Posner, the Outsider's favorite demon, calls the *Benetton* story the "rhetorical highlight of the book." He praises its compression, the use of Williams's rejection as a metaphor for social exclusion, and the irony of a teenage bubble-gum-chewing clerk's exercising power over a law professor. Posner reverts to the demon: "Yet here at the very pinnacle of Williams's art, the careful reader will begin to feel a sense of disquiet."

Posner is bothered because the Benetton episode does not hang together as a story. There are lapses and gaps; Williams leaves the reader dangling. What exactly led her to know that she was excluded because of her race? This is glitzy Benetton, located in Soho, a place that makes a profit catering to fashion-conscious people like Williams. Why would that type of store have a teenager handling the critical screening device? Was anyone else turned away? These are basic story facts that we need to know in order to appreciate her rage and frustration. According to Posner, "Williams has promised to get the particulars of an event or situation right, rather than submerging them in a generality, such as that whites hate blacks."

When Williams used the story in speaking engagements, the audience often raised the issue of generality, accusing her of filtering out the white story, thereby privileging her story. As one law professor reprovingly said, it was Williams's own interpretation, with no counterstory. Then came the rumor that the Benetton story was not true: "that I had made it up, that it was a fantasy, a lie that was probably the product of a diseased mind trying to make all white people feel guilty."

William's accusing her doubters of racism suggests a failure to appreciate the nuances of storytelling and techniques of narrative. Williams has gone beyond autobiography to embrace a diverse range of techniques: "To this end, I exploit all sorts of literary devices, including parody, parable, and poetry." By "reconceptualizing from 'objective truth' to rhetorical event," that is, blending law with story, Williams is assuming a heavy burden and risk. The burden is derived from the aesthetic component of storytelling; the risk is the failure to fulfill aesthetic criteria.

Narrative is a medium defined by the aesthetics of plot, character, and closure. "All short stories," according to Thomas Leitch, "proceed to a revelation that establishes a teleology, or retrospective sense of design, informing the whole story." Structural analysis describes the elements of the narrative form as consisting of actions, happenings, characters, settings, and a discourse of expression. Action is some change produced by a character or agent, with the character serving as a connecting thread that orients the reader. According to Seymour Chatman, structure establishes coherence: "in the beginning anything is possible; in the middle things become probable; in the ending everything is necessary."

Much of the disquietude and doubt over portions of Williams's narratives are due to their aesthetic failure. When critics complain that she suppresses a white vision or omits counterimages, they are referring to the absence of effective character development. We get to know Williams, with her eccentric TV habits and journal entries, and the family history, but everyone else is identified by initials as they dart in and out of shadows. Plots—"a narrative without a plot is a logical impossibility"—can never develop and live without the interaction of characters. As Robert Gordon Davis says: "The characters must be at once individuals of the most concrete sort and yet types, 'so strangely, fascinatingly particular, and yet so recognizably general.'" Filtering out oppositionalist voices leaves the *Benetton* story with an aesthetically defective, one-sided, and incomplete plot. In addition, without a dynamic exchange between Williams as narrator and her characters, she condemns the self to one-dimensional, albeit eccentric, rigidity.

The negative effects of aesthetic failure are played out in Williams's ongoing battle with her students. In a chapter from *Alchemy* subtitled "A Reflection on Law-School Pedagogy," a student identified as B confronts Williams, charging her with losing control of the class and making B feel guilty by implying that her uncle, who owns rental property, is a slumlord. Several days later the associate dean sends Williams a memo chastising her for silencing the more moderate students in her class. Back in class, Williams tells her "angry students" a story about the homeless of New York City; the students "are hungry and edgy. They grow with the restless urge to go shopping." After class, they complain to the dean that they are not learning real law and demand they get remedial classes from someone other than Williams.

While all of this confrontation and complaining is going on, Williams is lecturing the readers on the homeless, the corrupting effects of money, TV, advertising, and materialism, apparently oblivious to the opportunity to engage the students in a dialogue over race. Why were they angry—was it due to racial tension? There must have been minorities in her class. What was their reaction? Were they also angry? With an injection of some depth to her profile, B could have been a resource for counterperspectives that would allow Williams to escape the constraints of lecturing. Given the subtitle of the chapter, it is surprising that Williams gives her dean the character of a skeleton. After he says that money is real, Williams says, "I fail to heed the warning in his voice and continue rashly." Warning about what? This is yet another aesthetic gap. The most egregious aesthetic failure of the chapter is her complete silence on the request for a remedial course. How could she not offer a lengthy response to such a racially charged demand? This is exactly the type of incident she has used to build a reputation. She must have known about the controversy that erupted when, in the spring of 1986, Stanford Law School capitulated to a similar demand by students who were complaining about visiting professor Derrick Bell's constitutional law class. Bell had circulated an essay describing his humiliation over the incident to law schools throughout the country, explaining: "I publicized the incident in the hope that other minority law teachers would not be subjected to similar experiences."

Apology Autobiography, the Critical Reader, and Fictive Insertions

Anne Coughlin attributes the one-dimensionality of Williams's narratives and her exultation of self to the use of apology autobiography. *The Alchemy of Race and Rights* "is an example of an apology, a conventional autobiographical form in which the author undertakes to defend her intellectual career." Coughlin sees an extensive diary of aggrandizement of self in Williams's narratives: an impressive publication record, laudatory reviews of her scholarship ("my work has been described as a 'sophisticated frontal assault' on laissez-faire's most sacred sanctum, as 'new-age performance art,' and as 'anecdotal individualism'"), numerous invitations to conferences, plus other signals of a successful career.

To give B, the dean, or other characters a role in the stories would distract from the narrator's achievements. Williams takes the additional step of using interlocking narratives to denigrate her characters. She often starts with an experience (the experiential narrative), which is then included in a second or framing narrative. For example, Williams encounters a homeless bum on the streets, then describes her feelings and views to a group of listeners (students and colleagues), whose reactions she also describes. The framing narrative enables Williams to influence the reader to accept her interpretations by marginalizing the responses of the listeners. Coughlin concludes that "[v]irtually without exception, the listeners are flat, unreflective, ill-educated and bigoted characters," like B and the dean.

What distinguishes Williams from other storytellers is literary style. The consensus among her admirers is that her unorthodox composition technique gives her messages a singular resonance. When, however, it comes to describing her technique, consensus crumbles into terms like postmodernism, innovative, great literature, interdisciplinary, provocative, and, most often, transformative. There is good reason for a variety of descriptions; Williams's style is helterskelter, a style that defies traditional literary characterization. It is similar to William S. Burroughs's cut-up method in which he cut out sentences, words, and paragraphs from newspapers to compose stories. With Williams, it is a jumble of stream of consciousness, recitations from newspapers and television, encounters, lectures, and imagery. Williams likes imagery: "I dream that I'm teaching my Uniform Commercial Code class. My students are restless and inattentive, bored to death with the sales of chattels. Suddenly, from somewhere deep in my psyche, polar bears rise."

Literary people would label the Burroughs style open and unplotted. Unlike conventional linear narratives, open and unplotted stories are indeterminate, a series of unresolved conflicts that requires the reader to make inferences. Even for a professional writer, this is an extremely difficult style to master. Signals to readers have to be discernible, but not obvious. Also, there is the stress of closure; the author assumes the burden of bringing the collection of unplotted narratives to a final resolution. Effective closure is critical to the success of a story: Barbara Herrinstein Smith says, "closure announces and justifies the absence of further development; it reinforces the feeling of finality, completion, and composure which we value in all works of art; and it gives ultimate unity and coherence to the reader's experience. . . ."

The history of closure in the Benetton episode is a story of overenthusiasm and, ultimately, aesthetic failure. The original version appeared as a 1987 article in the *Miami Law Review* with the title "Spirit-Murdering the Messenger: The Discourse of Fingerpointing as the Law's Response to Racism." It was a very short story. The narrator goes to Benetton, rings the buzzer, the boy rejects her, she fumes, the end. Closure. The master of short stories, Edgar Allan Poe, would like its compression: a gesture by a punk kid that registers on the narrator and the reader as a shattering racial slur—a spirit murder. As Estrich used rape, Williams uses the incident as a preface to a conventional (for her) legal analysis.

When *Alchemy* came out in 1991, the Benetton plot had been embellished with sequels. Still furious, Williams made her famous poster and pinned it to the store's door. Poe would not have objected—it makes sense as a manifestation of the revenge motive. Professor Culp describes the reaction of a Duke colleague: "No lawyer I know would have assumed that the actions of a seventeen-year-old store clerk were reflective of the actual policies of Benettons. She should have gone to the store clerk's supervisor, written to the company headquarters, or sued, but she should not have responded by putting up a poster board and writing about it in her diary." To Culp, this was an example of racial division: "What my colleague wants Professor Williams to do as a lawyer is act like my colleague, a white privileged law professor, would have acted. Professor Williams's point is that in her reality such actions are often not effective."

Culp offers us the ubiquitous colleague from the shadows to play the privileged insensitive white male role. In this case, Culp's colleague rings true; that is precisely the reaction I would expect from the typical white male Liberal law professor. It is, likewise, the reaction I would expect from Professor Culp. On the other hand, Williams's reaction was inevitable and consistent with her cathartic inclinations. As a white male law professor, I would have pounded on the door until I got an explanation.

Aristotle warned authors about episodic plots in which the succession of incidents is neither likely nor necessary. Whatever compression and unity Williams had achieved was subverted by the addition of another sequel. Williams submitted an account of her experience to a law review and encountered the cultural bias of editors who expunged her rage. "My rushing, run-on-rage had been reduced to simple declarative sentences." Next, they deleted reference to Benetton on the grounds it could be defamatory. Finally, the ultimate insult: "All reference to my race had been eliminated because it was against 'editorial policy' to permit descriptions of physiognomy."

Why the episodic addition? Williams had communicated a taut message with the story of a redneck teenager's power over a Black law professor. The sequel was a journey into the abstract world of symbolism: the white male law review as a bastion of the tyranny of neutrality that "acted either to make me look crazy or to make the reader participate in old habits of cultural bias." Aristotle blamed episodic plots on "bad writers because they cannot help it and by good writers to please the actors." Williams answers Aristotle with yet another sequel. The next telling of her Benetton experience is at a law school conference on equality and difference. This time she is misquoted by newspaper coverage, which converts her pro-affirmative action presentation into an attack: "Affirmative action promotes prejudice by denying the status of women and blacks, instead of affirming them as its name suggests." Williams vows to write another law review article.

Coughlin suggests that Williams's squabble with the law review editors was over the interpretation of the autobiographical contract. Under the accepted reading of the contract, the narrator assumes responsibility for an accurate account of self and experience. This offer subsumes the right to verification by the readers. When the editors raised the issue of verification, Williams saw blatant racism: to question her story is to deny that Blacks have the authority to complain about racism, and to assert that if they do, they are likely to misrepresent or exaggerate the seriousness of the complaint. To Coughlin, Williams's assumption that racism lay behind efforts to verify creates a Catch-22 dilemma for readers. Since personal experiences and interpretations of encounters are virtually unverifiable, any challenge by the reader is destined to trigger a defensive response. Coughlin says: "[P]ersonal stories tend to pre-empt responses other than sympathy or silence, precisely because any critical commentary or desire for clarification may be dismissed as ad hominem—and any criticism necessarily is ad hominem, since the material available for criticism is the scholar's personal experience."

If Coughlin is correct and reader criticism or the questioning of experience narratives will unleash charges of racism, the reader is in an untenable position. As a vehicle for legal advocacy, autobiography is inherently flawed by the disquietude problem. Where the issue is the use of personal experiences as a guide for legal policy, doubts over authenticity are inevitable. Viewed from a different perspective, an aesthetic failure can become an authenticity problem. Suspicions come easy. Why, for example, did Williams mention the students' request for remedial classes and ignore Professor Bell's Stanford experience? She pinned a poster of indignation on the Benetton door but took a more direct insult from the students without a whimper. The reasonable reader would charge her with a responsibility to publicize the event. There is also the aesthetic failure of prolonging an effective closure by adding new encounters to the first version of the Benetton story. A critical reader would be justified in wondering about the new experiences. Were they added for the lecture circuit to enhance the range of racial implications of the story, like adding new scenes to improve the appeal of a new play?

In concluding "A Reflection on Law-School Pedagogy," Williams announces that she used the notes and thoughts that were incorporated into the chapter for an article published in the *Maryland Law Review* in which "neither deans nor the dissatisfaction of my students" was mentioned. However, the student-dean encounters *were* included in the law review article in virtually the same form as the subsequent book descriptions. There was one notable absence in the article: student B, who had directly challenged Williams in the book and was responsible for the memo from the associate dean, was not mentioned. Why would Williams omit B, a person who pushed her into an "unprofessional" response and served as an opening for a discussion on the oppressive social and economic system? Viewed from one angle, the gaps and omissions may be memory lapses, but viewed from a different angle it could be dramatic embellishment; adding B to the book creates a more gripping agony effect.

Coughlin says that dramatic embellishment creates "nagging ambivalence over the truth of [the] episode." She also gets a case of nagging ambivalence over Williams's sausage-machine story, which is second only to Benetton as a model for Outsider narrative scholarship. In this case, a sausage manufacturer charged with selling contaminated products argued that sausage meant pig meat and lots of impurities. In her argument to the jury, Williams debunked the notion advanced by the defense that because it is a sausage machine, whatever comes out is by definition sausage. She urged them to revolt against the "tyranny of definition machines and insist on your right to name what your senses will know." As with Benetton, Williams uses the sausage machine on the speaking circuit to attack the Reagan Court's "dominant social contract."

Coughlin is troubled because the sausage metaphor predates Williams's narrative and is traceable at least back to Bismarck. It was also included in Ambrose Bierce's *Devil's Dictionary:* "Litigation, n. A machine which you go into as a pig and come out as a sausage." This revelation opens up a variety of interpretations; it may have been nothing more than a lapse, that is, Williams simply assumed the reader would know she was not declaring originality. On the other hand, Williams is a law professor and knows the importance of citing sources. Ultimately, according to Coughlin, "if we conclude that this particular autobiographical representation was false and that the sausage story did not occur, we must decide whether that conclusion suggests that other personal experiences reported by Williams likewise did not occur."

The dilemma for the critical reader is that there is a trail of too many lapses, too much dramatic embellishment and too many fictive insertions, to let the matter drop. Williams's encounter with the student editor appears to be an irrefutable agony experience. The first edit deletes her rage and anger and replaces it with impersonal declarative sentences. The second edit cut out the identification of Benetton for lack of verification. At this point, there is no more agony than is usual in dealing with student editors. One would be hard pressed to detect racism in an edit that addresses possible legal liability. So far, Williams is entitled to be angry, but only for overzealous editing, not for racism. Then comes the race factor: the Benetton incident started when "I pressed my round brown face to the window and my finger to the buzzer, seeking admittance." Reference to her physiognomy is eliminated in the final page proofs. In "a voice gummy with soothing and patience," an editor explains that it's just a matter of style, and, moreover, the reference has nothing to do with "any principle." After numerous phone conferences, the reference was reinserted in the proofs.

The critical reader could uncover at least three things to undermine Williams's version of the events. Any of these factors supports Coughlin's nagging ambivalence over the truth of the story. First, there are nagging doubts over the occurrence of an acrimonious and nasty series of exchanges over the brown face deletion. Why would the editors go to the mat over this phrase in an article that explicitly deals with racial oppression in a symposium on excluded voices? The second problem comes from her rage at the conversion of her angry prose into an impersonal objective style. A comparison of the law review story with the version in the book shows a striking similarity in syntax, indeed, often a verbatim tracking. Williams's book account never acknowledges this similarity, leaving the impression her law review article was published with the student editorial revisions. A critical reader could rationally conclude that the revisions never occurred.

Williams's version of her relationship with the law review is further delegitimized by the Introduction to the symposium, written by a student editor. The objective of the symposium was to explore how the dominant white male language oppresses minorities. According to the editor's introduction: "By manipulating language to create self-serving labels for social conditions, the elite ignore the repressive conditions under which society's less influential groups suffer." As a Black woman, the editor establishes the context for the symposium with a brief agony experience narrative. As a first-year law student, she hears a white female student tell some other white students that she, the editor, "is not going to make it in law school; she doesn't have what it takes." When asked by the editor to explain herself, the student replies: "You don't have the same mastery of the English language as I do."

It is hard to imagine a more congenial project and a more sympathetic editor. The student editor not only understood the voice struggle against the dominant language and patriarchy but also practiced the same storytelling genre as Williams. The editor even extended a special invitation to Williams and her run-on-rage style: "In this Symposium, those participants unwilling to communicate in the dominant language were encouraged to speak in a voice they found most comfortable." Given this supportive and appreciative environment, why would editors revise Williams's prose from something she "found most comfortable" to the neutral style of the dominant language? After encouraging the symposium participants to redefine words "in order to empower the excluded," why would the editor turn on Williams and seek to regulate her writing under the tyranny of neutrality?

Autobiographical Storytelling: Fad or the Future?

The volume of autobiographical storytelling production is a modest part of the total body of Outsider scholarship. Williams and Culp have few duplicates. It is more difficult to compose a narrative than one might expect; from experience I agree with Bell, who says, "there's some creativity in trying to balance out and review the points that have to be made in a traditional law article. But there is more creativity in trying to make those points within a story that people will—and can—read as a story." Voice storytelling is largely indigenous to Blacks, numerically the smallest group in the Outsider movement. If the volume of the genre is increasing, it is in small increments. Nevertheless, it would be a mistake to assume from these factors that there is a leveling off of the genre's influence or a diminishing commitment by storytellers. What makes autobiographical narration so influential is its strong resonance.

Most law review articles are never read and have zero resonance. A select few rise to the top and are read and cited, but only within a narrow field of specialization. Grazing law people read grazing law articles. With some exceptions, even the popular articles have short life spans, quickly falling into the scrap heap of string citations or periodic recognition for obsolete or idiosyncratic views. In voice narrative, the resonance meter flashes. There is not a CRT member or sympathizer who has not empathized with Paulette Caldwell over wanting to know her hair again or who is not familiar with Jerome Culp's narrative that begins: "I start many of my law school courses with a description of myself. 'I am,' I say slowly, 'the son of a poor coal miner.'" Not to have committed Williams's stories to memory is unpardonable. Professor Abrams's reaction is typical: "In short, I believe Williams's stories the way I believe a good piece of literature."

What gives punch to the resonance is the eclecticness and the scope of voice stories. Voice stories can be assigned to practically every course and are automatic for use in minority or feminist oriented seminars. Culp uses his narratives in many of his courses, while Williams has produced a collection of stories to cover almost every law school course. Since racial oppression is assumed to be a fixture in our society, a voice story has timeless relevance and, unlike doctrinal work, never becomes obsolete. Resonance comes from another source: critical evaluation by CRT and sympathetic writers. Although not storytellers, Jane B. Baron, Alex M. Johnson Jr., and Kathryn Abrams have written articles promoting the credibility of voice scholarship. Favorable promotion in a top law review such as Harvard's or Stanford's is similar to a review in the *New York Times Sunday Book Review* section—it expands the audience, while adding a new layer of credibility. Promotion has also triggered a growing body of antistorytelling criticism, adding to the dialogue and giving the movement even more credibility as something to be taken seriously.

The debate over voice narratives helps storytellers connect with law reviews. All law reviews look for hot controversies, and anything involving race is hot. The best way to get into the debate is to publish a narrative. Student editors are increasingly receptive to storytelling; to them, voice narratives are another participant in the market of pop legal culture, feminist advocacy, and law and a banana topics. Stories are easy to edit and do not require *Bluebook* work. Even if some reviews are reluctant to publish narratives, articles about storytelling are typically written in doctrinal style, rendering them acceptable as traditional scholarship.

The ongoing feminization of the law academy enhances the prospects for autobiographical narrative. The priority on hiring women and minorities is not likely to be affected by the efforts to terminate affirmative action, thereby ensuring more feminization successes. A body of white female autobiographical storytellers like Robin West is already in place. Her autobiographical essay breaks ground, with its focus on her sexual experiences. "[Should I talk about this? Does adolescent and post-adolescent promiscuity make me exceptional, and therefore—again—marginal? (You've got to be kidding.)]" Marie Ashe's narrative on her birthing is a minor classic: "I scream to them then, How much longer? Just tell me how much longer. I beg them. I push his hand away. He is pressing something steel inside me." They are supported by the promotional writing of other white feminists like Abrams and Baron. The symbolism of Columbia Law School's inviting Williams to join the faculty puts the imprimatur of an elite law school on the work of a pure autobiographical storyteller.

A silent guerrilla war is being conducted behind the lines of the protectors of doctrinal scholarship. Law students are being trained to be storytellers. It is fashionable among feminists and CRT people to require their students to keep personal journals of their reactions to the class. Techniques vary: weekly readings in class followed by discussion, periodic review with written comments by the professor, completed journals exchanged among the class at the end of the semester. In his seminar Civil Rights at the Crossroads, Derrick Bell required his students to submit two-page papers of reflections on the weekly assignments. Students were encouraged to integrate their personal experiences with doctrinal analysis. Like all journals, reflections are narratives that cover the personal views of students on course content, on fellow students, and on professors. The message to the student is unmistakable: the subjective trumps the rational, while narration is preferred over doctrinal analysis. Bell incorporated a collection of student reflections into a law review article, combining personal experiences with confessions: "When I was a little girl, I used to wrap a towel around my head, or a shirt, or any flowing piece of material to enable me to have long flowing blonde hair." "I have a very hard time formulating a single opinion on the interracial romance debate." "As I enter the gym, I notice that everyone is black." As Frances Lee Ansley, another practitioner of the reflections technique, observed: "The rewards of the underground classroom can also be real."

Autobiographical storytellers have a lot of friends in the American Association of Law Schools. If anything, Snopes undervalued the extent of the AALS's drift into political correctness. He had seen it coming from the subtle changes in nuance and in focus and in a declining interest by old-line Liberals. It was a changing of the guard precipitated by the go-go years of the 1980s when schools were hiring large numbers of young faculty. Snopes remembered one of his Harvard friends complaining about being peppered with questions by "some crazy Crits" after he gave a paper titled "The Unconscionability of the Unconscionable Contract under the UCC." But the organization may have survived, stumbling along as a hiring meat market, inspired by cocktail parties, along with some boring presentations, had the Anita Hill–Clarence Thomas confrontation not occurred. This spark energized the race and feminist movements in legal education, with the AALS serving as the logical melting pot for the dissemination of change. Since that event Outsiders have been the dominant voice, and storytellers now have an influential forum for circulating their story.

8

The Abyss of Legal Scholarship

The Scholarship Game

It is not service to the community, and despite the self-serving spin in the catalogues, it is surely not teaching. The name of the game is scholarship. Publish or perish is a nonnegotiable law of academe. Do it if you want a chance at tenure; otherwise, hit the road. The problem is not getting published (a cynic said: "I am not sure that we have reached the point where you could jot something down on a cocktail napkin and get it published, but we're close"), but getting it approved by the Promotion and Tenure Committee and ultimately by the faculty. It is a torturous and demeaning process. As Tenured Radical said with considerable bitterness shortly after his approval by a narrow margin, "It's worse than spending six years on a capitalist gulag. It's worse than being a stockbroker."

It's like walking through a minefield blindfolded (an odd thing to run through Tenured Radical's mind, since he had never been in the service and, until Clinton's election, hated the military). I knew from day one I had to adhere to the conventional doctrinal style that was familiar from my law review experience, but it was different now. My law review Note was a committee project; now I was on my own and the stakes were a helleva lot higher. This is what the Faculty Handbook said:

> *Standards for evaluating teaching and scholarship sufficient to support a promotion or tenure are not readily reducible to words or formulae. The scholarship must reflect substantial research, a thorough understanding of the subject, and an insight into the issues and problems that contribute substantially to available knowledge. It should, in other words, make a significant advance to our understanding of the field. The most important aspect is the depth and reach reflected in the scholarship. Descriptive analysis is often a useful contribution, but the grant of tenure normally requires that the scholarship also include the development of a systematic approach or analytical rigor of a higher order.*

This didn't give me anything close to a clue as to what they wanted. I got some strange answers—mostly bafflegab—when I asked my senior colleagues to explain what it meant. "It's what it says." "Your last article has to be over fifty pages with at least 300 footnotes." "Take an obscure little problem that no one has thought much about, blow it out of all proportion, and solve it, preferably several times, in prestigious law reviews." A few of the more prolific writers gave me a stack of reprints with the advice, "Read these, and it's a cinch." Like hell, not a chance. No way. The criminal law guy turns out short pieces with titles like "Police Plus Perjury Equals Mistrial," in specialized journals like Criminology. *How can you get tenure by stringing a few cases together to state the obvious? He must be one of those quantity-equals-quality promotions. Then there was Moot's pile of crap. He got tenure the old-fashioned way— long, tedious articles recapitulating what someone else had said. I couldn't believe that they wanted me to waste my time with plagiarism. The tax reprints from, I can never remember his name, defied reading—too damned boring.*

Snopes suggested I ask a few of the recently tenured people to let me scan the outside reviews of their scholarship. They were glad to comply but, again, it was a collection of mixed signals. "She has chosen to write on issues of great difficulty and importance in the law and society field, issues requiring a broad approach." "Professor Syzygy comprehensively researches and treats the issues and critically analyzes legal doctrines and policy positions of courts and commentators." "The articles did not show a fully developed scholar; their best parts were descriptive, and they stopped short of grappling with the important issues." "He also has a tendency to list arguments made in briefs, paraphrasing them in a relatively uninteresting fashion." "There are some original points here, but they get obscured in the setting of the discussion." "His carefulness and thoroughness make him a little too restrained in his imagination." "Footnotes are often irrelevant, incomplete, or not connected to the text. The syntax is awkward and, at times, borders on the spastic." "She said that she was going to apply economic theory to duress—but where, I can't find it. Whatever she is trying to say is hidden in bizarre syntax."

It didn't take a genius to fathom that the outside reviewers were playing games to justify the fees they received. The primary objective of the review is to make sure that the audience knows that the reviewer is a star, someone who is a player. It is common to say something positive and then, to let people know who they are dealing with, to insert a zinger, a paragraph that gives the dean the option to stiff the promotion. Deans like zingers. Putdowns are common: "Professor X's scholarship justifies tenure at your school. (But not at mine.)" And God help the poor unfortunate candidate who has not profusely cited the reviewer. But all of this was irrelevant to my problem. I was still in a fog over tenure strategy.

Of all people, it was Snopes who saved my ass. It started late on a rainy Friday afternoon when we were the only ones left in the faculty lounge. "Who the hell are you?" he said in that soft gravely voice. "You're not one of those visitors the dean keeps dragging in, are you? No, you couldn't be; you're not female or Black." Then he squinted at me and said: "Are you gay?" When I identified myself, he chuckled and sarcastically observed, "Oh, you are one of our brilliant new assistant professors." We had a congenial conversation for about forty minutes, during which I did the smartest thing I have ever done—I complimented him on his famous tenure article. Two weeks later I got the following letter:

My young friend,

I appreciate your kind remarks about my scholarship; it is obvious that you have a feel for what writing is about. I think that I can return your courtesies. It was evident from our conversation that you are in a state of shock over the impending adventure of promotion and tenure. It is not an easy time, especially at a school like Scoff, with its fractious and silly faculty. Egos and oddballs. Tugwell says that we should change our name to Sloth Law School. I want to offer some advice. First, let me disabuse you of the common assumption around here that it was my article that knocked the tenure door off the hinges. That helped, but there was more, much more.

This is not Harvard Law School; we do not have the Dalton type of embarrassments. Here, like most law schools, promotion and tenure is a private affair; Moot compares it to adultery: "It has to be cultivated with discretion." Your youthful instincts are good—by scoping out your seniors you made all the right sucking gestures. They think you respect them. That and a ten-dollar-bill will get you a cup of coffee. Notice they couldn't tell you a substantive thing about scholarship or what it takes to get a union card. Forget about the presence of objective and neutral criteria for judging scholarship. Unlike scientific research, which solves problems, our written work doesn't add anything to the universe of knowledge. I was in your position, but I had ten years of trial experience before I came to Scoff, so I was not as naive as you. It took me less than a month to realize I was in the company of deadbeats. A bunch of egomaniacal wimps. If you understand that, then you can start the first phase of strategy: compose a psychological profile of the opposition—the dean and the tenured faculty.

1. The Dean. Here we are dealing with facts. First, the average tenure of a dean is around three and one-half years. Normally you could expect the guy who approved your hire to stand behind your promotion, but the odds are that he will not even be around. Regardless, deans don't count much in P and T matters; they are hired to look good and raise money. Another fact: there is no such thing as a scholar dean. That is why they become deans. They all put the same spin on scholarship. Our good ol' vacuous Dean has written: "Scholarship is not necessarily long or short; it is not necessarily frequent or infrequent; it is not necessarily footnoted or footnote free. But good scholarship always has one essential ingredient—it poses and comes to grips with an issue, articulates and supports a meaningful thesis." He actually put that mush on paper. Fact three: They lie. It is an implicit term of the job description. Fact four: Remember fact three: never believe a thing they say.

2. The Faculty. *The reason you get grunts when you query your senior colleagues about scholarship is that they do not have the foggiest notion of what to say. This is a fact of life. Once they get tenure, most law professors retire to a quiet career of work-in-progress. Some of my colleagues, like Moot, put me in this category, but I really do have a manuscript. Every faculty, bar none, can be broken down into two categories of shirkers, the career shirker and the vocationalist.*

Every other office on faculty row is occupied by a career shirker. After tenure, they never make a gesture toward an article or even an op-ed piece. These people simply do not have an interest in writing; they do committee work, are big on retreats, and enjoy AALS meetings. They like to talk about teaching but are lousy in class and big on multiple-choice exams. Like Lester B. Bile, they use the same exam every year and make the secretary do the grading. Notice who does a lot of talking at faculty meetings, and you have identified a career shirker. The interesting thing is that after ten years they go from being tolerated by the administration to being esteemed by everyone for their success in beating the system. Be careful how you handle this group. Under no circumstances should you discuss scholarship or research with them—it makes them edgy. Also, it won't hurt to criticize Moot for being too productive; the phrase they want to hear is: "He spreads himself too thin, too superficial. Moot doesn't care about students."

The other shirking group is the vocationalists. To them, real scholarship is writing briefs, memoranda, and court opinions. They exalt how-to-get-to-the-courthouse articles. Whatever you do, do not produce anything that comes close to interdisciplinary work. Every chance you get, say something nasty about law and economics. Vocationalists tolerate doctrinal work, but only because they know that it is what young law professors have to write if they want tenure. But do not get fancy; keep it basic and you can count on their vote.

The people who control the tenure gate are the Moots of the world—doctrinalists who constitute a third of this faculty. Despite diminishing numbers, they still set the agenda for legal scholarship. Let me explain what motivates these people. Doctrinalists are the Puritans of legal scholarship, people of darkness who champion pain over pleasure. One writes because one is forced by academic convention to write. It is an unpleasant chore. I call them Hunger Artists.

Puritan writing is conducted according to a cluster of pain factors. The first Rule of Pain is that the longer the article, the more intense the suffering of the author and hence the greater the accomplishment. The same rule applies to footnotes—a high number of notes indicates that the author has forced himself to go through long hours of searching for fugitive sources. Footnoting is one of the Puritan's more ingenious ploys. The brute numbers of a high count demonstrate classic Puritan masochism. It conjures up an image of the dedicated scholar spending endless hours searching for the most comprehensive support. All this means is that the poor student assistant will suffer the pain of doing the research. Puritans defiantly reject the notion that writing can produce pleasure; therefore, until you have tenure avoid "fun" things like blistering op-ed pieces, nasty book re-

views, or criticism of the sorry condition of legal scholarship. Stick with the pain of the bland and boring doctrinal article. Complain about long hours dedicated to getting it right. Be a Hunger Artist.

The Objectification of Scholarship

Scholarship has been carefully analyzed and thoroughly dissected, yet it remains a puzzle floating in an abyss. Scholarship leads a chameleon existence, with the rules for determining quality generally bending to the politics of community judgment. In Ralph Waldo Emerson's time, scholarship served a teaching function, the collection of facts to inculcate students with morals. "The office of the scholar is to cheer, to raise, and to guide men by showing them facts amid appearances." The scholar "must be a university of knowledge." Shortly after the Civil War, state subsidization of higher education redefined and refocused scholarship to mean service and the use of skills to solve practical problems. Charles Eliot, while president of Harvard, described the impact of utilitarian scholarship: "At the bottom most of the American institutions of higher education are filled with the modern democratic spirit of serviceableness. . . . All the colleges boast of the serviceable men they have trained."

The dichotomy between the Emerson's "knowledge for the sake of knowledge" model and practical problem solving is the difference between the Liberal Arts and the sciences. The Liberal Arts people accuse the science community of pounding out useless and often destructive research, while the sciences disdain the Liberal Arts for wasting time and resources chasing the illusory holy grail of good and beauty. The influence of these conflicting views has a critical relevance to legal scholarship. The Empire people aspire to produce problem-solving scholarship and condemn the Outsiders for their affinity for good-and-beauty work. The Outsiders counter by claiming to produce a more authentic vision of law, race, and the experiences of gender by reference to various subjective factors.

In early civilization, scholarship was the recording of advances in astronomy and other forms of science. Recording methods became more sophisticated as technology and scientific discovery proceeded through the Industrial Revolution. Much of the scholarship described experiments, individually recorded and communicated within the narrow confines of fields of common interests. By modern standards, it was an extremely primitive process. World War II drastically changed the scientific process to create the richest and most powerful scholarship industry in the history of civilization.

Starting with the federal government's role as an entrepreneur in the Manhattan Project, the war effort created a cluster of new science communities. The legacy of the Project was the success achieved by collecting the world's top talent into teams and subteams to create efficiencies in problem solving and in recording accomplishments. After the war, this lesson became standard operating procedure in various projects such as those conducted by NASA. The creation of the National Science Foundation converted the federal government into a major science entrepreneur whose basic responsibility was to provide funding to universities for research. Initially focused on defense (which was kept at a fever pitch by the Cold War), government subsidization became the sugar daddy to every conceivable project that could be described in a proposal.

For the new elite class of scientist researchers, it was fame and money, money, and more money. The primary path to money was the grant spigot, a process that elevated the role of scholarship and publication. First, the applicant's chances of approval were contingent on a solid publication record. Even having one's articles cited in the footnotes of colleagues' articles was factored into the evaluation process. Second, the applicant's grant proposal could get an edge if the applicant had published work done under earlier grants.

The content, direction, and definition of contemporary scholarship qua scholarship comes from the symbiotic relationship between the government and the academy. The G.I. Bill converted the quiet life of the colonial model of the academy into a group of university nations, some with budgets greater than those of Third World countries. It was a domestic Marshall Plan that subsidized a building and hiring boom that lasted until the 1980s. Generally overlooked in the boom is the exponential elevation of the political clout of the members of the academy. They became skilled artists in working the politicians to produce a flow of tax money to academe.

The bulk of the money went to the sciences. Liberal Arts got a dribble: English lit or sociology hadn't produced the atomic bomb, a trip to the moon, and other high-tech ventures. From this point on, the academy was divided into the elites of research and money and the impoverished pipe-and-tweed-jacket types of Liberal Arts. A Carnegie Foundation Report summarized: "Thus, in just a few decades, priorities in American higher education were significantly realigned. The emphasis on undergraduate education, which throughout the years had drawn its inspiration from the colonial college tradition, was being overshadowed by the European university tradition, with its emphasis on graduate education and research."

It is a humbling experience for people in the humanities who have to accept the painful fact that the prestige of their school is dependent on scientific research more than on the Liberal Arts. Over a glass of sherry, many a Liberal Arts professor complains that grantsmanship is a critical factor in promotion and tenure and that, because their work is not objective, practitioners of the Liberal Arts are at a disadvantage. The success of science as a cash cow was like a stone hitting in the middle of a quiet pond, with a ripple effect of disciplines trying to objectify their work, exhorting their people to make it look scientific, make it sound objective. Sociologists became statisticians, counting and charting everything that moves. Political scientists reinvented polling techniques and other mathematical ways of measuring human relationships. Historians went on an empirical kick, dusting off voting records, counting minnieballs, and transcribing names off tombstones. English professors tried to uncover science in new forms of criticism such as New Criticism. According to Terry Eagleton, New Criticism's "battery of critical instruments was a way of competing with the hard sciences on their own terms, in a society where such science was the dominant criterion of knowledge." The most devoted and successful converts to scholarship objectification have been economists. They have proved that the dividends are worth the effort.

Economists brag that their field is the oldest of the arts and the newest of the sciences. This is hyperbole; it overstates the science part. While Adam Smith gave the discipline credibility with *The Wealth of Nations* in 1776, he also defined its content: economics is history, prediction, tendencies, psychology, and creative imagination. Years later, Kenneth Boulding restated the eclectic range of the field: "Economic problems have no sharp edges; they shade off imperceptibly into politics, sociology, and ethics. Indeed, it is hardly an exaggeration to say that the ultimate answer to every economic problem lies in some other field." Under these circumstances, it is not surprising that economists are an extremely contentious group of people, each one defending his judgment as the final word. When they want more action, they can join one of the schools—Keynesian, Marxist, populist, Chicago School—for more vicious battles.

Controversy and fighting do not constitute good public relations for an academic discipline; neither is the public perception that economics is "a fertile ground for quacks and charlatans." Economists became the butt of jokes typically suggesting faddish behavior. The solution: get rid of the muddy image of uncertainty by objectifying the discipline's scholarship into a science.

Boulding contends it was a trade-off: exchanging the responsibility for making moral judgments for the certainty of mathematics in order to achieve status as a science. "Even economics, we learn in the history of thought, only became a science by escaping from the casuistry and moralizing of medieval thought. Who, indeed, would want to exchange the delicate rationality of the theory of equilibrium price for the unoperational vaporings of a 'just price' controversy? In the battle between mechanism and moralism generally mechanism has won hands down."

It was a rational response to the marketplace. Objectification increases income. Who will get the high-paying consulting job—the econometrician or the holistic generalist? Another factor that appeals to the young, ambitious economist is the opportunity for model building; it is a way to break out of the middle of the pack with original and counterintuitive predictions supported by copious mathematical equations. Model creation and tinkering allows one to get on a power kick. "You can't argue about what's inside my black box [i.e., economic model] because I made it. The God's truth isn't in the black box. I am the God's truth."

Equations, as black-box symbols, are de rigueur for publication. The *American Economic Review* sets the agenda; every article opens with an introductory text describing the subject, then presents the equations (the black box), and ends with a short summary of what the box (God) has decreed. Wassily Leontief, the Nobel prize winner for economics in 1973, surveyed the *Review* over a four-year period and concluded that the black-box equations had no nexus with the real world except for an article about the utility maximization of pigeons. "Page after page of professional economic journals are filled with mathematical formulas leading the reader from sets of more or less plausible but entirely arbitrary assumptions to precisely stated but irrelevant theoretical conclusions."

The greater the success of the objectification of economics, the greater the opposition. Moral economists attacked the accepted wisdom of classical and neoclassical economics, charging that models objectifying consumer sovereignty, supply and demand, and profit maximization were misleading masks for capitalist control and exploitation. No one understood the oppositional function better than J. K. Galbraith, who incites disgust and jealousy among the objectivists by making money writing best-selling books in comprehensible syntax that expose the fictions of economic determinism. Objectivists mislead, Galbraith said, by diverting attention from the fact that the real issue is ideas, not the abstractions of the black boxes. "What was elaborated in the world of ideas could be destroyed in the world of ideas; what economists gave they could take away."

By adopting the scientific method as a model, Dean Christopher Columbus Langdell gave legal scholarship the advantage of objectification and status. What separates legal scholarship from studies in the arts and the humanities is the doctrinal article and its analytical and neutral method. To the doctrinalist, any deviation in the form of advocacy writing, narrative, or allegory is subjective and therefore nonscientific. To the Outsider, law, like economics, has appropriated the scientific method to cover a variety of subjective value judgments. Both the economist and the doctrinalist play the same tune: "You can't argue what's inside my black box because I made it."

The Voice of a New Paradigm

Voice writers are not in the objectification business. The credibility of voice writing depends on the unique subjectivity of Outsider perception and experience. Any effort to seek objectification would necessarily concede the credibility of the Langdellian scientific method and of the doctrinal article. The voice strategy is straightforward: attack the objectivity thesis as a fraud used to disguise indeterminacy and to create an asymmetrical forum in which the dominant group uses doctrinal scholarship to exclude minorities and women from recognition. An important element of the Outsider attack is the paradigm argument: the doctrinal paradigm is unresponsive to new problems and tensions and is in the process of being replaced by a more relevant and representative voice paradigm.

Paradigm is a boilerplate reference to Thomas Kuhn's *The Structure of Scientific Revolution*, which has been praised as "the single most cogent description ever written about the sociological nature of intellectual change." The popular interpretation of Kuhn is that science progresses in conceptual leaps instead of in a steady linear cumulative progression. The results of the leaps are paradigms; a new paradigm replaces an old paradigm. A shift in a paradigm is precipitated by a scientific crisis in which existing rules are incapable of solving emerging puzzles. "Puzzles are," according to Kuhn, "recognized anomalies whose characteristic feature is their stubborn refusal to be assimilated to existing paradigms." The next step is a revolution in which an alternative paradigm competes with the existing paradigm for support within the community. "Conversions will occur a few at a time until, after the last holdouts have died, the whole profession will again be practicing under a single, but now a different paradigm."

The Empire's model assumes a linear form of scholarship that meets the criteria of analysis, rationality, and objectivity. An Outsider application of Kuhn's thesis turns the majoritarian assumption on its head by arguing that a paradigm shift is in motion, with nontraditional forms of writing, such as storytelling, in the process of becoming the new paradigm, or at least a parallel paradigm. Voice advocate Alex Johnson Jr. says: "A new paradigm must be employed—one that recognizes the existence and the worth of the voice of color. This new paradigm must not supplant, but must supplement the majoritarian paradigm." Because of the oppressive objectives and consequences of majoritarian scholarship, most Outsiders would reject Johnson's compromise, opting to hold out storytelling as *the* new paradigm.

To rationalize a paradigm change, the Outsider starts with the existence of a clear conflict between the doctrinalists' and the storytellers' vision of what scholarship should be and do. It is a conflict similar to a Kuhnian crisis that divides the community into two factions—in Kuhn's words, "one seeking to defend the old institutional constellation, the other seeking to institute some new one." The choice will not necessarily be resolved according to objective or rational criteria. Kuhn wrote: "There must also be a basis, though it need be neither rational nor ultimately correct, for faith in the particular candidate chosen." Like Stanley Fish's interpretative community, success for acceptance depends on persuasion. "As in political revolutions, so in paradigm choice—there is no standard higher than the assent of the relevant community." Finally, a change in paradigms means different evaluative standards, in this case a switch to the subjective. "Therefore, when paradigms change, there are usually significant shifts in the criteria determining the legitimacy both of problems and of proposed solutions." To the Outsider, we are in the midst of a classic paradigm change.

Kuhn's paradigm analysis is typically used for what Tushnet calls "a canned footnote," meaning that he is cited without explaining how his message supports the text. The reason for the lack of explanation is that Kuhn's description of changing scientific paradigms does not relate to, or support, the assumption of a new voice paradigm.

The Kuhn paradigm thesis is concerned with scientific problem solving, or what he describes as a crisis in puzzle solving. During the paradigm revolution, everyone in the community is trying to solve anomalies. No solution, no new paradigm. This process challenges the storytellers with this question: Where is the puzzle? What exists is a disagreement over what constitutes legal scholarship. The dominant group relies on an objective form of scholarship that Outsiders reject, preferring the subjective storytelling method.

Storytellers reject objective criteria but are vague on evaluative criteria. This is an argument over perspective, not a contest to solve a puzzle. Even if we assume a puzzle, where is the consensus for a new voice paradigm? As Gary Gutting observes: "But the sign of Kuhnian consensus is not just some sort of general endorsement of a super-theory but an acceptance that is so strong it eliminates the need for further discussion of foundational questions about subject-matter and methodology of the disciplines and enables the discipline to devote most of its energy to puzzle-solving." When it comes to promotion and tenure, there is still a consensus in support of the doctrinal article as the paradigm.

Advocates of the existence of a Kuhnian paradigm effect in legal scholarship misread—or don't read—Kuhn. In a postscript to his book, Kuhn disavowed making science "rest on unanalyzable individual intuitions rather than on logic and law." Disturbed at efforts to use his thesis in nonscientific fields, he said: "My methodological prescription is, however, directed exclusively to the sciences and, among them, to those fields which display the special developmental pattern known as progress."

Despite Langdell's efforts, law is not a hard science and is not amenable to the puzzle-solving imperatives of Kuhn's paradigm model. This does not preclude the voice people's arguing the relevance of Kuhn for analogy purposes. Like sociology, law can use the paradigm thesis to provide perspectives. Douglas Eckberg and Leslie Hill say: "When used by sociologists, however, the term [paradigm] most often comes to mean no more than a general theoretical perspective, or even . . . a collection of elements from several more or less distinct perspectives." While voice scholarship does not solve puzzles, it does illuminate tensions, expose the politics of the establishment, and serve as a counter to doctrinal scholarship.

Scholarship Criteria: From Abstraction to the Particular

Scholarship should increase knowledge. This goal subsumes evidence of knowledge of the field and an ability to communicate with sufficient clarity to enable critical evaluation and response. When it comes time to add substance to these truths, the discussion disintegrates into the typical faculty brawl. To the scholar, those who merit the designation, they know it when they see it. Even the scholars cannot evade the eternal problem: if the objective is to increase the storehouse of knowledge, how much of an increase is necessary? What is an acceptable incremental increase? To Professor Moot and to many doctrinalists, it is a modest burden: a new interpretation, restatement of an existing rule, or a switch in emphasis on a topic.

Stephen Carter sees how much as a critical issue. The issue is not genre, whether voice, vocational, or doctrinal, but whether a particular work marks a sufficient advancement in knowledge. The fact that Shakespeare is a better playwright than Tennessee Williams doesn't mean that *A Streetcar Named Desire* is not a better work than *Hamlet*. "No matter the *probable* value of any particular scholarly contribution, one must still finally evaluate it; and it is in the process of that evaluation, I contend, that standards can and should be universalized."

Carter offers a scathing criticism of the present state of scholarship for its shoddy research and its politicized footnoting. He is, as a colleague of mine preaches, "tough on scholarship"; the Moots of the world would never survive his rigorous agenda. While some derivative work may be "very good" or, like Moot's articles, "novel," it is not scholarship. The test is "originality" and "is not whether the scholar's idea would have been obvious to the very best scholar in the field, but whether it would have been obvious to the ordinary scholar in the field." If the scholarship is within the contemplation of the ordinary scholar, it is not, under Carter's definition, scholarship.

Carter patterned his test on patent law, which denies protection if the difference between the invention and the prior art would have been obvious to a person with ordinary skill in the relevant art. It is a test that transfers a system designed to objectively evaluate advancement in technology to one intent on evaluating the issue of how much in legal scholarship. Because anything that Professor Moot writes would have been obvious to the ordinary professor in his field, his work does not make a sufficient contribution. According to Carter, it is "a perfectly competent treatment that any scholar of ordinary skill would have done by applying the same tools to the same problem." Under the Carter test, quality is determined by the nonobviousness of the problem or the solution. The ultimate question is whether the scholarship is "distinctive and unusual."

This is a demanding test that would elevate the barriers to tenure. To the tough-on-scholarship people like Professor Snopes, it would motivate faculty to a higher level of writing, while eliminating the redundancy of the incremental work of the Moots of legal education, perhaps ultimately reducing the number of law journals. The Carter test would make explicit what everyone knows: the bulk of legal scholarship is trivial and should never see the light of day. It resides in what is known as the Junk Stream.

Farber and Sherry criticize reliance on a nonobviousness test for two reasons. First, the best scholarship often makes its solution seem obvious. Good scholars do have this trait, but this is exactly the type of result that the process of comparing the prior art with the invention—the scholarly work—is specifically designed to catch. It is through the comparison that the examiner distinguishes trivial, incremental, or derivative writing from scholarship that makes an addition to knowledge. The second objection is that in critique scholarship it is necessary to state the obvious. True, but the focus of the Carter test is on the critique, and the comparison is between existing critical work and the new critique.

It is not that the test cannot work or that it is impractical but that it is too rigorous, too intolerant of mainstream scholarship, to gain acceptance. It would virtually close down an industry. Carter acknowledges this by suggesting that his test can best be used as a starting point, especially when debating the relative merits of scholarly works. As a guide to evaluation, the test shifts the focus from the type or method of scholarship to the question of how much. It is not whether "some scholarly modes are superior to others"; "rather, the relevant question should be what has resulted from the particular mode that the scholar has selected for work." The Carter test does not privilege method, be it vocational, interdisciplinary, doctrinal, or storytelling. According to Carter, this process would promote diversity, "rather than pushing people toward replicating the style or conclusions of those who have gone before."

"There is nothing out there. There is a pile of articles on what legal scholarship is, on the various genres such as law and literature, and on the historical development, but I can't pick up much on the process of actually evaluating someone's work." This is the lament of a young colleague serving for the first time on the Promotion and Tenure Committee and in the process of reviewing the work of several candidates for promotion. "Not only that, but my field is commercial law—how am I supposed to assess the work of someone who writes on feminist issues?" He was correct: there is not much literature on the nitty-gritty of evaluation. Fortunately for my troubled colleague, I could direct him to Edward L. Rubin's thorough set of directions.

When I mentioned the "nothing out there" lament to a senior colleague, he grunted: "So what, who cares? How is an evaluation theory going to improve quality? My evaluation criteria are in my articles." Anticipating this reaction, Rubin reverses the question to ask, How can we not have a theory?

He answers by pointing to the negative effects of idiosyncratic evaluation techniques, which can be unjustifiably harsh on the individual or corruptive to institutional aspirations. There are significant benefits from the presence of an acceptable test. In the process of applying an evaluation agenda to someone else's work, the reviewer would be forced to reexamine his own work. An evaluation theory can play a critically important role in assessing nonmainstream fields like CRT and CLS, where the absence of formal criteria results in recriminations on both sides. The Outsiders see the dominant group as idiosyncratic or ideologically biased, unreceptive to new ideas. To the dominant group, the Outsiders practice reverse bias, categorically rejecting mainstream writing while refusing to make critical assessments of their own work.

Rubin starts with the proposition that law is not a science; legal scholarship does not deal with the truths of casual relationships and predictions based on descriptions of observable phenomena. Legal scholars compose prescriptions of normative statements addressed to decision makers—judges, legislators, and regulators. The objective is to produce agreement; therefore, the first criterion for excellence is clarity: "The legal scholar can achieve understanding only by identifying his controlling norms with clarity and by explaining their relationship to his specific arguments." The next criterion is persuasiveness; the argument must succeed in justifying the norm or the means of implementing the norm. To discourage an evaluator from succumbing to bias, Rubin transfers the judgment on persuasiveness to the decision maker: would a rational public decision maker accept the author's norm or accept the argument for implementing the norm?

Rubin gives a practical demonstration of his test by applying it to several articles, including Charles Reich's "The New Property." Reich's normative premise was that, as a basic moral value, property rights are a source of liberty protected by the Constitution. With clarity and persuasiveness, his new property argument demonstrates that this norm has been subverted by the federal government's creation of new property rights, jobs, subsidies, contracts, and so on—a cluster of rights that lacks the legal protection afforded other property rights. Reich concludes with a constitutional interpretation, a message to the decision makers, convincing "us to see the document as he sees it, and thus contributes to our understanding of it."

In the promotion-and-tenure process, the audience factor is finessed by review opinion letters from the top names in the candidate's field. As anyone who has plowed through these messages knows, they have to be read with great care and healthy skepticism. As a practical matter, legal scholars face a layer of audiences: the profession (the practicing bar), law professors as a group and in specialties, and self-designated groups based on race and gender. Rubin deals with the audience factor by characterizing scholarship as a type of "performance," with an audience of other scholars, that is, the scholars from the author's field who act as onlookers to the author's prescription to the primary audience of decision makers.

It is a parallel test, applied simultaneously with the clarity-persuasiveness criterion. The observer scholars expect "significance," which is determined by the work's relationship to the ongoing historical development of the field. Rubin asks: "Is it in the field's mainstream, or on its advancing edge? Is it a side-eddy, a backwater, or entirely out of the channel?" A work that belongs to the development of the field earns a minimal score; if it rationalizes the continuation of a trend, it gets a higher score; and it goes to the top of the heap if it is "highly original and adventuresome." The evaluation is completed by the reviewer who is determining "applicability," Rubin's version of answering the question How much? The work has to furnish an "identifiable insight that adds to the reviewer's understanding of the field." "[T]he operative question is whether the evaluator would apply the work or the idea that it contains in her own thinking process."

Within the audience of law professors, differences and disputes between subdisciplines can get nasty: constitutional law is a collection of packaged value judgments, corporate law is capitalist protectionism, criminal law is oppression, and so on. Where a lack of shared understandings inhibits evaluation, Rubin recommends that the reviewer assume doubt, "a consciously adopted mindset," and anxiety, "a response elicited by experience." Rubin wants the reviewer to reexamine any preexisting assumption in order "to stand apart from it [and] see it as merely one position among many." If the reviewed work creates doubt and anxiety about the credibility of the reviewer's assumptions, it has value. "Thus, the very process of formulating counter-arguments, which is a mechanism for outright rejection of the author's work when uncritically performed, becomes a datum for assessing that work's quality in the context of a more disciplined evaluative theory."

Outsider Evaluation Strategies

Agitation for acceptance of storytelling as legal scholarship assumes the existence or potential existence of evaluative criteria. With its recommendation for tolerance for nontraditional work ("The school should commit itself to avoid prejudice against any particular methodology or perspective used in teaching or scholarship"), the American Association of Law Schools has furnished institutional support for new criteria.

Nevertheless, storytellers and their supporters appear to be playing a loser's strategy. They argue vehemently in support of the values and transformative wonders of narrative, but when it comes time to come together on evaluative criteria, they splinter. It opens them up to the criticism that if they cannot set up an evaluative agenda, maybe it cannot be done.

Delgado accuses the dominant group of a bias against counterstories because they "jar, mock, or displace a tenet of the majoritarian faith," which puts them beyond Empire comprehension. "Majoritarian tools of analysis, themselves only stories, inevitably will pronounce Outsider versions lacking in typicality, rigor, generalizability, and truth." Rather than counter the anticipated dominant group bias with a set of standards, Delgado calls for a truce. "Sometimes it may be better to live with uncertainty a little longer, tolerate a degree of experimentation, rather than shut off a world crossing experiment that may one day benefit us all."

Calling for a truce is a surprising and prejudicial concession from one of the movement's most influential advocates, one who preaches the essentialist argument that voice storytelling derives special status from the communal and cumulative experience of oppression. To Delgado, the fact that it is an Outsider's story validates it as scholarship. Mary Coombs has added a gloss to essentialism by arguing that it is incumbent on Outsiders to adopt their own criteria to "insulate our work from the imposition of inappropriate criteria developed by and for other scholarly communities, such as traditional legal scholarship." Coombs then goes on to promote the passion and subjectivity of Outsider work, which "helps us produce better scholarship." She concludes that scholars unfamiliar with voice narrative should rely on "those they recognize as experts in the genre for their assessment." In other words, leave evaluation to the storytellers who would become the new Imperial Scholars.

The first step in Coombs's evaluation process rejects abstraction and objectivity as criteria. Coombs assumes narrative is directed to a range of disparate audiences with the intention of increasing the audiences' understanding of the storyteller's culture. The reviewer's responsibility is to determine the work's suitability for the audience "in terms of its language and its sensitivity to the audience's relevant pre-understanding." Examined from the perspective of women and minorities, the issue is whether the story advances the interests of these groups. As scholarship, personal narratives should embody truth, but the rejection of objectivity requires a redefinition of that term. The new definition is not universal truth, that is, objective truth, but a truth that is "true to the vision of those for whom the work purports to speak."

In her influential article "Hearing the Call of Stories," Kathryn Abrams also backs off from definitive evaluative criteria, instead opting to provide perspective and advice. Her objective is to educate the dominant scholar to the new storytelling genre by anticipating and responding to criticisms. A commitment to the subjective means the reader will never get deterministic answers commonly produced by objective scholarship. Truth is determined by credibility as measured by the response evoked in the reader by the narrative, that is, "some quality or qualities that, if present, incline the reader to credit the account of reality being advanced through narrative." Must the storyteller's experience be typical if it is to provide a basis for remedy or a new rule? Not necessarily. It depends on the group and the scope of the prescriptive proposal.

The problem with Abrams's multiple criteria is they are so finely nuanced as to be meaningless. The burden shifts to the readers, who "must learn to be sensitive to the distinct voice of the author." She then advises that "no two narrative essays can be read with precisely the same questions." Readers from the Empire also must learn "to discern the unifying threads of a nonlinear argument, or draw out the narrative implications of a richly detailed story, or group the similarities in diverse accounts presented sequentially." This is not a trivial challenge to Empire evaluators. First they must reject tradition criteria; then they must learn a new language of judgment that somehow enables them to uncover the messages of nonlinear arguments.

The ultimate in subjectivity is essentialism—the story of the experience validates it as legal scholarship. In a footnote to a poem describing her interview at a law firm, the author explains: "I will not engage in discourse in which I alone transmit a scholarly but false analysis of the abstraction of my experiences. Rather, I will strive to engage you in a conversation between my words and your memories, as I relay my own. In this dialogue I seek to cultivate a unique theory of combined reality." This combined reality between narrator and each reader creates a distinctive experience that defies objective evaluation. As a vision of Outsider "combined reality," the poem satisfies the essentialism criterion and hence qualifies as scholarship.

The circularity of the essentialism argument has counterproductive effects. It creates an atmosphere in which rejection of voice storytelling triggers accusations of racism, already an implicit accusation in the general dialogue about storytelling. In this highly charged atmosphere, the most inno-cent gesture can become racial. The rejection letter from the *Journal of Legal Education* to one of the coauthors of a poem describing their experiences as Blacks going through the tenure process had this line: "The ideas in the Hol-low Piercing Scream have been advanced many times." The poem, with the rejection, was published in another journal with this footnote: "A recent ex-ample of the denial of the Black experience was the tone and content of a rejection letter from the *Journal of Legal Education*." The obvious message is: criticize Outsider work at the risk of being labeled racist.

Coombs recognizes the political advantages of essentialism. The objective of her "criteria for judgment" is to erect a barricade of scholarly respectabil-ity around the assumption that the work validates itself. Criteria of judgment are, she says, "politically valuable . . . to insulate our work from the imposi-tion of inappropriate criteria" of the dominant group. It is a transparent fa-cade, laced with nebulous advice: "standards must grow organically"; "crite-ria are already implicit" in the canonical works of Bell and Williams; "stan-dards of judgment must develop out of the discourse of the Outsider communities"; "outsider scholarship is defined by its commitment to the in-terests of people of color and of all women"; and "narrative . . . is intended to transform the understanding of its audience."

"Unique vividness of detail." "Inspire and punctuate." "Creates the im-pression of a voice being overheard." "Complex image." "Emotional reso-nance." "Complexity of the human beings." While these phrases may have come from the *New York Times Book Review* section, they are Abrams's com-ments on feminist narratives. Like Coombs, she fears that the application of dominant group criteria would in fact constitute a pretext to subvert the sto-rytelling movement and argues that to ignore criticism would lead to "the marginalization of our innovations." Abrams's efforts to apply literary critical phraseology to feminist narratives demonstrates what Coombs implies: sub-jective Outsider criteria virtually compels favorable reviews—or silent ac-quiescence.

Objective Evaluation of Narrative

Rubin's analysis of criteria suggests the problem is not the storyteller's mes-sage but its medium. He endorses a mediation approach that seeks inclusion by putting the burden of adaptation and reconciliation on dominant schol-ars. They must adapt to "complete subdisciplines" that have both different normative visions and methodologies and to "partial subdisciplines" that have either different norms or different methodologies. With norms based on criticism of presumed dominant-group racial and gender oppression, Critical Race people and feminists obviously are not mainstream. In fact, Rubin gives the two groups high marks for normative clarity. "[T]hese works consciously separate themselves on normative grounds, in part because this very separation is an element of their substantive position." Since storytelling is idiosyncratic to the doctrinal method, narrative falls within the complete-subdiscipline characterization and must be subjected to a more careful evaluation.

The first factor is the significance of the subdiscipline to the overall development of legal scholarship. Rubin is practical on this issue: he suggests counting noses to determine the number of adherents. Rubin concludes that both Critical Legal Studies and Law and Economics would qualify as significant subdisciplines. Next, the work under review must be significant within its own subdiscipline. The operative question is whether a decision maker would be persuaded and whether the work contains insights that a scholar could apply. It is a judgment guided by doubt; if the work creates doubts in the evaluator's mind about his own work, it deserves respect.

As significant subdisciplines, feminism and Critical Legal Studies scholarship are amenable to Rubin's expanded evaluative process. Critical Race Theory, on the other hand, turns out to have hybrid methodological characteristics that produce two different results. While Critical Race norms are clearly nonmainstream, the methodology of much of CRT scholarship adheres to the traditional doctrinal model. Rubin cites an article by Mari Matsuda on Critical Legal Studies that includes arguments for reparation for Native Hawaiians. By stating that the article will adopt "the perspective of those who have seen and felt the falsity of the Liberal promise," the author suggests a voice perspective, yet proceeds to employ doctrinal argument. As a result, the article would be evaluated as partial subdiscipline scholarship. Because the article is connected to the mainstream through methodology, the evaluator is permitted to directly address the question of significance, rather than first assessing the significance of the subdiscipline. Rubin concludes that Matsuda's arguments are "too familiar and diffuse" to have influence on the field. Her article stands in contrast to Regina Austin's "Sapphire Bound!", an analysis of the imposition by white male middle-class appellate courts of their perspectives on inner-city Black teenage girls. Rubin says the article strikes a major theme as a challenge to the dominant group's insensitivity to the values of minorities and women.

How about voice storytellers like Williams and Culp; how would they fare under Rubin's three gates to evaluation? Not very well, in fact. Rubin closes the gates to narrative, leaving storytellers in a state of limbo. Narrative "functions as specific technique for the presentation of substantive views, not as a comprehensive system that generates its own scholarly approach." The conclusion that narrative is not methodology renders it inadequate or defective for evaluation as legal scholarship.

Rubin defines methodology as "an interlinked set of consciously articulated procedures that generates research and resolves substantive uncertainties in that subject." The methodology of Law and Economics uses microeconomic techniques to compose a norm, a black box, and then proceeds to argue for its application to a legal problem. Likewise, doctrinal methodology enables scholars to select cases, laws, and principles to use in analysis and synthesis to produce prescriptions. In "The New Property," Charles Reich examined a group of cases to demonstrate fundamental changes in the relationships among property rights, the interests of citizens, and the government, concluding with a new normative premise.

Scratch methodology, and it bleeds ideology. Doctrinal methodology is a commitment to the ideology of legal scholarship and law as science. This, in part, accounts for the dominant group's intense protectionism and contempt for other methodologies. Resistance to the Law and Economics movement softened only when it became evident that the prescriptions derived from microeconomics would be filtered through the doctrinal form. Unlike the voice storytellers, Law and Economics prescriptions have been generally consistent with the dominant group's Liberal vision.

It is because of the tight identification of methodology with ideology that Rubin separates them. This ensures a more effective and credible evaluation process and forces the evaluator to consider the distinction in comparing different methodological approaches to problems in the same field, for example, a Law and Economics work compared with doctrinal responses to an issue in real property. In addition, recognition of the methodological factor eliminates the confusion that results from the impressions generated by advocates of an ideology that their norms and prescriptions own the methodology, as the Chicago school's efficiency norm asserts ownership of the Law and Economics methodology.

Rubin rejects narration for its failure to satisfy his criteria without an explanation. Perhaps under his objectivist criteria he assumes it is self-evident that autobiography or agony experiences do not generate research or solve problems. There is no evidence that Williams's Benetton story triggered anything other than visceral reactions—some favorable, some critical. A story of an agony encounter is a form of research on self, but, by Outsider acknowledgment, it is a private inquiry into the author's personal world of alienation. How does a voice autobiography solve problems like racial oppression or the evils of objectivity and patriarchy other than by describing subjective reactions? The transformative thesis that stories can rehabilitate oppressors remains unproven and, if the literature is any indication, may have hardened resistance to Critical Race sermons. Rubin is correct; his criticism is self-evident, at least under objective criteria. But this is exactly the storyteller's point: objective criteria are irrelevant to what they do. That is why they call it the tyranny of objectivity.

Outsiders could deflect these criticisms by adopting literary critical techniques to guide evaluation of their work. This would entail reliance on the subjective criteria used by literary critics to make judgments on a work's merit. The evaluator would start with an identification of the work's school, such as Realism or Naturalism, and ask how it compares with the dominant works of that movement. For example, the Literature of Psychology and Analysis was a reaction to Realism, producing writers like Fyodor Dostoyevsky and James Joyce, who wrote about human motivations from the inside rather than from the point of view of the objective outside observer. This could constitute a point of reference for the methodology of voice narrators, like Williams, who explore internal psychological agonies. Evaluators could compare her Benetton story with similar works from the Psychology and Analysis school. The voice narration methodology favors specific modes, mostly autobiography, along with allegory and parable. With a long history in the development of literature (parable dates back to biblical times), these modes supply another set of references for evaluation of voice stories.

An interdisciplinary evaluation that incorporates literary criticism exposes storytelling to the threatening burdens of aesthetic judgment. Comparing Outsider work with the canon of literature and measuring the storyteller's performance against acceptable critical criteria could be embarrassing for the law professor as writer. Moreover, storytellers would have to relinquish autonomy to unpredictable and sometimes whimsical people who take aesthetics very seriously.

Lurking in the disputation over evaluative criteria is a stubborn barrier, the intuitive rejection of storytelling as scholarship. It does not look like scholarship. *Lord of the Flies* may be a great thinkpiece on leadership, but it is not research and scholarship. I once gave a luncheon talk to members of a law firm on the new legal scholarship to bring them up to date on advocacy and narrative writing. They were talented, successful, and up to date on events. Several had serious literary interests. I described Bell's "Civil Rights Chronicles" and the Benetton incident. Most of the younger lawyers had been exposed to Bell, but not to Williams. They were more amused than agitated. A securities lawyer said: "So what? At our school we knew that the faculty was playing the seventies song, but that sort of thing doesn't affect my work. It's irrelevant." The elders were not amused. After expressing his disgruntlement, a senior partner asked: "What does narrative allow you to do that cannot be more effectively done in the normal doctrinal style?"

Senior Partner mouths the views of Farber and Sherry, who argue that acceptance of storytelling as legal scholarship is a rejection of basic institutional values. Like Senior Partner, they cannot discern a connection between doctrinal work and Benetton. Farber and Sherry have been the storyteller's worst nightmare. They reject the assumption that Outsiders speak in a distinctive and unique voice. They refuse to accept the premise that stories strengthen community among minorities and feminists, thereby converting the stories into scholarship. They disdain the transformative thesis that stories can have a rehabilitation effect on the dominant group, nor do they buy into the assumption that middle-class minority law professors can convey the feelings, voice, and experiences of ghetto people.

Criteria for scholarship emanates from institutional imperatives. One essential imperative is scholarly dialogue: whatever the field or subdiscipline, scholarship has to engender dialogue in the form of criticism, disagreement, and counteranalysis. There is, under the rules of scholarly dialogue, an obligation by the community to test a colleague's work. Success is measured by the existence of critical reaction. The silence of colleagues is torture to a scholar. Farber and Sherry tell us that storytellers seal off the opportunity for critical dialogue by politicizing narratives in order to engage in community building instead of seeking the truths of analysis. The agony experiences of narratives are used to advance the political interests of Outsiders by establishing their identity as a separate community. This means that members of the Outsider community are obligated to refrain from publishing anything that deviates from the accepted political vision. "If community building is the highest form of legal scholarship, then presumably the *worst* form of legal scholarship would be divisively undermining or disrupting the community." Randall Kennedy violated a political contract of the Critical Race community when he disputed CRT claims in "Racial Critique of Legal Academia."

The only way to provoke critical reaction is to engage the community of scholars in analysis and reasoned argument, to titillate and challenge them with ideas. Narratives lack this provocative factor; the readers are purposely denied the opportunity to open a dialogue with the storyteller. It is authoritarian writing—love it or leave it. Loving it is not an option if, as is often the case, the reader cannot detect a legal connection. At this point, the gate comes down on voice narrative: "In other words," Farber and Sherry conclude, "can an unadorned account of personal experiences, standing alone, constitute good scholarship? Unlike many current legal storytellers, we conclude that it cannot."

9

Comments and Conclusions

A Topic for the Public Intellectual Circuit

Objective and analytical scholarship that contributes to knowledge is a working description of the goal of the legal scholar. The doctrinal methodology incorporates a communication apparatus that extends from law school to practice to judicial decision making. The similarity between a well-reasoned article and a quality appellate decision is no accident. Objectivity and analytical reasoning criteria are practical vehicles for problem solving—the fundamental mission of lawyers. Consistent with this responsibility, the doctrinal model constitutes the most efficient way for law professors to advise judges and lawmakers.

Doctrinal evaluation is a process that consists of a thorough analysis and exposure of all relevant ideas and issues. Law problem solving often involves choosing among normative prescriptions with varying levels of ideological content. The virtue of the doctrinal methodology is that it has the flexibility to communicate a variety of competing ideologically based prescriptions. This explains why the dominant group considers the Outsider plea for new evaluative criteria to be disingenuous, if not cynical; why do they need new standards when they already have access to the community under the traditional methodology? This methodology served the ideology of the Realists and, most recently, the prescriptions of Law and Economics, psychology, literature, and so on.

Like the M-1 rifle of World War II, doctrinalism is a deceptively simple methodology. Even blindfolded, one could disassemble and assemble the M-1 within sixty seconds; yet the rifle performed on any terrain regardless of weather and packed the punch of an elephant gun. The same characteristics account for the persistent success of the doctrinal methodology. Despite Tenured Radical's initial frustrations over criteria, he quickly learned that anyone can master the technique; it can be used to generate articles on any topic. It is a method that permits the author discretion to reach a preferred result. Like the economist who uses mathematical equations to construct Black Boxes, the law professor uses objective analysis to produce Black Boxes for legal problem solving.

The analogy of doctrinal writing and the Black Box explains the recognition by the university that legal scholarship can be serious, justifying the law school's status as a member of the community. One side effect is an ironic reversal of roles. People in the humanities who criticized law schools as trade schools and law professors as vocationalists now have to endure unfavorable comparisons between their subjective work and legal scholarship. Unlike work in literature or history, legal scholarship produces Black Boxes to solve problems. At least that is the image carefully nurtured in the 1970s and 1980s.

Randall Kennedy's "Racial Critiques of Legal Academia" galvanized the debate by challenging the Outsiders to prove their case. His forthright rejection of the claim that minority scholars "produce a racially distinctive brand of valuable scholarship" announced the opening of a debate that is still in progress. The sometimes testy debate was an internal affair conducted in typical academic somnolence, largely ignored by the public and by colleagues in other parts of the university. The competing arguments would have stayed sequestered in the cloistered world of law journals had not Johnnie Cochran been accused of using storytelling techniques to convince the jury that O. J. Simpson was innocent. In 1996, Jeffrey Rosen, the legal affairs writer for the *New Republic*, wrote that "the defense strategy in the Simpson case was textbook implementation of the premises of the critical race movement."

Rosen's thesis is that Cochran's defense was predicated on Black essentialism; Blacks and whites see the same thing differently. When Black jurors view the evidence and hear the witnesses, their impressions are shaped by the cumulative experiences of racial oppression. Essentialism made the suggestion of a Los Angeles police frame-up plausible, even though it was factually impossible. Cochran converted the "N word" used by whites to commit spirit murder, and the ultimate in the CRT lexicon of hate speech, into the moral equivalent of the two murders. Realizing that O. J. was not authentic (his wife and friends were all white), Cochran revised his image. Before a visit by the jury to O. J.'s home, all pictures of white people were removed and replaced with photographs of Blacks, including Norman Rockwell's poignant painting of a Black schoolgirl being escorted to class by federal marshals.

Rosen condemns the use of storytelling as a subversion of truth. He is troubled by the emphasis on stories of "group grievances" as a substitute for the facts of a particular case. Race storytelling usurps reason: "Reasoned arguments depend on things such as truth, evidence, logic, objectivity and the rest of the anachronistic apparatus of the critical mind. Stories, by contrast, appeal to the heart. They are designed to edify, and to confirm the prejudices of a community of listeners."

In a sixteen-page criticism, Rosen did what Bell, Williams, and Delgado had not done; he made CRT storytelling a topic for the public intellectual circuit. The debate is now filtered into a more populous, diverse, and less discriminating audience. The revival of the public intellectual started with the publication of Allan Bloom's *Closing of the American Mind* and blossomed to include three categories: *Highbrow, Lowbrow,* and *Shock. Highbrow* is populated with people like Bloom, Henry Louis Gates Jr., and Mary Ann Glendon, who speak to an educated audience on topics of general interest. They are critical, seeking to expose the discrepancy between reality and conventional wisdom. *Lowbrow* includes vivid personalities such as Camille Paglia ("Male urination really is a kind of accomplishment, an arc of transcendence"), Stanley Fish, and Alan Dershowitz, best described by a Harvard Law School student newspaper cartoon in which he peers into a TV camera, only to be reminded by a student: "Damn it, Dersh. It's just an elevator security camera. . . . Stop panning!" *Lowbrows* seek to convert the academic mundane into notoriety and celebrity. The third level is *Shock*: people like Geraldo Rivera and Charles Grodin, who are celebrities but aspire to be taken seriously. Geraldo endeavors to elevate his image with *Lowbrow* guests like Dershowitz.

The public intellectual sphere is an unregulated forum, lacking the discipline and focus of academe. Anyone can play, and no one has to worry about the rigors of a peer review. It gives Rosen the forum to make a tenuous connection between legal storytelling and the Simpson verdict. What most lawyers saw as Cochran's following his litigation instincts to play the race card, Rosen connected to the narrative movement to come up with the conclusion that Cochran's use of the storytelling technique "transgressed the boundaries of acceptable advocacy and shook the color-blind aspirations of American law more profoundly than any murder trial in the post–civil rights era." This is a heavy responsibility to lay on Delgado and Williams, but certainly an acceptable piece of public intellectual criticism. It would make an ideal topic for a Geraldo show featuring a panel composed of Alan Dershowitz, Chris Darden, and the Reverend Al Sharpton.

Rosen describes storytelling as more than a method of education and a vehicle for transformation of white Liberals. It is an amorphous multipurpose tent, subsuming indeterminacy, nihilism, emotion over truth, racism, authenticity, and jury tampering. If one accepts Rosen's perspective that storytelling is a big-tent public intellectual issue, the question looms: Is story-telling simply too illusive, too leachy, too irrelevant, for academic evaluation?

The Edwards Circle

The purpose of scholarship is dialogue and debate. The transcript of the dialogue determines the credibility of a scholar's career. George Stigler describes how he earned a Nobel prize in economics: "The new ideas will normally require much repetition, elaboration, and, desirably, controversy, for controversy is an attention getter and sometimes a thought getter." The thoroughness of the criticism determines the value of the scholar's ideas and recommendations. The debate is conducted within a community of peers. For the law professor, the community is composed of peers within his specialty, lawyers who practice in his field, and regulators or judges who look to him for advice.

To Judge Harry Edwards, it is a simple and rational journey from the mind of the law professor to the minds of the community. As a professor specializing in labor relations, he wrote for other labor law people. It has never been that simple or direct. William Douglas, Thurman Arnold, and the other New Deal advocates wrote with a split vision of the law community and the Liberal public intellectual audience of the 1940s. People who write on constitutional law target everyone, especially readers of the *New Republic* and the *New York Times*, as subscribers to their views. The Yale law professor who wrote *Trial by Ordeal*, accusing a New York City judge of Bible Belt justice for his treatment of Bertrand Russell, sought the applause of the enlightened readers of *The Nation*. Jurisprudents write for the world.

At tenure, law professors get tunnel vision and adhere to the Edwards script. Edwards's Circle of scholarship incorporates the trenchant standards of Rubin and Farber and Sherry. The judge is practical: keep your eye on law and ignore the glitter of chic irrelevancies. The Edwards Circle also has the advantage of precedent in a library of role models of classic doctrinal writers. Doctrinal writing is the bulls-eye; Don Turner and Derek Bok hit the bulls-eye. Nimmer, who wrote in the classic vocational style, resides at the outer edge of the Circle. Anything beyond his methodology is not scholarship. The interdisciplinary movement is located between the bulls-eye of doctrinal work and Nimmer.

The bulk of legal scholarship is doctrinal. While Empire traditionalists reject the content of Professor Kathryn Abrams's "Hearing the Call of Stories," they nevertheless concede that the methodology is acceptable. She follows the standard style form sheet: linear text, with the requisite 250-plus footnotes packed with pithy commentary. Moot would no doubt dismiss the article as a wasteful diversion of talent on an irrelevant topic. On the other hand, Moot would be more generous to Professor Alex Johnson's advocacy in "The New Voice of Color," which he would include in the Edwards Circle as a contribution to the race theory debate initiated by Randall Kennedy's "Racial Critiques of Legal Academia."

An article must analyze of a problem with sufficient clarity to enable criticism to meet the threshold criteria for acceptance into the Edwards Circle. Do the Blair narratives of Norvel Morris sufficiently identify the legal issues for a dialogue? It's a close case. Fuller's "Speluncean Explorers" left a clear trail of messages that continue to spark debate; he is in the Circle. What about "Roll Over Beethoven"? This is a classic example of a genre that Judge Edwards criticizes: advocates writing about theory in private code to fellow true believers while purposely obfuscating the message so that even they cannot respond.

Bell's Civil Rights parables and Delgado's Rodrigo narratives are candidates for the Circle. Both write in the linear style, rely on numerous footnotes, and deal with the legal implications of race. Both provide sufficient argumentation, research, and interpretation to provoke a dialogue. As an incrementalist, Moot would exclude much of Delgado's Rodrigo pieces, especially the recent ones, on the grounds of their relentless advocacy, their use of ideologically charged footnotes, and the author's obvious efforts to preach to the Lowbrow public intellectual market. "That's why," insists Moot, "Delgado started publishing Rodrigo stories in books. He is imitating Bell. He is going public. There is no question about it—he is bored with the academic community. Delgado wants to be the Alan Dershowitz of race. He is headed for the Geraldo call girl circuit."

A parable in doctrinal form does not assure inclusion in the Circle. Bell's parable about the passage of a constitutional amendment to enable a barter with the space invaders for the entire Black population is a lesson in racism. As the instrument for enforcing civil rights laws, the legal system has an interest in race conflicts. But the parable is not directed to the specifics of remedial legislation and, other than noting the irrelevance of *Brown v. Board of Education*, has virtually no discussion of laws and cases. The message from the Space Invaders parable is clear, but it is not legal scholarship.

The difficulty of engaging in critical dialogue with narrative is dramatized by Marie Ashe's "Zig-Zag Stitching" agony experience. The first part of the article reveals Ashe's rage over the legal regulations of motherhood, an intertwined network where if "I loosen a single thread, it tightens the others." For the past thirty-five winters, Ashe has spread her grandmother's coverlet over her bed. She concludes: "It has seemed to me that the major attributes of legal discourse concerning women and mothers are these: it originates in men, it defines women with certainty, it attempts to mask the operators of power, it silences other discourse." Next comes birthing. "He slit my vagina." "Calm, peaceful and in no hurry, my doctor urged me to adopt whatever posture felt most comfortable." "Four weeks on my back in bed while the bleeding continued, its cause unknown." "Incident with the prosecutor—I ask him to refer to me, before the jury, as 'Ms.' not as 'Mrs.' I can't understand that, he says, given your condition." "The last three of my five birthings have occurred at home."

Ashe generalizes on birthing regulations. "The pressures against birthing at home, in the sites where our mothers and grandmothers birthed, are enormous." She never describes these pressures. Medical-legal regulation of pregnancy is "so pervasive that we often fail to recognize them as in fact regulations." "I have experienced a number of spontaneous abortions—miscarriages—and one intentional abortion." "Every abortion involves violence and bloodiness." "I ask whether *any* legal regulation of 'reproduction' can avoid a perpetration of violence against women." Ashe's conclusion: "I want a law that will let us be—women."

Like Williams, Ashe relies on a heavy dosage of metaphors to deliver her message. It is a high-risk technique; metaphors can add layers of subtle nuance to the message, but they can also create impenetrable static between readers and meaning. They are an open invitation to a diverse range of interpretations. The focus of the reader-critic inevitably shifts to the effectiveness of the metaphor. Kathryn Abrams praises Ashe's metaphors for their "pungency, intimacy and dominance over the landscape of her article." Abrams detects a "new feminist method of discourse" and expressed satisfaction and amazement "that such a relentlessly physical and concrete account had ever made it into the pages of a legal periodical." Yet she acknowledges that she had to read "Zig-Zag" three times before she could uncover clues to its meaning. Even with clues, the best she could discern were "possibilities" of legal visions, perhaps a plea for nonregulation. Professor Caldwell's *I Want My Hair Back* is a similar puzzle, indecipherable to the Kingsfields and uncharted territory for sympathizers like Abrams. Narrators like Ashe, Caldwell, and Williams consciously create static between their work and their readers. In doing so, they reject the conventional role of the scholarly audience as a source of criticism and debate.

Whatever the genre or field, Outsiders seek to create controversy. Controversy, crisis, and trashing are assumed to be the agents of paradigm change. By taking trashing to the fringes of acceptable dialogue, the Crits self-destructed by exposing CLS's empty vessels. In the context of the Edwards Circle, it is a disjunction between the rational and the irrational. Rubin addresses this as an issue in deviant scholarship. How should the community deal with discourse or prescriptions that are deviant from mainstream scholarship? He uses Catharine MacKinnon's work as an example of a clear and comprehensible message with such an extremely negative view on the sexual relationship between men and women "that no decision-maker would be persuaded by her and that no scholar who did not already agree with her substantive position would find her insights useful."

It is a problem with an analogy to the junk science controversy: Should scientific conclusions so at odds with mainstream peer-group judgments be admitted for jury consideration? In the scholarship context, the issue is whether to include the work as part of the ongoing dialogue or to ignore it as too extreme and dissonant. Rubin waffles on MacKinnon, observing that some of her prescriptions, such as those on sexual harassment, seem more persuasive if the evaluator recognizes his self-doubts over his reaction or "recognizes a personal reaction as an anxiety indicating the force of her argument."

Although she often gets carried away with shock imagery ("You grow up with your father holding you down and covering your mouth so another man can make a horrible shearing pain between your legs"), MacKinnon's prescriptions are comprehensible. With her success in influencing pockets of decision makers, Rubin is correct in including much of her work is part of an ongoing dialogue. On the other hand, how should (or would) Rubin or other evaluators respond to Mark Tushnet's screed against Clarence Thomas in which he posited that Thomas lied during his confirmation hearings, justifying indirect impeachment?

The Tushnet article was a light version of public intellectual writing, designed to amuse a sympathetic audience by dumping on the moderates and conservatives while getting fifteen minutes of media attention. It is not intended to be taken seriously. "Roll Over Beethoven" also falls within the foolish genre, with Duncan Kennedy and Peter Gabel thumbing their noses at the Empire—two youthful elitist revolutionaries playing intersubjective pod games. While insulting the doctrinal methodology, "Roll Over"'s incomprehensibility obscured whatever law message it contained.

The race separatist assumption translates into an aggressive message that condemns the dominant group. Bell and Williams use stories to engage in uncompromising attacks on the oppressors. Other scholars use the linear advocacy technique without the doctrinal methodological restraints of objectivity, neutrality, and thoroughness. To the Kingsfields of the Empire, failure to rely on the discipline of the doctrinal method fosters advocacy writing that espouses norms or policies with counterproductive social and political consequences. The delivery of the message is clear, but the message is countermainstream propaganda.

When a juror believes a defendant is guilty of a criminal violation but votes to acquit, it is called jury nullification. By voting to acquit, the juror ignores the facts and the judge's instructions on the law. Because a not-guilty verdict is not subject to review or reversal, the Supreme Court has noted, a juror has the "physical power" to nullify even though there is no moral right to do so. In "Racially Based Jury Nullification: Black Power in the Criminal Justice System," Paul Butler argues that, legally and morally, it is the "responsibility of black jurors to emancipate some black outlaws." Butler acknowledges that his "goal is the subversion of American criminal justice."

Nullification is a byproduct of the historical tension between the judge as the source of authority and the jury as representative of the people. The tension has been resolved by a division of labor: the judge instructs the jury on the applicable law to be applied to the facts; the jury determines the facts. Nullification usurps the function of the judge. Law students learn of nullification from the 1735 John Peter Zenger trial where the jury ignored the judge's instructions regarding the charges of seditious libel. Since *Zenger*, nullification has been used in the prosecution of defendants charged with aiding escaping slaves, by Southern juries in cases where whites were charged with crimes against Blacks, and in trials involving Vietnam protesters. With the exception of the state courts of Indiana and Maryland, judges are not permitted to inform jurors of their right to nullify.

Butler gives three justifications for Black-on-Black nullification. First, the legal system is used by a white supremacist political system to maintain the status quo of capitalism. The laws of capitalism favor whites at the expense of Blacks, who are marginalized by exclusion from educational and employment opportunities. Materialism corrupts Black youths into equating property with success, resulting in the illegal appropriation of material resources, even at the expense of other Blacks. The inevitable result is an abnormally high percentage of young Black men under the supervision of the criminal justice system, comparable to that found in a police state.

The second justification is Butler's response to the contention that nullification constitutes a betrayal of democratic principles. To Butler, this assumes a democracy that represents the interests of all groups, which it does not for Blacks. Black interests are subordinate to the majority tyranny of a white oligarchy. Under these conditions, nullification is a form of self-help that gives Blacks the power to mete out justice in a way the system does not.

Finally, there is what Butler calls "the rule of law as myth." He is referring to the Realist-Crit indeterminacy thesis, which rejects the neutrality of judges. The judicial correction of prior racial injustices demonstrates indeterminacy; the courts first created the injustices. Butler's point is that law is a myth; hence, nullification is not nullification, because there can be no nullification of indeterminate laws.

Popular legal culture is the fashion at the *Yale Law Journal*; it publishes poetry, music, photography (which they call art-commentary), and articles by death-row prisoners. With Butler's essay, Yale makes another venture into popular culture with its radical-chic public intellectual journalism. It is a replay of Don Cox, Field Marshal of the Black Panther Party, who, at Lenny Bernstein's cause party, said: "We want all black men who are in jail to be set free." Butler tops Cox with his goal of subverting the criminal justice system: "I want to dismantle the master's house with the master's tools." White supremacy accusation is Lowbrow public intellectual rhetoric, typically used on the talk shows to establish turf and to put the opponent on the defensive.

Public intellectual writing provides a forum for using generalizations without supporting documentation. Over time, the generalizations often become truisms. The white supremacy thesis, the theme of Butler's first and second justifications, is a truism among CRT members. On a point so vital to his nullification proposal, one would expect Butler and his editors to provide more support than a laundry list of "examples of racism in criminal justice." It is a short list—fifteen lines of text, starting with the Scottsboro case of the 1930s, the Rodney King case (reference to the second trial is omitted), the O. J. Simpson trial, "including the extraordinary public and media fascination with it," and concluding with "the extraordinary rate of incarceration of African-American men."

The third justification, law as myth, is another CRT generalization as truism. With the CLS movement dead as a doornail, the indeterminacy thesis is a truism only to a dwindling group of true believers. Even among true believers, one would not expect Butler and his editors to cite as support for his truism an article that criticizes indeterminacy as "problematic," incapable of contributing to substantive change, and that concludes "critical scholars should put away the dogma of indeterminacy, and try their hands at tasks more difficult than deconstruction."

The issue is not that the piece is thinly researched and full of generalizations as truisms—it is. The question is whether Butler's proposal is too dissonant and antagonistic to the views of the community and therefore irrelevant to the dialogue. While a provocative contribution to the public intellectual circuit (it was abridged for an article in *Harper's Magazine*), no decision maker would be persuaded by Butler's proposal, and no scholar who did not already agree with him would find his insights useful.

Once Butler gets into the details, things fall apart. He isolates murder, rape, and assault as offenses that Black jurors should convict on the evidence; after that, he offers fuzzy qualifications, ifs, context, and sociology. Theft or robbery is in the gray area of context; when a poor woman steals from Tiffany's, a juror "might" nullify, but not when she robs her next-door neighbor. There is a presumption of nullification for narcotics offenses. While ghetto drug dealers should normally be convicted, the juror should retain discretion to nullify if there is reason to believe the dealer would cease doing business once back on the street. To help drug dealers and other defendants cease doing business, Butler proposes that jurors who nullify "might be morally obligated to participate in black self-help programs, such as those proposed by Louis Farrakhan." Stealing from a "rich family" is "troubling" and is clearly wrong. But if it is done to support a drug habit, Butler sees a moral case for nullification, at least until drug rehabilitation is available to inner-city residents. Because of the gross economic inequities that exist between Blacks and whites, Butler "encourages" nullification of theft from "very wealthy" whites.

Butler's proposal creates two trials, the case-in-chief to determine the factual issue of guilt or innocence and the second nullification trial to apply the Butler instructions. He challenges Black jurors with the formidable, if not impossible, tasks of distinguishing between drug pushers who are incorrigible and those who can be rehabilitated; of determining whether the defendant stole to support a drug habit and whether the person he robbed was poor, middle class, or wealthy; and of making findings of fact that address guilt or innocence. In his haste to open prison doors, Butler ignores a serious problem: the relevant facts for nullification are inadmissible. This is no incidental procedural failure; it undermines the moral underpinning of Black-on-Black nullification by forcing Black jurors to guess as they decide whether to let criminals back into the community. Responding to Andrew D. Leipold's criticism of his failure to discuss this problem, Butler candidly admits that "the jurors' difficult job of assessing blameworthiness might be, in part, a shot in the dark, given that, I think it is better to err on the side of emancipation of African-American people."

Point by point, Leipold exposes the defects of Black-on-Black nullification: Butler overstates Black alienation from the criminal justice system, invokes the false assumption that drug crimes are victimless, misreads the history of nullification, fails to recognize the negative effects on enforcement and prosecution, and ignores the likelihood of a negative reaction from legislative bodies. He could have added the judicial reaction; subsequent to his article, the Second Circuit Court of Appeals said: "We categorically reject the idea that, in a society committed to the rule of law, jury nullification is desirable or that courts may permit it to occur when it is within their power to prevent." Leipold concludes that Butler's nullification strategy is "immoral, unethical, and undemocratic." While valid, these criticisms miss the point; Butler is not playing the role of the law academic, while Leipold, with his efforts to identify operational flaws in the same way that the scholar breaks down a decision or an article, is making an academic response. Butler is not talking to his brethren who specialize in criminal justice; his proposal is directed at a broader public intellectual audience whose members are uninterested in the fine details of the rules of evidence. He writes in the postmodern style in which, as he says, "knowing what you know gives law review editors headaches because it does not lend itself to formal citation."

Unintended Contradictions

All literary vehicles, such as novels, short stories, and biography, are subject to criticism. Criticism of doctrinal work conforms to the analytical model; the critic uses the analytical technique to expose defects or lapses. Literary criticism is political, whether it takes the Marxist slant or follows the psychological (Freudian), sociological, impressionistic or some other splinter school. Literary critics are subjective. T. S. Eliot admits there is no answer to the question "what use, or uses, is literary criticism" and concludes that "criticism may be, what F. H. Bradley said of metaphysics, 'the finding of bad reasons for what we believe upon instinct, but to find these reasons is no less an instinct.'" Except for Coughlin, narrators have not been challenged by literary critics. Rubin, Farber, and Sherry criticize narration on the basis of doctrinal and objective criteria. Outsiders may claim exclusivity over Black experiences; they can claim neither exclusive rights to the autobiographical technique nor immunity from literary criticism.

Coughlin criticizes Outsider autobiography for its contradictory self-portraits. Williams's narratives depict experiences of oppression by the dominant group as she describes her accomplishments and success in that same group. To Coughlin, the unintended story that emerges is that Williams's identity and self have been created by the very system she seeks to revolutionize. "In this way, the autobiographical performance undercuts the critical rhetoric by insisting on the validity of the evaluations produced by the very standards that Williams intends to oppose."

Delgado succumbs to self-tarnishment. In justifying his attack on the Imperial Scholars for excluding minorities from the scholarship loop, Coughlin concludes, Delgado was compelled to create "a narrative self, ironically, as possessed by the same imperial motivations and practices for which he rebukes the despots of the inner circle." Robin West's autobiographical confessional of her sexual experiences as a forum for sexual politics reinstates the status quo by describing what already exists. Coughlin's discussion of Professor Culp's narratives flushes out the dynamic and inevitable tensions that come from autobiographical criticism and confirms the impossibility of settling on common criteria for evaluation of Outsider experience narratives.

"'I am . . . the son of a poor coal miner,'" Culp says on the first day of class. He does it to claim a life rooted in his parents' struggle, to contrast the past with the future, and to inform his Black students "that they too can engage in the struggle to reach a position of power and influence." In response to the white students' suspicion of his credentials, he adds a "truncated autobiography" of his background. After an education at Chicago and Harvard, we learn, Culp taught at "three very good law schools" and was the first Black law professor at Duke. "I am," he says, "one of the relatively small number of black people who, through measures of luck, hard work, and government policy, have 'made it.'"

While Delgado and Williams were coopted by autobiography into self-parody, Culp's fate is worse. Coughlin concludes that Culp's autobiography robs him of his Black experience. His elevation from a lowly background to a successful position of influence mimics the Horatio Alger rags-to-riches story, told "without a trace of irony." Culp's autobiographical approval of self-help as the way to overcome adversity, including institutional racism, rejects the Black perspective. He has adopted the dominant group's belief in individualism. Coughlin notes an irony; Culp criticizes Justice Thomas for his rejection of Black perspective but seemingly overlooks the Horatio Alger parallels in their life stories. "Before we participate in Culp's autobiographical program, it would be useful to know why Justice Thomas's rags-to-riches story promotes a racist ideology, while a seemingly identical story narrated by Professor Culp opposes, and even overthrows, that ideology."

In reaction, Culp's bristles with indignation; Coughlin is trying to tell him and his audience what he meant! Her problem is that she does not listen; instead, she appropriates his stories for her "tortured interpretation." She ignores his instructions on the correct interpretation of what he is saying when he uses autobiography to teach students that there is a "'me' in the law" and that "black professors of law use their autobiographies in a number of ways to illuminate their teaching and scholarship."

Culp is caught in the dilemma of autobiographical storytelling. He is not offering the audience a doctrinal analysis with a concluding statement of the author's interpretation and an invitation to readers to show why and where he is wrong. He is using the autobiographical narrative, which after publication belongs to the reader as much as to Culp. Implicit in the autobiographical contract is the audience's right to supply whatever interpretation it deems appropriate. Culp is entitled to the support of favorably inclined interpretative communities, but he lacks the power to determine the correct interpretation. Coughlin relies on her understanding of autobiography to come up with an Horatio Alger interpretation, implicitly extending an invitation to her audience to join her interpretative community. At the core of this imbroglio over who controls interpretation is the irony of Culp, a member of a group that invokes deconstruction to attack the status quo of the dominant message, yet rejects deconstruction when it is directed at his work.

A Glimpse into the Future

The Edwards Circle and voice storytelling are incompatible, a head-on crash of methodology, substance, and ideology. Going from a burpgun Williams narrative of spiritual homicide to a taut Richard Posner article on antitrust is like getting an electric shock treatment. Doctrinal articles speak in one voice, and storytellers speak in multiple voices. Outsiders detect self-serving manipulation in doctrinal neutrality and objectivity; doctrinalists scorn voice autobiographical tales as exaggeration or fuzzy fiction. Storytelling is a submarket of memoir chic in which "true torment sells." What storytellers offer as personal agony experiences triggers nagging ambivalence from critics seeking truth. The dominant scholar writes to inform; the Outsider writes to transform. "Storytelling may be fun, but it is not legal scholarship." "Experience stories resonate for everyone; doctrinal articles join the Junk Stream." The longer the crossfire goes on, the more unpleasant the exchanges get, further distancing the two sides.

The race factor imposes a pervasive and unremitting stress on the discussion. Storytellers are angered by the refusal of the dominant group to acknowledge that their experiences are distinctive and that as stories they can constitute a form of legal scholarship. This rejection is considered irrefutable evidence of the slavemaster mentality of critics. In response, Liberal critics seek to deflate the race issue by commending narratives for providing informative insights into the effects of racial subordination. Posner praised Williams for her use of metaphor and irony in the Benetton story. Doctrinal scholars argue that race is irrelevant to the issue of scholarship criteria.

What do Outsider and dominant scholars see as they peer over the ramparts? It must be disconcerting for the Empire to confront the reality of Outsiders as insiders in the university community. Within the larger universe, they are part of the diversity and multiculturism agenda in which race and gender experiences have for a long time been decreed distinctive and credible subjects for scholarship. The work of Bell and Williams has currency in undergraduate race and gender classes. The importance of the multicultural ethos cannot be underestimated; its agents provide support for race and gender exclusivity and separateness on the lecture circuit and in journals, thereby conditioning the public and undergraduates who go on to law school and law review. In addition, the prevailing mood of hate-speech censorship tends to dampen the vigor and scope of criticism from the dominant group. Anti-storytelling people like Moot are not going to risk being called racist; he prefers to dispense his venom at tenure time behind closed doors.

While CLS is defunct, its anti–Empire views are being sustained through the influx of youthful Tenured Radicals who disdain the practice of law, the Socratic Method, and the curriculum canon of contracts, torts, property, and procedure. They gravitate to constitutional law (to impersonate Larry Tribe), labor law (to Naderize the corporate hegemony), professional ethics (to discuss the practitioner as crook), poverty law (the homeless as hero), plus an assortment of nonlaw seminars. Educated at prestigious schools, they are well versed in political correctness and instinctively support race and gender causes. While many support voice storytelling as scholarship, the depth of their influence is problematical. As a group, Tenured Radicals are more trivial than Crits. They see the doctrinal piece as an easy path to tenure, after which they do radical things like circulating memos demanding retreats to discuss phallogocentricism in Posner's economics.

Outsiders are benefiting from the deteriorating relationship between doctrinalists and law reviews, at least among top-tier journals. Until the 1970s, the reviews were totally dependent on the doctrinal article as the lifeblood of survival. Then the publish-or-perish tenure requisite triggered a massive growth in the supply of articles. Whereas they once begged and scrounged for material, top-tier journals now receive thousands of submissions yearly. It is a buyer's market, with student editors in control of a bottleneck monopoly that holds the path through the Promotion and Tenure Committee for young professors.

Student editors have become as arrogant as the people with whom they are dealing. The umbilical cord between student editors and doctrinalists has been severed. Over the past ten years editorial boards have been dominated by people with politically correct agendas, people trained in undergraduate programs in which objectivity, elitism, and hierarchy are scorned. To the chagrin of the doctrinalist, this translates into an affirmative action program for Outsider storytelling and popular legal culture articles playing at deconstruction.

As Spock might say, it was the logical thing to do. By objectifying their writing to satisfy doctrinal criteria, Bell and Delgado endorsed a system they were challenging. While Rodrigo was promoting the demystifying effects of narrative and the superiority of the subjective over the analytical, he was simultaneously submitting to the ultimate in authoritarianism—*The Bluebook*—while making anti-Empire arguments in a conventional linear doctrinal style. Bell's dialogue with Geneva Crenshaw reads like a legal brief. Sensing the irony of their position, Bell and Delgado did the logical thing; they expanded their crusade into the public intellectual sector. This shrewd move can only help the movement. By entering the public realm, Bell and Delgado challenge a much wider audience while attracting the attention of a media system that welcomes provocative, even inflammatory, rhetoric.

The Outsiders are a much more threatening movement than CLS. While Crit goals were quixotic, Outsiders have set targets that can be written in concrete: autonomy in scholarship, a stake in defining legal education, and, eventually, a role in reshaping society. They want tangible changes, not the vapor of intersubjective zap. Instead of talking about frivolous distractions like paying professors and janitors the same salary, Outsiders are focused on the bad guys sitting in the corridors of power. They adhere to the golden rule of not engaging in internal criticism and hence never trash a colleague's work, instead saving their rage for someone who criticizes an icon like Bell. When Randall Kennedy broke the golden rule, the Outsider palace guard laid down a barrage of retaliatory rebuttals, serving notice that his right to speak in a Black perspective voice had been revoked. The Outsiders have the bonding glue of race that neither the Crits nor the Empire can duplicate. As Farber and Sherry observe: "Don't let all the *isms* fool you; their basic theory is both simple and astoundingly powerful."

Luck and genius defines the Empire. It invented a system that eliminated the competition. Success started with Christopher Columbus Langdell and his objectification of law. The Langdell paradigm functioned like a finely tuned watch: the science of legal analysis was transmitted in a disciplined message to students through Socratic discourse. Until recent times, law reviews were mail drops for faculty-produced doctrinal articles, another byproduct of the scientific model. The doctrinal form of scholarship perpetuated the Langdellian system, demonstrating resiliency by assimilating New Deal advocacy, white male storytelling, interdisciplinary articles, and the Junk Stream.

Snopes blames it on *One L, L.A. Law*, and the Wall Street leveraged-buyout binge of the 1980s. "Too much money and too many young professors coming in. We never got the opportunity to give them individual counseling and we never detected their deep resentment of us and what we had done. Like Tenured Radical, they were sitting ducks for Critbabble. Seminars are the leukemia of legal education: they give these young people a forum to relive what they imagine the 1960s was like—a poor effort at Oliver Stone revisionism. The prevailing wisdom for rationalizing the law and a banana curriculum was that it was a way of demonstrating to the outside community that we were teaching theory, that we were actually academics like everyone else. But it was a lie; there never was any theory, just radical value judgments. No question about it, the fissures and crevices in the system were there but no one wanted to acknowledge what was going on. Now, it's too late."

It may be, as Snopes surmises, too late to halt the deterioration of the Empire, but as a practical matter there is no choice for the Liberals but to resist voice storytelling. At stake is the future of the law school as a credible academic institution within the university community. The objectification of law and the doctrinal method pulled legal education out of vocationalism and rationalized its acceptance as a legitimate academic field. University administrators and the community still assume that doctrinal writing is the accepted method. A compromise with the Outsiders that permits storytelling to serve as a license for promotion and tenure would have devastating consequences.

It would be difficult to account for a retreat from such a fiercely defended position. After successfully weathering the CLS rebellion, it doesn't make sense to fold to CRT, a movement whose goals are even more anathema. Law and Economics and its objectivity was easy to absorb, but not a methodology that flaunts subjectivity and emotion. Practical problems are associated with acquiescence. Administrators are familiar with the doctrinal criteria, understand it, and concede the credibility of the criteria. Narrative would challenge them with vague subjective criteria that defy commitment to paper. How can the law school's Promotion and Tenure Committee explain, on rational and analytical grounds, its decision to approve narrative work to the university people? The outside review letters, likely from sympathetic Outsiders, would be couched in effusive praise of the candidate's works, for its transformative effects (without verification), for its new insights into spirit murders, and for its pungency and intimacy. Defending or explaining experience as legal scholarship would create intolerable static in the promotional process.

The autobiographical narrative as truth is a black hole. Autobiography involves two categories of truth: the truth of the author's self-portrait and the truth of the referential facts. Self-portrait puts the reader at the discretion of the author's perception of self, subject to an obligation not to intentionally misrepresent. Referential facts are generally on the record and verifiable. The black hole is the acceptance of the autobiographer's subjective "truth," a truth that is dependent on the whim of the author, a whim that can be a collection of convenient revisions of history or misrepresentations. Disquietude over a Mary McMarthy autobiography may pique the interest of literary critics, but disquietude over a voice narrative undermines the integrity of the experience as the message. Creating further disquietude is the tendency of voice writers to use unverifiable referential facts, exchanges with faceless people like students or people walking dogs.

It's trickle-down economics. Doctrinal objectivity has won recognition from the university community for the idea that legal education is a discipline that contributes to its field by producing problem-solving scholarship. This recognition justifies supracompetitive salaries and subsidies for research, elevates the status of the profession, and rationalizes barriers to entry. It is at risk, however, if Outsiders' "I know what I know" form of subjectivity and emotion is accepted as a legitimate vehicle for legal scholarship. To extend recognition to Outsider voice writing is a return to vocationalism or, even worse, to the level of the humanities.

The possibility of an Empire collapse prompts an intriguing question: Do Outsiders want to gain parity with the doctrinal model and in the process pull the house down on their careers? Outsiders benefit from the prevailing status of the law academy. Because of the law of supply and demand in minority hiring, one can assume that minorities are better compensated than similarly situated white males. Success would therefore be a pyrrhic victory; Outsiders would get parity on a sinking ship. Moreover, if Outsiders are admitted to the Club, what is left to criticize; where is the oppression? Outsiders would be insiders, fair game for the next Outsider movement. It is deconstruction: the marginalized deconstruct the privileged into irrelevance; the marginalized become the privileged, only to get deconstructed.

It is the best of times for those who enjoy academic controversy and follow squabbles over scholarship as an avocation. Never in the history of legal education have the arguments over what constitutes legal scholarship been so heated. Realism's challenge to Liberal doctrinalism was powderpuff compared to what is going on now: parable, allegory, storytelling, hair experiences, birthing, voice narratives, agony experiences, doctrinal advocacy—even a painting submitted as an exam answer. To make things more interesting is the Balkanization of scholarship by race (e.g., white, Black, Asian), gender, sexual orientation, ideology, and discipline, each group having its own tradecraft. Even technology contributes to separateness. Ten years ago faculty debated the issues of the day in the hallways or faculty lounge; now, with word processors at home, faculty rarely come to school except to teach, which, given their self-serving scheduling, may be limited to two times a week.

There are signals that justify speculation over how some of the differences separating Outsiders and the Empire will be resolved. Legal education is experiencing serious market problems: applications and enrollment continue to drop. Money is getting increasingly scarce, particularly at state schools. (Ohio is considering closing two of its five state law schools.) The best and the brightest no longer aspire to enter practice as the image of the lawyer hovers near that of the used car salesman. With salaries and benefits losing to inflation, teaching is not as attractive as formerly, which is a moot point to the many schools subject to a moratorium on hiring. Once given autonomy status as cash cows, budgets now are subject to close review by the university administration.

As the budgetary crunch continues, the gap will widen between the wealthiest, top-tier law schools that can rely on endowment support and the rest of the academy. Over the short run, the effects on scholarship at the financially resilient schools will be marginal; law reviews will continue to be eclectic in the selection of manuscripts, and alternative journals will survive to engage in advocacy. The faceoff between Empire and Outsiders will continue unabated. Over the long term, however, the advantage will shift to the keepers of the Empire. While a tight budget burdens everyone, it falls hardest on those in the periphery of influence. The allocation of resources is determined by the self-interests and political judgment of the decision makers. Under these conditions, faculty hiring, already a sensitive topic, takes on even greater implications. "Compromise hiring," where a Liberal is balanced with an Outsider, will not pass budget scrutiny. Since it is improbable that an Empire administration will make a selection against its own self-interest, we can expect a gradual reduction in the population of Outsider faculty. This translates to a reduction in the number of minorities who have access to prestigious schools as vehicles for circulating voice scholarship.

Austerity and retrenchment are facts of life at mainstream schools. Every line of the budget is scrutinized. The new priority is a leaner, more efficient profit center, with fewer frills and more substance. This back-to-the-basics core curriculum trains lawyers, not psychologists or sociologists. The pressure will grow for more trial practice courses, less law and a banana seminars. Under a no-frills agenda, deans eschew faculty candidates who specialize in nontraditional scholarship that invites accusations of waste from the provost's office. This is especially true in state law schools, which are dependent on cost-conscious legislatures. With the new emphasis on a basic curriculum, the path to promotion will reside in articles about law written in the analytical style of the doctrinal method. The tighter the budget squeeze, the more dominant the Empire's position vis-à-vis the Outsiders.

Although not as ideologically radical as the students attending top-tier law schools, mainstream-school students have been receptive, if not supportive, of Outsider causes. This includes the law reviews and alternative journals that compete to publish nontraditional articles. During the first half of the 1990s, there was a significant interest in ideologically correct careers: public-interest law (on the left-Liberal side), government service (environmental law), and correct areas of practice such as labor (representing unions). For the new wave of mainstream students of the second half of the decade, the glamour of politically correct law has faded. They are a more practical group, entering school with an eye cocked toward the placement office. It appears to be the start of a new cycle in which students want to learn law to practice rather than to change society. Overall, it is a revised atmosphere in which visits by celebrity activists like Duncan Kennedy and Derrick Bell have been replaced by lectures by well-known lawyers and judges. The Tenured Radical type of seminar, "Phallogocentricism in Military Law," is out, while corporate and commercial law courses are in. Faculty who consult or have connections with law firms, the nerds of the early 1990s, are now favored over the Crit types.

The overall effects of a more traditional focus, a mild revival of the classic Langdellian analytical methodology, is not good news for Outsiders. The news gets worse. Judge Edwards's complaint is being heard. He first spoke while hostilities between the law academy and the bar were at their peak. The Outsiders were hurling charges at the practitioner for profit-mongering, ignoring the poor, and using legal ploys to help rich clients, while people that Edwards called faculty dilettantes were accused of being more interested in law and a banana subjects than teaching law. The estrangement is now over; the Outsiders are more interested in race and gender than in going after lawyers, while deans and faculty see law firms and alumni as sources of needed funding. It is quid pro quo—if the schools want money, they have to "talk and act traditional." No more indeterminacy, deconstruction, or lawyer bashing.

Predicting the impact of an analytical problem-solving curriculum on law review policy is a venture into speculation. Autonomy and the unchallenged discretion to publish whatever strikes the board's fancy is a powerful ego aphrodisiac and will not be surrendered without a fight. On the other hand, there are factors that could lead to modifications, especially among mainstream schools. The conditioning influences of a problem-solving curriculum will over time produce student editors less inclined to publish nontraditional work. This suggests the revival of a closer editor-faculty relationship, with both groups favoring the doctrinal methodology. The long-term effects will be the publication of scholarship directed at an Edwards audience of lawyers and judges.

There is an important change coming to law schools and the university that will drastically alter the professor's status. Tenure as we now know it will no longer exist. Tenure termination was off in the future, but the budget squeeze has moved it to the present. Schools cannot subsidize that large mass of shirkers who occupy space as unproductive fixed costs. The most likely modification will be a multiple-year contract, lasting probably five years, with renewal conditioned on a peer review. To ensure renewal, faculty will adopt the risk-averse strategy of writing conventional doctrinal articles, rather than taking a chance on nontraditional work. The termination of tenure will also end the practice of writing doctrinally for tenure and shifting over to narratives or poetry.

The Most Likely—and the Worst-Case—Scenario

Critical dialogue defines scholarship. It is a challenging and elusive responsibility, often succumbing to skulduggery, humbug, or circuitous sleight of hand. In *Beyond All Reason*, a synthesis of their law review criticisms of Outsider voice scholarship, Daniel Farber and Suzanna Sherry call for a "dialogue." They concede the pressure of "urgent problems" involving race and gender; agree that the concept of merit needs "reappraisal;" and then conclude with a call for a spirit of compromise. "Those of us in the mainstream must remain open-minded; we must not be afraid to learn from others."

As a guide to an offer of political pardon the two critics profile a special invitation list of a group they identify as "reconstructive" Outsiders—people like Lani Guinier, Martha Minow, and Robert Gordon, who are committed to "transformation and emancipation." Working together as a community of mainstream and reconstructive scholars the group could transcend "the battle between radical multiculturalism and the Enlightenment tradition."

A plea for a friendly dialogue is seemingly incongruous in the face of the heated exchanges recorded over the past decade. There are the Posner-West exchanges, Coughlin vs. Delgado and Culp, Culp vs. Posner, the numerous angry responses to Randall Kennedy's seminal article, Delgado's "Reply" to Farber and Sherry, plus a thick layer of crossfire occurring in the public intellectual circuit. However, Farber and Sherry make a distinction—these sometimes testy exchanges are attributable to radical multiculturalists, a cluster of subversives excluded from the invitation list. Instead of progressive reconstructive thoughts, they are "deconstructivists" who harbor "a paranoid mode of thought that sees behind every social institution nothing but the tracks of white supremacy and male oppression." They preach "totalitarianism" as they seek to subvert the Empire's truth.

For extending a peace offer to the progressives while ignoring the hardcore radicals, Farber and Sherry are accused by the *National Review* of being gullible and undiscerning. "Such naiveté, to the contrary, shows that the authors fail to see that the radicals' position, by definition, has no limiting principle that would make common ground possible." I disagree. It is *not* a matter of naiveté; instead Farber and Sherry acknowledge reality—the radical Outsiders are not interested in making concessions and are therefore beyond redemption. Why waste time on unworthy incorrigibles that can best be spent on enticing progressive radicals back to the enlightened truth of the Empire?

There is another reality that Farber and Sherry fail to acknowledge: Why should the radical Outsiders shoot themselves in the foot by compromising? They are now an Institution, conducting careers both in law and in the public intellectual sector supported by the imprimatur of the law academy. As Outsiders they are the beneficiary of a symbiotic relationship with Empire critics like Farber and Sherry, who, incidentally, devoted a book to them— and not to the respectable progressive reconstructivists. The effect of the stinging crossfire critiques is to validate the resonance of the radical multiculturalist voice. To engage in a transformative dialogue would fatally compromise their role as oppressed victims and concede that the days of the Empire plantation are over. It is the total exclusion by the mainstream Empire that confirms oppression status.

A safe prediction is that hostilities between the radical Outsider wing and Empire scholars will continue unabated. There is too much at stake and, for many, it is a lot of fun. The forum will embrace more public intellectual exchanges, especially from Outsiders. It is a medium with the advantage of a quick line of communication to a wider audience than readers of law journals. For the meanspirited, going the public intellectual route is a passport to invective advocacy. The feminist movement will become more focused on defining its identity to further Balkanize legal education. Already a significant influence, feminism is forcing a debate on the Tyranny of Objectivity. The ultimate result will be a fractious, distracted, and demoralized environment, with the students, and eventually the profession, paying the price.

Bibliography

Abrams, Kathryn. "Hearing the Call of Stories." *California Law Review* 79 (1991): 971.

Allen, Francis. *Law, Intellect, and Education.* Ann Arbor: University of Michigan Press, 1979.

Altman, Andrew. *Critical Legal Studies: A Liberal Critique.* Princeton: Princeton University Press, 1990.

Ashe, Marie. "Zig-Zig Stitching and the Seamless Web: Thoughts on 'Reproduction' and the Law." *Nova Law Review* 13 (1989): 355.

Auchincloss, Louis. "The Senior Partners' Ghosts." *Virginia Law Review* 50 (1964): 195.

———. "Abel Donner." *Virginia Law Review* 75 (1989): 1.

Austin, Arthur. "Footnotes as Product Differentiation." *Vanderbilt Law Review* 40 (1987): 1131.

———. "Footnote Skulduggery and Other Bad Habits." *University of Miami Law Review* 44 (1990): 1009.

———. "Political Correctness Is a Footnote." *Oregon Law Review* 71 (1992): 543.

Arnold, Thurman. "Trial by Battle and the New Deal." *Harvard Law Review* 47 (1934): 913.

Barrett, Lindon. "Self-Knowledge, Law, and African American Autobiography: Lucy A. Delaney's 'From the Darkness Cometh the Light,'" in *The Culture of Autobiography: Constructions of Self-Representations,* ed. Robert Folkenflik. California: Stanford University Press, 1993.

Bell, Derrick. "The Civil Rights Chronicles." *Harvard Law Review* 99 (1985): 4.

———. "Forward: The Civil Rights Chronicles." *Harvard Law Review* 99 (1985): 4.

———. "The Final Report: Harvard's Affirmative Action Allegory." *Michigan Law Review* 87 (1989): 2382.

———. "After We're Gone: Prudent Speculation on America in a Post-Racial Epoch." *St. Louis University Law Journal* 34 (1990): 393.

———. *Faces from the Bottom of the Well.* New York: Basic Books, 1992.

———. *Gospel Choirs: Psalms of Survival for an Alien Land Called Home.* New York: Basic Books, 1996.

Bell, Derrick, Tracy Higgins, and Sung-Hee Suh. "Racial Reflections: Dialogues in the Direction of Liberation." *University of California at Los Angeles Law Review* 37 (1990): 1037.

Bok, Derek C. "Section 7 of the Clayton Act: The Merging of Law and Economics." *Harvard Law Review* 74 (1960): 226.

———. "Reflections on the Distinctive Character of American Labor Law." *Harvard Law Review* 84 (1970–71): 1394.

Boulding, Kenneth E. "Economics as a Moral Science." *American Economic Review* 59 (1968): 1.

Bowman, Cynthia. "Street Harassment and the Informal Ghettoization of Women." *Harvard Law Review* 106 (1993): 517.

Bradbury, Malcolm. *My Strange Quest for Mensonge.* New York: Penguin Books, 1987.

Brown, Wendy. "Guns, Cowboys, Philadelphia Mayors and Civic Republicanism: On Stanford Levinson's The Embarrassing Second Amendment." *Yale Law Journal* 99 (1989): 661.

Brudnoy, David. "One, Two, Many Consciousness III." *National Review* (December 1970): 1354.

Bruner, Jerome. "The Autobiographical Process," in *The Culture of Autobiography: Constructions of Self-Representations,* ed. Robert Folkenflik. California: Stanford University Press, 1993.

Butterfield, Fox. "Parody Puts Harvard Law Faculty in Sexism Battle." *New York Times* (April 1992): A8.

Cain, Patricia A. "Teaching Feminist Legal Theory at Texas: Listening to Difference and Exploring Connections." *Journal of Legal Education* 38 (1988): 165.

Caldwell, Paulette M. "A Hair Piece: Perspectives on the Intersection of Race and Gender." *Duke Law Journal* (1991): 365.

Carter, Stephen L. "Academic Tenure and 'White Male' Standards: Some Lessons from the Patent Law." *Yale Law Journal* 100 (1991): 2065.

Carrington, Paul D. "Of Law and the River." *Journal of Legal Education* 34 (1984): 222.

Chatman, Seymour. *Story and Discourse: Narrative Structure in Fiction and Film.* Ithaca, N.Y.: Cornell University Press, 1978.

Collier, Peter. "Blood on the Charles." *Vanity Fair* (October 1992): 144.

Coombs, Mary I. "Outsider Scholarship: The Law Review Stories." *University of Colorado Law Review* 63 (1992): 683.

Coughlin, Anne M. "Regulating the Self: Autobiographical Performer in Outsider Scholarship." *Virginia Law Review* 61 (1995): 1229.

Culp, Jerome McCristal, Jr. "Posner on Duncan Kennedy and Racial Difference: White Authority in the Legal Academy." *Duke Law Journal* 41 (1992): 1095.

———. "You Can Take Them to Water. But You Can't Make Them Drink: Black Legal Scholarship and White Legal Scholars." *University of Illinois Law Review* (1992): 1021.

————. "Voice, Perspective, Truth, and Justice: Race and the Mountain in the Legal Academy." *Loyola Law Review* 38 (1993): 61.

Dalton, Clare. "An Essay in the Deconstruction of Contract Doctrine." *Yale Law Journal* 94 (1985): 997.

Delgado, Richard. "The Imperial Scholar: Reflections on a Review of Civil Rights Literature." *University of Pennsylvania Law Review* 132 (1984): 561.

————. "The Imperial Scholar Revisited: How to Marginalize Outsider Writing, Ten Years Later." *University of Pennsylvania Law Review* 140 (1992): 1349.

————. "On Telling Stories in School: A Reply to Farber and Sherry." *Vanderbilt Law Review* 46 (1993): 665.

————. "Coughlin's Complaint: How to Disparage Outsider Writing, One Year Later." *Virginia Law Review* 82 (1996): 95.

————. "The Colonial Scholar: Do Outsider Authors Replicate the Citation Practices of the Insiders, but in Reverse?" *Chicago-Kent Law Review* 71 (1996): 696.

de Man, Paul. "The Jews in Contemporary Literature." *Le Soir* (March 1941); reprinted in appendix to David Lehman, *Signs of The Times*. New York: Poseidon Press, 1991.

————. *Allegories of Reading.* New Haven: Yale University Press, 1979.

Derrida, Jacques. "Of Grammatology," in *A Derrida Reader: Between the Blinds*, ed. Peggy Kamuf. New York: Columbia University Press, 1991.

Douglas, William O. "Law Reviews and Full Disclosure." *Washington Law Review* 40 (1965): 227.

Dunn, John Gregory. "The Secret of Danny Santiago." *New York Review of Books* (August 1984): 17.

Eagleton, Terry. *Literary Theory: An Introduction.* Minneapolis: University of Minnesota Press, 1983.

Edwards, Harry T. "The Growing Disjunction between Legal Education and the Legal Profession." *Michigan Law Review* 91 (1992): 34.

Ellis, John. *Against Deconstruction.* Princeton: Princeton University Press, 1989.

Emerson, Ken. "When Legal Titans Clash." *New York Times Magazine* (April 22, 1990): 26.

Emerson, Ralph Waldo. *The American Scholar.* Ithaca, N.Y.: Cornell University Press, 1955.

Erkridge, Williams N., Jr. "The Case of the Speluncean Explorers: Twentieth-Century Statutory Interpretation in a Nutshell." *George Washington Law Review* 61 (1993): 1731.

Estrich, Susan. "Rape." *Yale Law Journal* 95 (1986): 1087.

Farber, Daniel A. and Suzanna Sherry. "Telling Stories Out of School: An Essay on Legal Narratives." *Stanford Law Review* 45 (1993): 807.

————. *Beyond All Reason: The Radical Assault on Truth in American Law.* New York: Oxford University Press, 1997.

Farrell, John Aloysius. "Reich Redux." *Boston Globe Magazine*. (April 2, 1995): 26.

Frank, Jerome. *Law and the Modern Mind*. Garden City, N.Y.: Anchor Books, 1963.

Franks, Lucinda. "The Seeds of Terror." *New York Magazine* (November 22, 1981): 35.

Frug, Mary Joe. "A Postmodern Feminist Legal Manifesto (An Unfinished Draft)." *Harvard Law Review* 105 (1992): 1045.

Fuller, Lon. "The Case of the Speluncean Explorers." *Harvard Law Review* 62 (1949): 616.

Gabel, Peter, and Duncan Kennedy. "Roll Over Beethoven." *Stanford Law Review* 36 (1984): 1.

Gass, William. "The Art of Self." *Harper's Magazine* (May 1994).

Gates, Henry Louis, Jr. "'Authenticity,' or the Lesson of Little Tree." *New York Times Book Review* (November 1991): 1.

"Gender, Race, and the Politics of Supreme Court Appointments: The Impact of the Anita Hill/Clarence Thomas Hearings." *Southern California Law Review* 65 (1992): 1279.

Gillers, Stephen. "Taking *L.A. Law* More Seriously." *Yale Law Journal* 98 (1989): 1607.

Gilligan, Carol. *In a Different Voice*. Cambridge, Mass.: Harvard University Press, 1982.

Glendon, Mary Ann. *A Nation under Lawyers: How the Crisis in the Legal Profession Is Transforming American Society*. New York: Farrar, Straus and Giroux, 1994.

Glendon, Mary Ann. "What's Wrong with Elite Law Schools." *Wall Street Journal* (June 8, 1993): A14.

Golden, Daniel. "An Unconventional Traditionalist." *Boston Globe* (March 1990): 12.

Goodrich, Chris. *Anarchy and Elegance: Confessions of a Journalist at Yale Law School*. Boston: Little, Brown, 1991.

Granfield, Robert. *Making Elite Lawyers*. New York: Routledge, 1992.

Greenfield, Meg. "Radio Free Beltway." *Newsweek* (June 1992): 68.

Gutting, Gary, ed. *Paradigms and Revolutions: Appraisals and Applications of Thomas Kuhn's Philosophy of Science*. London: University of Notre Dame Press, 1980.

"Harvard University." *American Law Review* 5 (1870): 177.

Hellman, Lillian. *Pentimento*. New York: Signet, 1974.

Jaszi, Peter. "Toward a Theory of Copyright: The Metamorphoses of 'Authorship.'" *Duke Law Journal* (1991): 455.

Johnson, Alex M., Jr. "Defending the Use of Narrative and Giving Content to the Voice of Color: Rejecting the Imposition of Process Theory in Legal Scholarship." *Iowa Law Review* 79 (1994): 803.

————. "The New Voice of Color." *Yale Law Journal* 100 (1991): 2007.

————. "Scholarly Paradigms: A New Tradition Based on Context and Color." *Vermont Law Review* 16 (1992): 913.

Johnson, Karl, and Ann Scales. "An Absolutely Positively True Story: Seven Reasons Why We Sing." *New Mexico Law Review* 16 (1986): 433.

Kahlenberg, Richard D. *Broken Contract: A Memoir of Harvard Law School*. New York: Hill and Wang, 1992.

Kelman, Mark G. "Trashing." *Stanford Law Review* 36 (1984): 293.

Kennedy, Duncan. "Form and Substance in Private Law Adjudication." *Harvard Law Review* 89 (1976): 1685.

———. "Rebels From Principle: Changing the Corporate Law Firm From Within." *Harvard Law School Bulletin* (Fall 1981): 36.

———. *Legal Education and the Reproduction of Hierarchy*. Cambridge: Afar, 1983.

———. "Psycho-Social CLS: A Comment on the Cardozo Symposium." *Cardozo Law Review* 6 (1985): 1013.

Kennedy, Randall L. "Racial Critiques of Legal Academia." *Harvard Law Review* 102 (1989): 1745.

Kornhauser, Anne. "GW Law Review Implements 'Diversity Criteria.'" *Legal Times* (May 1989): 6.

Kuhn, Thomas S. "Reflections on My Critics," in *Criticism and the Growth of Knowledge*, ed. Imre Lakatos and Alan Musgrave. Cambridge University Press, 1970.

———. *The Structure of Scientific Revolution*. Chicago: University of Chicago Press, 1970.

Lasson, Kenneth. "Scholarship Amok: Excesses in the Pursuit of Truth and Tenure." *Harvard Law Review* 103 (1990): 926.

Leatherman, Courtney. "Woman Who Took On Harvard Law School over Tenure Denial Sees Vindication." *Chronicle of Higher Education* (October 1993): A19.

Lejeune, Philippe. *On Autobiography*, ed. Paul John Eakin, trans. Katherine Leary. Minneapolis: University of Minnesota Press, 1989.

Lerner, Max. "The Demonizing of Bork." *Wall Street Journal* (October 1989): A18.

Lester, Julius. "James Baldwin—Reflection of a Maverick." *New York Times Book Review* (May 1984): 1.

Levine, Michael. *The Socratic Method*. New York: Simon and Schuster, 1987.

Macaulay, Stewart. "Symposium: Stewart Macaulay Popular Legal Culture." *Yale Law Review* 98 (1989): 1545.

Maguire, John M. "Hearsay about Hearsay." *University of Chicago Law Review* 8 (1941): 621.

Matsuda, Mari J. "Looking to the Bottom: Critical Legal Studies and Reparations." *Harvard Civil Rights-Civil Liberties Law Review* 22 (1987): 323.

———. "Affirmative Action and Legal Knowledge: Planting Seeds in Plowed-up Ground." *Harvard Women's Law Journal* 11 (1988): 1.

McFadden, Robert D., Ralph Blumenthal, M. A. Farber, E. R. Shipp, Charles Strum, Craig Wolff. *Outrage: The Story Behind the Tawana Brawley Hoax*. New York: Bantam Books, 1990.

Merton, Robert K. "Insiders and Outsiders: A Chapter in the Sociology of Knowledge." *American Journal of Social Law* 78 (1972): 9.

Miller, Mark. "Professor, Tell Us a Story." *National Review* (December 1997): 52.

Minow, Martha. "Incomplete Correspondence: An Unsent Letter to Mary Joe Frug." *Harvard Law Review* 105 (1992): 1096.

Monaghan, Peter. "Winner of National Book Award Won't Be a Voice of Black America." *Chronicle of Higher Education* (January 1991): A3.

Morris, Norval. "The Veraswami Story." *University of Chicago Law Review* 52 (1985): 948.

Nimmer, Melville B. "Inroads on Copyright Protection." *Harvard Law Review* 64 (1951): 1125.

Norris, Christopher. *Derrida*. Cambridge: Harvard University Press, 1987.

Pascal, Roy. *Design and Truth in Autobiography*. Cambridge, Mass.: Harvard University Press, 1960.

Passaro, Vince. "Black Letters on a White Page." *Harper's Magazine* (July 1997): 70.

Phillips, Harlan, ed. *Felix Frankfurter Reminiscences*. New York: Anchor Books, 1962.

Posner, Richard A. "The Present Situation in Legal Scholarship." *Yale Law Journal* 90 (1981): 1113.

———. *Economic Analysis of Law*. Boston: Little, Brown, 1992.

———. *Overcoming Law*. Cambridge, Mass.: Harvard University Press, 1995.

Pressman, Lee, D. William Leider, and Harold I. Cammer. "Sabotage and National Defense." *Harvard Law Review* 54 (1941): 632.

Swygert, Michael I., and Jon W. Bruce. "The Historical Origins, Founding, and Early Development of Student-Edited Law Review." *Hastings Law Journal* 36 (1985): 739.

Ramsey, Benita. Introduction to "Excluded Voices: Realities in Law and Law Reform." *University of Miami Law Review* 42 (1987): 1.

Redlich, Josef. "The Common Law and the Case Method in American University Law Schools." *Carnegie Foundation Bulletin* 8 (1914): 11.

Reich, Charles A. "The New Property." *Yale Law Journal* 73 (1964): 738.

———. *The Greening of America*. New York: Random House, 1970.

Rodell, Fred. "Goodbye to Law Reviews." *Virginia Law Review* 23 (1936): 338.

Rosenberg, Charles B. "An L.A. Lawyer Replies." *Yale Law Journal* 98 (1989): 1625.

Rubin, Edward L. "On Beyond Truth: A Theory for Evaluating Legal Scholarship." *California Law Review* 80 (1992): 889.

Scheppele, Kim Lane. "Forward: Telling Stories." *Michigan Law Review* 87 (1989): 2073.

Schlegel, John Henry. "Notes Toward an Intimate, Opinionated, and Affectionate History of the Conference on Critical Legal Studies." *Stanford Law Review* 36 (1984) 391.

———. *American Legal Realism and Empirical Social Science*. Chapel Hill: University of North Carolina Press (1995).

Sedgwick, John. "Beirut on the Charles." *GQ* (February 1993): 153.

Seligman, Joel. *The High Citadel: The Influence of Harvard Law School*. Boston: Houghton Mifflin, 1978.

Stevens, Robert. *Law School: Legal Education in America from the 1850s to the 1980s*. Chapel Hill: University of North Carolina Press, 1983.

Taylor, Stuart, Jr. "The Rule of Nonsense at Harvard Law." *Legal Times* (June 1992): 25.

Turner, Donald. "The Definition of Agreement under the Sherman Act: Conscious Parallelism and Refusals to Deal." *Harvard Law Review* 75 (1962): 655.

Tushnet, Mark V. "Critical Legal Studies: A Political History." *Yale Law Journal* 100 (1991): 1515.

―――. "Clarence Thomas: The Constitutional Problems." *George Washington Law Review* 63 (1995): 466.

Unger, Roberto Mangabeira. "The Critical Studies Movement." *Harvard Law Review* 96 (1983): 563.

Walsh, David. "What the Stories about Harvard Law Leave Out." *Boston Globe* (May 1992): 43.

West, Robin L. "Deconstructing the CLS-Fem Split." *Wisconsin Women's Law Journal* 2 (1986): 85.

―――. "The Difference in Women's Hedonic Lives: A Phenomenological Critique of Feminist Legal Theory." *Wisconsin Women's Legal Journal* 3 (1987): 81.

―――. "Jurisprudence and Gender." *Chicago Law Review* 55 (1988): 1.

Williams, Patricia J. "Alchemical Notes: Reconstructing Ideals from Deconstructed Rights." *Harvard Civil Rights-Civil Liberties Law Review* 22 (1987): 401.

―――. "Spirit-Murdering the Messenger: The Discourse of Fingerpointing as the Law's Response to Racism." *University of Miami Law Review* 42 (1987): 127.

―――. "Commercial Rights and Constitutional Wrongs." *Maryland Law Review* 49 (1990): 293.

―――. "Fetal Fictions: An Exploration of Property Archetypes in Racial and Gendered Contexts." *Florida Law Review* 42 (1990): 81.

―――. *The Alchemy of Race and Rights.* Cambridge, Mass.: Harvard University Press, 1991.

Wilson, Colin. *The Outsider.* Boston: Houghton Mifflin, 1956.

Wishik, Heather. "Reverie." *New Mexico Law Review* 16 (1986): 495.

"Women in Legal Education—Pedagogy, Law, Theory, and Practices." *Journal of Legal Education* 38 (1988): 1.

Wright, William. *Lillian Hellman: The Image, The Woman.* New York: Ballantine, 1986.

Index

About the Author

Arthur Austin is the Edgar A. Hahn Professor of Jurisprudence at Case Western Reserve University.